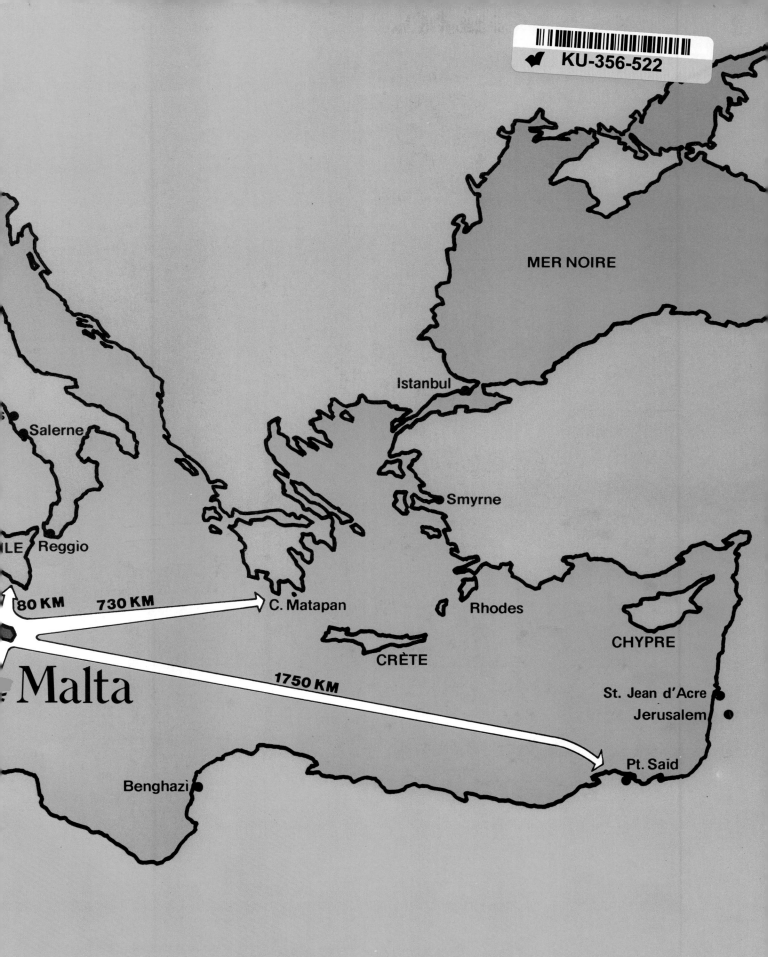

MER NOIRE

Istanbul

Smyrne

Salerne

Reggio

ILE

80 KM   730 KM   C. Matapan

Rhodes

CHYPRE

CRÈTE

Malta

1750 KM

St. Jean d'Acre

Jerusalem

Pt. Saïd

Benghazi

Bernard Nantet

MALTA

Editions Delroisse

NEW EDITION

Dghajsa, bateau maltais.
A dghajsa, or Maltese boat.
Ein Dghajsa, maltesisches Boot.

depuis 5000 ans, une île...

an island, for 5000 years...

Temple de Mnajdra.
Temple of Mnajdra.
Der Tempel von Mnajdra.

4

Sommaire

Fort Saint Ange.
Fort St Angelo.
Das Fort Saint Ange.

Contents

Enfilades de seuils, temple de Mnajdra.
Succession of thresholds, Mnajdra temple.
Schwellenreihen, der Tempel von Mnajdra.

← *Xaghra Valley, Gozo.*

LES TEMPLES DE L'ARCHIPEL DES GÉANTS
ET LES VÉNUS NÉOLITHIQUES
TÉMOIGNENT D'UNE PRÉHISTOIRE MÉDITERRANÉENNE

LES REMPARTS ÉLEVÉS PAR LES CHEVALIERS
RACONTENT UNE ÉPOQUE DE CORSAIRES,
DE RAZZIAS, DE SIÈGES ET D'ASSAUTS.

Environs de Mdina.
Near Mdina.
Umgebung von Mdina.

THE TEMPLES OF THE ARCHIPELAGO OF GIANTS AND THE NEOLITHIC VENUSES BEAR WITNESS TO MEDITERRANEAN PREHISTORY

THE RAMPARTS BUILT BY THE KNIGHTS COULD TELL A STORY OF RAIDS, SIEGES AND ATTACKS

Le Grand Port.
The Grand Harbour.
Der Grosse Hafen.

ILES DE DÉFENSE.
CONVOITISE DE CONQUÉRANTS.
SIÈGES DE BATAILLES GIGANTESQUES.

CHARLES QUINT
EN FIT DON AUX CHEVALIERS
POUR LE PRIX D'UN FAUCON.

Pêcheurs à Marsalforn, Gozo.
Fishermen at Marsalforn, Gozo.
Fischer in Marsalforn, Gozo.

**ISLANDS OF DEFENCE
THE ENVY OF CONQUERORS
THE SITE OF GIGANTIC BATTLES**

**CHARLES THE FIFTH GAVE THEM TO THE
KNIGHTS IN RETURN FOR A FALCON**

Eolienne à Marfa.
Water mill at Marfa.
Wassermühle in Marfa.

MALTE
Superficie: 246 km2
Longueur: 27 km
Largeur: 14 km
Périmètre côtier: 137 km
GOZO
Superficie: 67 km2
Longueur: 14 km
Largeur: 7 km
Périmètre côtier: 43 km
Pluie: 220 mm seulement par an
Température: en hiver 13.7°C
en été 22.6°C
Population totale: 320.000 habitants (presque
autant à l'extérieur)
Capitale: Valetta

Paysanne à Ghain Tuffeiha.
Countrywoman at Ghain Tuffeiha.
Bäuerin in Ghain Tuffeiha.

Cultures sur la côte nord.
Cultivated land on north coast.
Bestellte Felder an der Nordküste.

Maison à Mdina.
House at Mdina.
Haus in Mdina.

Entrée de porte à Sliema.
Doorway at Sliema.
Türrahmen in Sliema.

Fenêtre à St Julian.
Window at St Julian's.
Fenster in St. Julian.

TOUT COMMENCE A GHAR DALAM

Pendant des générations, des bergers ont utilisé comme parcs à bestiaux une grotte non loin de l'actuelle petite ville de Birżébbuga au bord de la baie de Marsaxlokk. Ils ne se doutaient pas que sous les litières de leurs bêtes des mètres de terre recélaient l'histoire très ancienne de leur île. Or un jour de 1865 un savant anglais, Arthur Issel, visita l'archipel à la recherche de fossiles . . .

Outre une confirmation des connaissances géologiques, la grotte de Ghar Dalam apporta la trace la plus ancienne de la présence de l'homme dans l'île.

Le rocher des îles maltaises est formé d'alluvions de l'époque tertiaire il y a de cela environ cinquante millions d'années. Ces dépôts se sont durcis en emprisonnant une multitude de coquillages comme on peut le constater en se promenant au bord de la mer, notamment en bas de la corniche à Sliema. Il y a un million d'années, au début des grandes glaciations, une érosion gigantesque dûe à des pluies diluviennes ravina le sol et commença à dessiner le relief.

Des savants prétendent qu'à cette époque – au pléistocène – les îles maltaises étaient jointes à la Sicile et à l'Afrique, la séparation d'avec l'Afrique ayant eu lieu en premier. Notons que les profondeurs entre l'archipel et le continent africain atteignent parfois 2500 mètres alors que vers la Sicile elles ne dépassent pas deux cents mètres.

La Méditerranée était alors un "vaste pâturage avec de grands arbres, des arbrisseaux et des grandes herbes de marais dans lesquels des oiseaux et de grands volatiles, des tortues d'eau douce, éléphants, hippopotames et de nombreux vertébrés allaient et venaient en quête de nourriture".

La côte à Sliema.

The coast at Sliema.

Die Küste bei Sliema.

Musée de Ghar Dalam - éléphant nain.
Ghar Dalam Museum - dwarf elephant.
Das Museum von Ghar Dalam - Zwergelefant.

Grotte de Ghar Dalam.
Ghar Dalam grotto.
Grotte in Ghar Dalam.

Musée de Ghar Dalam.
Ghar Dalam Museum.
Das Museum von Ghar Dalam.

Dans la grotte de Ghar Dalam, longue d'environ 90 mètres, les fouilles ont abouti à la découverte d'une impressionnante quantité d'ossements d'animaux de toutes sortes: herbivores comme les antilopes, carnivores comme des ours, loups ou hyènes, mais surtout des éléphants et des hippopotames dont la particularité est que ces deux derniers mammifères sont nains; le plus petit d'entre eux ne dépasse pas la taille d'un chien Saint Bernard. Par contre, il a été trouvé un cygne de taille gigantesque.

Ces découvertes étonnantes, spécifiques à l'île de Malte ont prouvé qu'il y a 250.000 ans l'île était encore reliée à la Sicile, mais coupée de l'Afrique du Nord. Le reste de l'Europe était couvert de glaciers et les animaux dans leur retrait vers les régions plus chaudes se sont trouvés coincés dans ce cul-de-sac. Ne pouvant atteindre d'autre rivage ils ont dégénéré sous forme de faune résiduelle pendant un grand nombre de générations avant de s'éteindre définitivement. Que l'on se souvienne simplement de l'existence en Afrique du Nord d'éléphants à l'époque romaine ou plus proche de nous des lions de l'Atlas à la fin du siècle dernier.

Pendant assez longtemps on a cru détenir la preuve de la présence sur l'île de l'homme de Néanderthal qui vivait il y a environ 100.000 ans. On avait en effet découvert dans la grotte deux dents humaines caractéristiques de l'homme préhistorique. Hélas, un jour un dentiste arracha de la mâchoire d'un homme du pays... une dent exactement semblable! Plus tard de nouvelles méthodes d'analyse confirmèrent les doutes résultant de cette opportune coïncidence.

C'est quand même la grotte de Ghar Dalam qui fournit les premiers vestiges irréfutables de la présence humaine. 3.800 ans avant Jésus Christ, des éleveurs seraient venus de Sicile; en effet, la poterie présente de grandes analogies avec des céramiques trouvées à Stentinello près de Syracuse. Par contre les motifs sont aussi très proches de ceux qui décorent des poteries de Dalmatie et de Méditerranée orientale. On pense que ces premiers habitants étaient aussi pêcheurs. Leurs premières habitations auraient été les grottes naturelles fort nombreuses dans ce pays calcaire.

Ghar Hassan, côte sud.
Ghar Hassan, south coast.
Ghar Hassan, Südküste.

La côte à Sliema - la côte nord.
The coast at Sliema. - North coast.
Die Küste bei Sliema - Die Nordküs

Les côtes

Malte a été dénommée par les premiers navigateurs "l'île des ports". Tout au long de son histoire, son destin a été marqué par sa situation stratégique en Méditerranée et par les refuges qu'elle pouvait offrir aux bateaux de toutes sortes.

Il y a peu d'endroits sur le pourtour des îles d'où l'on ne voit les tours de guet mises en place par les Chevaliers et destinées à prévenir toute attaque. Construites sur un modèle à peu près identique (une seule porte, forme carrée et base des murs renforcés), elles étaient visibles les unes des autres et pouvaient communiquer par signaux optiques.

To the first navigators, Malta was known as the "Island of harbours". Throughout its history, its destiny was dictated by its strategical situation in the Mediterranean and by the refuge it provided for ships of all kinds.

There are few places on the coasts of the islands from which the watch towers, set up by the knights to provide them with a warning against attacks, cannot be seen. They are built in almost identical style (a single door, square shape and with reinforced wall bases), are inter-visible and can communicate with one another by optical signals.

La Grotte Bleue

Autant la côte sud ouest est inhospitalière avec ses falaises de plusieurs dizaines de mètres qui surplombent la mer et rendent tout accostage extrêmement périlleux, autant les versants est et nord-est offrent de larges échancrures et des baies abritées. Les Phéniciens ne s'y sont pas trompés. Nombreuses sont les baies de ce côté de l'île dont le nom est composé de la racine sémitique "marsa" qui signifie port ou refuge: On trouve ainsi Marsaxlokk, Marsaskala, Marsamxett et à Gozo Marsalforn. Le développement côtier s'est évidemment effectué autour de ces pôles d'autant plus que les terres, descendant en pente douce vers la mer, permettaient une meilleure implantation des agglomérations, quand les problèmes de sécurité n'obligeaient plus les gens à vivre à l'intérieur des terres.

La mise en valeur des îles sur le plan touristique ne fait qu'accentuer cette tendance. Grands hôtels et clubs de vacances se sont élevés auprès de petites plages de sable situées à quelque distance de La Valette. Mais de nouvelles règles d'urbanisme doivent fort heureusement canaliser ce processus.

A part quelques criques, qui sont comme un coup de hache dans une falaise au pied de laquelle la mer continue à creuser sans relâche, la côte sud est propre à dérouter toute installation humaine qui tirerait une partie de sa subsistance de la mer. Les paysages y sont grandioses, les grottes profondes et pour ceux que n'effraient pas les promenades en Dghajjes (bateaux maltais) au pied des murailles qui s'élancent vers le ciel, la visite de ce que l'on appelle la "grotte bleue", est inoubliable. On peut ainsi se rendre compte de l'étonnante stabilité des barques, qui sont parfois de grande taille. Peintes de couleurs vives, elles comportent toujours une nuance bleue ou verte. Vers la proue, de chaque côté, un oeil est finement dessiné.

La Grotte Bleue.
The Blue Grotto.
Die Blaue Grotte.
→

Salines à Marsalforn.
Salt pans at Marsalforn.
Salinen in Marsalforn.
←

Gozo vue de Marfa.
Gozo seen from Marfa.
Blick von Marfa auf Gozo.

Comino Filfla

Si Malte et Gozo sont les deux îles importantes, il en existe une plus petite, Comino (Kemmuna). Sa soeur, petite Comino (Kemmunett) s'est détachée il n'y a pas tellement longtemps. Le bras de mer qui les sépare a reçu le nom de "lagon bleu" en raison de l'extraordinaire couleur turquoise de ses fonds et de la protection qu'il offre contre la houle.

Par endroit, la falaise de Comino tombe à pic dans la mer et on a l'impression, tant la découpe est nette, que la dégradation se fait avec une régularité constante. Les gens qui y vivent en permanence se comptent sur les doigts d'une seule main. Un hôtel construit il y a quelque temps donne un peu d'animation à l'îlot dont la longueur excède à peine un kilomètre et demi.

Face aux temples préhistoriques de Mnajdra et de Haġar Qim sur la côte sud, l'îlot de Filfla, chargé de mystères, est l'objet de plusieurs légendes. Très difficile d'accès, il a toujours été considéré comme porteur de malédictions. C'est bien la seule terre de l'archipel qui soit désormais inhabitée.

...mino et sa tour fortifiée.
...mino and its fortified tower.
...mino und sein befestigter
...m.

Rocher de Filfla.
Cliffs at Filfla.
Die Klippen von Filfla.

Le relief

Vu d'avion, l'archipel maltais ressemble à un continent qui se serait effondré ou qui aurait été envahi par la mer tant apparaissent importantes les failles, qui constituent le fait géologique marquant.

Blocs émergés où l'on aurait du mal à distinguer de vastes étendues de terres arables, les îles sont presque essentiellement constituées de roches calcaires. Presque toute la superficie est divisée en parcelles de dimensions réduites, ce sont les champs que les paysans ont constitué au cours des siècles en enlevant les pierres d'un sol qui devait, coûte que coûte, assurer leur subsistance. Ainsi, le plan général des zones rurales n'a certes pas beaucoup changé depuis de nombreux siècles. Quelques champs abandonnés ont laissé la place aux courtes herbes de garrigue comme le thym, très serré, d'une forte odeur épicée. Les champs sont cultivés d'une manière intensive, parfois au rythme de trois récoltes par an. On cultive surtout la pomme de terre.

Le relief très arrondi, bouleversé par l'érosion, ne présente pratiquement pas de surface qui n'ait jamais été travaillée par l'homme.

Le nord de Malte est constitué d'une série de failles qui donnent à cette partie de l'île des allures d'immenses "montagnes russes". Dans le fond des vallées ainsi créés, les cultures viennent bien, tandis que les sommets sont d'une aridité impitoyable. On y fait des tentatives de reboisement.

The Problem of Water

Le problème de l'eau

The highest point in Malta is 258 metres (198 metres in Gozo). The rivers, like the wadis of North Africa, flow only for a few hours after the rains, and the water, absorbed by the chalky soil, provides the scanty replenishment of a few sources which serve for the remainder of the year. Since the problem of drinking water is crucial for the population, the collection and distribution of rain and well water is a state monopoly. Sea-water desalination plant provides the extra amount required. Even at the time of the Knights of Malta, the island experienced water shortages, and Alof de Wignacourt, one of the Grand Masters, built an aqueduct to provide Valetta with drinking water at the beginning of the seventeenth century.

Le point le plus haut de Malte est à 258 m (198 m à Gozo). Les rivières sont plutôt des oueds qui ne coulent, comme en Afrique du Nord, que pendant quelques heures après la pluie. Le sol calcaire absorbe cette eau qui alimente chichement quelques sources le reste de l'année. Ce problème de l'eau potable étant crucial pour les habitants, la récupération des eaux de pluie et de source, ainsi que leur distribution, est un monopole d'état. Des usines de déssalement de l'eau de mer fournissent au pays le complément indispensable. Le manque d'eau existait déjà à l'époque des Chevaliers puisque l'un des Grand Maîtres, Alof de Wignacourt, construisit au début du 17ème Siècle un aqueduc destiné à alimenter La Valette en eau potable.

Everything starts in Ghar Dalam

For generations a grotto not far from the small town known today as Birzebbuga, to the north of Marsaslokk Bay, was used by shepherds as a sheepfold. Little did they think that a few feet of earth under their animals' litters hid the very ancient history of their island. And then, one day in 1865, Arthur Issel, an English scientist, came to the archipelago looking for fossils.

Apart from confirming certain geological knowledge, the grotto of Ghar Dalam provided the very oldest evidence of man's presence on the island.

The rock of the Maltese Islands consists of alluvial deposits from the tertiary era about fifty million years ago. As they hardened, these deposits imprisoned a vast number of shells, as can be seen from walking along the sea shore, particularly below the corniche at Sliema. A million years ago, at the beginning of the ice age, a gigantic erosion caused by torrential rains channelled the ground and began to form the relief.

Scientists claim that at this epoch — the pleistocene — the Maltese Islands were joined to Sicily and Africa and that the separation from Africa took place first. It is worth noting that, whereas the sea between the archipelago and the African continent sometimes reaches depths of 400 fathoms, between it and Sicily it never exceeds 70 fathoms.

At that time the Mediterranean was a vast pastureland with large trees, bushes and marshland grass in which birds and other large winged creatures, freshwater tortoises, elephants, hippopotamus, and many other vertebrates roamed about in search of food.

Excavations in the grotto of Ghar Dalam, which is about 90 metres long, resulted in the discovery of an impressive quantity of the remains of animals of all sorts — herbivora such as antelopes, carnivora such as bears, wolves and hyenas, and above all elephant and hippopotamus. The two last-named species of mammal are distinguished by the fact that they are dwarves; the smallest is no bigger than a Saint Bernard dog. On the other hand, a swan of gigantic size was also found.

These astounding discoveries, which are specific to Malta, proved that 250,000 years ago the island was still connected to Sicily but cut off from North Africa. The remainder of Europe was covered with an ice cap, and in retreating towards warmer regions the animals had been "trapped" in this dead-end. Being unable to reach the further shore, they degenerated for a large number of generations before becoming finally extinct. It should not be forgotten that there were elephants in North Africa in Roman times and lions in the Atlas mountains at the end of the last century.

For a long time it was believed that there was proof of the presence on the island of Neanderthal man, who lived about 100,000 years ago, since human teeth characteristic of prehistoric man were found in the grotto. Unfortunately, one day a dentist extracted a tooth from a local inhabitant and found it was exactly the same! The doubts which then arose were later confirmed by modern scientific methods of analysis.

Nonetheless, it was the grotto of Ghar Dalam which furnished the first irrefutable evidence of human presence. About 3800 BC shepherds, probably from Sicily, arrived; at all events, their pottery is very similar to that found at Stentinello near Syracuse. On the other hand, the decoration is very similar to that used for the pottery of Dalmatia and the eastern Mediterranean. It is believed that these first inhabitants were also fishers. Their first homes were the natural grottoes in which this chalky country abounds.

Relief

Seen from the air, the Maltese Archipelago looks like a continent which has sunk into or been invaded by the sea, owing to the size of the faults which are its main geological characteristics. The islands, emerging from the sea like blocks of stone on which it is difficult to distinguish the vast extent of arable land, essentially consist of chalky rocks. Practically the whole area is divided into small plots; these are the fields which have been laboriously made over the centuries by removing the rocks from a soil which had to provide the peasants with a living, cost what it might. The result is that the overall plan of the rural areas has certainly changed very little over the centuries. A few neglected fields have given way to stunted garrigue herbs such as thyme with its very spicy odour. But most fields are cultivated intensely, sometimes providing three crops a year. The chief crop is the potato.

Over the surface of the islands, worn smooth by erosion, there is practically no area which has never been cultivated.

The north of Malta consists of a series of faults which impart an aspect of a huge scenic railway to this part of the island. In the bottoms of the valleys thus formed crops grow well, whereas the summits are mercilessly arid. There are projects for retimbering them.

The coast

The first navigators called Malta the "island of harbours". Throughout its long history, its destiny has been bound up with its strategic situation in the Mediterranean and the shelter it could provide for boats of all kinds.

There are few places round the islands from which the watch towers built by the Knights of Malta to guard against attack cannot be seen. They were all built in more or less the same way (a single door, square shape and reinforced wall bases), were within sight of each other and could communicate by visual signals.

While the south-east coast is inhospitable, with its cliffs a hundred or more feet high overhanging the sea and making any approach to the shore a very dangerous business, the gentle slopes at the east and north-east provide wide indentations and sheltered bays. The Phoenicians made no mistake! A large number of the bays on this coast bear names partly consisting of the Semitic root "marsa", meaning harbour or refuge. Examples are Marsaxlokk, Marsaskala, Marsamxett and Marsalforn (on Gozo). The development of the coastal region was obviously carried on from these focal points, particularly as the land, sloping gently down towards the sea, was especially suitable for the building of dwellings when security problems did not compel the people to live in the interior.

The development of the islands for tourists merely accentuated this trend. Large hotels and holiday centres have risen up around the small sandy beaches some distance from Valetta. However, new town-planning regulations should keep this development under control.

Apart from a few creeks cut, as though with an axe, into cliffs at the feet of which the sea continues to dig relentlessly, the south coast is such as to discourage any human settlement depending partly on the sea for a living. Here the landscapes are grandiose and the grottoes are deep, and for those who are not afraid of sailing in dghajjes (Maltese boats) at the foot of the rocky walls reaching up to the sky, a visit to what is known as the "blue grotto" is an unforgettable experience. The stability of these vessels, which are sometimes very large, is amazing. They are painted in bright colours, one of which is always blue or green. On each side of the prow, there is the delicately drawn picture of an eye.

The Islands

While Malta and Gozo are the two largest islands, there is also a smaller one known as Comino (Kemmuna), from which its even smaller sister Cominotto (Kemmunett) was separated in comparatively recent times. The narrow strip of sea between them is known as the "Blue Lagoon" owing to the extraordinary turquoise colour of the sea bottom and the protection provided against swell.

In places the cliffs of Comino rise straight up from the sea and are so cleanly cut that they give the impression that weathering has taken place at a constant rate. Only a handful of people live here permanently. A certain amount of animation is provided by a hotel built there fairly recently; the island is less than a mile long.

The tiny island of Filfla facing the prehistoric temples of Mnajdra and Ħaġar Qim on the south coast is full of mystery and is the subject of many legends. It is very difficult to reach and has always been considered as bringing bad luck. It is the only land in the archipelago which is completely uninhabited.

MALTA
Area: 246 square kilometres
Length: 27 kilometres
Width: 14 kilometres
Length of coastline: 137 kilometres
GOZO
Area: 67 square kilometres
Length: 14 kilometres
Width: 7 kilometres
Length of coastline: 43 kilometres
Rainfall: only 220 mm per annum
Temperatures: Winter 13.7°C
Summer: 22.6°C
Total population: 320,000 (nearly as many living abroad)
Capital: Valletta.

Pwales Valley, au fond Manikata.

Pwales Valley; in the distance Manikata.

Pwales Valley, im Hintergrund Manikata.

Vénus préhistorique - Musée National.
Prehistoric Venus - National Museum.
Prähistorische Venus - Nationalmuseum.

Le voyageur qui fera escale à Malte pour les Chevaliers et leur histoire sera étonné d'y trouver des vestiges de constructions gigantesques. Ici, en effet, s'est épanouie pendant des millénaires une étonnante civilisation méditerranéenne.

Les légendes disent que l'archipel a été dans le lointain passé habité par des géants. On s'en douterait presque en passant sous le linteau de plusieurs tonnes du temple d'Ħaġar Qim ou en atteignant les autels de sacrifice de Mnajdra par les extraordinaires portes monolithiques en pierre. Il n'y aurait pour s'en convaincre qu'à mesurer les hauts murs de Ġgantija dont le seul nom est une évocation.

ARCHIPEL DES GEANTS

The traveller who disembarks at Malta in search of the Knights and their history will be astonished to find there vestiges of gigantic buildings. For a surprising Mediterranean civilisation blossomed here for many thousands of years.

Legend has it that the archipelago was once occupied by giants. One might have suspected this when passing under the lintel, weighing several tons, of the temple of Ħagar Qim or when arriving at the sacrificial altar of Mnajdra through the extraordinary monolithic stone-doors. To be convinced it would only be necessary to measure the high walls of Ggantija, whose name alone suggests their size.

ARCHIPELAGO OF GIANTS

The first inhabitants

SKORBA

A new type of population appears to have arrived from Sicily about 3600 BC. The first Maltese dwellings have been discovered at Skorba, on the outskirts of the village of Zebbiegħ. These are round huts all of which that remains today are the barely discernable stone footings; this certainly remained the typical house throughout the prehistoric period, apart from certain minor changes. For two hundred years the inhabitants made grey pottery (the grey Skorba period), and then began covering it with a coating of red (red Skorba).

ŻEBBUĠ

About thirty years ago a series of tombs, the oldest of the island, were discovered at Żebbuġ, not far from Mdina. The contents provided useful information regarding the transition from the neolithic age to that of copper and bronze (building of temples). Since scarcely any metal has been found on the islands, it is thought that the archipelago had a particular religious significance. Might it not have been a major centre of pilgrimage where the use of metal – which is practically non-existent inside the temples – was forbidden? The soil of Malta, meagre as it was, could scarcely have excited the envy of conquerors greedy for land for the agriculture which was coming into being.

Apart from pottery, the tombs of Żebbuġ also contain very stylized representations of human forms, including a stone stele of which famous modern sculptors would not be ashamed.

MĠARR

With the Mġarr period begins that of the temples (on the island of Malta). The re-positioning of the enormous blocks of stone forming the temples was facilitated and rendered more exact by the discovery, at different sites, of tiny scale models such as that shown opposite.

When the first research took place in 1925, it was thought that the crude aspect of the Mġarr pottery was due to degeneration and therefore representative of a more recent period; but as a result of datings by new methods of analysis carried out in 1953, the Mġarr period was situated at the time of the building of the temples. There are a number of temples, the largest of which belongs to the Ġgantija (Gozo) epoch.

Les premiers habitants

C'est un nouveau type de population qui serait arrivé vers 3600 avant J.-C. en provenance de Sicile. A Skorba, en bordure du village de Zebbiegħ, on a découvert les premières habitations maltaises. Ces huttes rondes dont seules subsistent les bases de pierres à peine discernables ont certainement été la forme courante des maisons durant toute l'époque préhistorique, avec quelque évolution sans grande importance. Pendant deux cents ans les habitants ont fabriqué de la poterie grise (période dite de grey Skorba) qu'ils ont recouvert ultérieurement d'un enduit – un engobe – de couleur rouge (red Skorba).

A Żebbuġ, non loin de Mdina, on a découvert il y a une trentaine d'années une série de tombes, les plus anciennes de l'île, dont le contenu a donné d'utiles renseignements sur le passage de l'époque strictement néolithique à celle du cuivre et du bronze (construction des temples). Le peu de métal jamais trouvé sur les îles a fait émettre l'hypothèse d'un caractère particulièrement religieux de l'archipel. N'aurait-il pas été un grand centre de pélerinage d'où l'usage du métal – qui s'est révélé quasiment absent à l'intérieur des temples – était banni? Le sol déjà ingrat de Malte, n'a pas dû exciter les convoitises de conquérants en quête de riches terres pour une agriculture en pleine naissance.

Les tombes de Żebbuġ, outre de la poterie originale, ont révélé des représentations de figures humaines très stylisées dont une stèle de pierre que n'aurait pas désavouée nos plus grands sculpteurs contemporains.

Avec la période de Mġarr (dans l'île de Malte) commence celle des temples. La remise en place des énormes blocs de pierre constituant les temples a été facilitée, notamment pour l'exactitude du "remontage", par la découverte sur différents sites de minuscules modèles réduits.

On crut, lors des premières recherches en 1925, que l'aspect grossier des poteries de Mġarr représentait une dégénérêscence, donc une époque plus tardive; mais des datations faites en 1953 grâce aux nouvelles méthodes d'analyse permirent au contraire de placer la période de Mġarr au début de la construction des temples. Plusieurs temples constituent l'ensemble. Le plus important d'entre eux appartient à l'époque de Ggantija (île de Gozo).

Modèle réduit de temple
Stèle de pierre de Żebbuġ
Ci-dessous: céramiques de Skorba

Scale model of temple
Stone stele at Żebbuġ
Below, Skorba ceramics

Kleines Modell eines Tempels
Steilsäule von Żebbuġ
Unten: Keramiken von Skorba

They say on Gozo that a woman of enormous size bore on her head the stones for the temples which stand along the northern coast of the island, while at the same time carrying and feeding her baby.

Two thousand years before Christ the Maltese built the first monuments both on Malta itself (at Ħaġar Qim and Mnajdra) and on Gozo (at Ġgantija). This latter gave its name to the entire period, but the others are just as gigantic and interesting.

The existence of the ruins of a huge building near the village of Xagħra has been known of for a long time. The megaliths are known as the "Giants' Towers".

There are two temples at Ġgantija surrounded by a protective wall, one corner of which, completely restored, is twenty feet high. What strikes the visitor at first in most of the Maltese temples is the long central corridor opening out on each side onto a number of apses opposite one another, while the end of the corridor itself consists of an opening which usually contains an altar. Looking at the plan of a temple, we are reminded of the more than generous shapes of the goddesses of fecundity.

It is thought that the entire building was covered with a roof (of wood?) and reproduced the appearance of a cave converted into a place of worship. To judge by the objects found in temples of this type, the worship of ancestors and the goddess of fecundity was also practised.

Traces of plaster have been discovered inside joints between stones and the walls may have been covered with some kind of rendering. The temple on the left is the older and bigger; it has four apses. A few spirals engraved on blocks can be faintly seen. The total area is 85 square metres, and the corridor is 27 metres long. the distance covered by the two main apses is 23 metres 50.

On raconte sur l'île de Gozo qu'une femme de grandeur gigantesque avait transporté sur sa tête les pierres des temples qui se trouvent sur la côte nord de l'île. En même temps, elle portait son bébé dans ses bras en le nourrissant.

Deux mille cinq cents ans avant Jésus Christ les Maltais érigeaient les premiers monuments de l'archipel tant à Malte même (Ħaġar Qim, Mnajdra) qu'à Gozo (Ġgantija). Ce dernier site a donné son nom à l'ensemble de la période mais les autres le valent autant en gigantisme qu'en intérêt.

On connaissait depuis longtemps, près du village de Xagħra, l'existence de ruines d'un bâtiment gigantesque. On appelait les grandes pierres les "Tours des Géants".

Il y a deux temples à Ġgiantija entourés par un mur d'enceinte dont l'un des angles entièrement restauré atteint six mètres de haut. Ce qui frappe en premier lieu dans la majorité des temples maltais est le passage central, long couloir qui donne de chaque côté sur plusieurs grands alvéoles - des absides - se faisant face, l'extrémité du couloir étant lui-même constitué par un alvéole abritant généralement un autel. Un temple, vu en plan, fait penser aux formes plus que généreuses des déesses de fécondité.

On pense que l'ensemble était recouvert d'un toit (de bois?) et était censé reconstituer l'aspect d'une caverne transformée en lieu de culte. D'après les objets qui ont été trouvés dans les temples de ce type on y aurait de même rendu le culte aux ancêtres et à la déesse de fécondité.

Des traces de plâtre ont été décelées à la jointure intérieure des pierres et auraient pu recouvrir les murs à la manière d'un crépi. Le temple de gauche, le plus grand est le plus ancien. Quelques spirales très effacées sont gravées sur des blocs. La surface totale est de 85 mètres carrés, la longueur du couloir atteint 27 mètres.

La distance correcte pour les deux principales est de 23 mètres 50.

Mnajdra

Les temples de Mnajdra.
The Mnajdra temples.
Die Tempel von Mnajdra.

If any proof is required that the Maltese were builders, you only have to visit some of the largest of the thirty or so prehistoric temples in the archipelago. Some of the restored walls of Ġgantija are twenty feet high, and blocks weighing several hundredweight must have been transported. Fairly sophisticated hoisting techniques must have been used. Professor Atkinson has calculated that a block weighing one ton, placed on wooden rollers on flat ground could be moved by two men using levers. For a slope of one in 11, seven more men would be required. For positioning the enormous stones forming pillars or door lintels, an earthen ramp was probably built, and the material was pushed up on rollers to the required position. Whatever the method used, the population at the time must have been sufficiently numerous to provide the necessary manpower.

Porte monolithique de Mnajdra.
Monolithic door at Mnajdra.
Monolithische Tür in Mnajdra.

Mnajdra

A few hundred yards below Ħaġar Qim, not for from Qrendi, are the three temples of Mnajdra, the smallest of which has only two apses but three thresholds. It would appear to be the oldest.

The one on the left has four apses facing one another two by two but containing a number of niches, some of which are decorated while others are at two levels, the upper one being supported by a central column. Monolithic doors lead to the "oracle chambers" situated behind the apses. The columns of the doors of the central aisle support lintels of impressive dimensions. The main portal is nearly ten feet high.

The central temple, which was the last to be built, includes an artificial terrace. The stone blocks of the inside walls are nearly all of the same dimensions and give the impression of being huge paving stones stood on edge; each weighs several hundredweight. The temple has two pairs of apses and is certainly the most regular in construction and choice of materials.

Situé à quelques centaines de mètres en bas de Ħaġar Qim, non loin de Qrendi, l'ensemble de Mnajdra montre trois temples dont un petit à deux alvéoles seulement, qui a la particularité d'avoir trois seuils. Il semble être le plus ancien.

Celui qui est situé à gauche présente quatre absides se faisant face deux par deux mais comportant tout un ensemble de niches, certaines décorées, d'autres à deux niveaux, le dernier étant supporté par un pilier central. Des portes d'un seul bloc mènent à des "chambres d'oracle" situées derrière les alvéoles. Les montants monolithiques des portes du passage central soutiennent des linteaux aux dimensions impressionnantes. Le portail d'entrée mesure près de trois mètres de hauteur.

Le temple central, construit en dernier, comporte une terrasse artificielle. Les blocs de pierre des murs intérieurs sont pratiquement tous de mêmes dimensions et l'on croirait de grandes dalles dressées, gigantesque jeu de construction où les éléments se pèsent par centaines de kilos. Composé de deux fois deux absides, c'est très certainement celui qui est le plus régulier dans la construction et le choix de ses matériaux.

Ħaġar Qim

The most complex and elaborate of the Ggantija epoch temples is built exclusively of limestone blocks. It would, in fact, be more correct to speak of a group of temples, an examination of which shows that there were profound upheavals in a lay-out which initially must have been very similar to other monuments of the same type. The impression is gained that neighbouring temples were made to communicate by eliminating contiguous apses or merely by piercing openings. A main central corridor thus formed allows of access to the various parts of the monument. There are also interior doors consisting of a single block of carved stone and classical markings on the walls.

One of the original features of Ħaġar Qim consists of a number of small altars of carved stone. One of these, now in the National Museum, represents the tree of life holding up a shallow bowl. It was damaged by tourists who carved their initials on it while it was still on the site.

Statues of "fat" women such as that shown opposite (height 18") have been found. All the heads have disappeared. They were separate from the bodies and were fixed in position by a hole in the neck. It is thought they may have been of wood, which would explain their disappearance.

An exhibit at the National Museum consists of a scale model of the facade of the temple as it is today.

Ħaġar Qim raises unending questions such is the complexity of altars, "oracle chambers", breaks in the architectural continuity and the re-use of these elements at different periods.

Le plus complexe, le plus élaboré des temples de l'époque de Ggantija est entièrement composé de pierres calcaires. Il serait même plus juste de parler d'un ensemble de temples dont l'examen fait apparaître de profonds bouleversements dans un plan qui aurait présenté dès le départ de profondes analogies avec les monuments de même type. On a l'impression qu'on a fait communiquer des temples voisins par suppression des absides qui étaient contiguës ou par simple percement des seuils. Un grand couloir central ainsi formé permet d'accéder aux différentes parties du monument. On retrouve également des portes intérieures d'un seul bloc de pierre sculpté, ainsi que le classique piquetage sur les parois.

L'une des originalités de Ħaġar Qim est la présence de petits autels de pierre sculptés. L'un d'entre eux, maintenant au Musée National représente l'arbre de vie soutenant un bol peu profond. Il a été endommagé par les multiples visiteurs qui y gravèrent leurs initiales alors qu'il était encore sur le site.

Des statuettes de femmes "obèses" comme celle que nous montrons ci-contre (hauteur 45 cm) ont été trouvées. Toutes les têtes ont disparu. Elles étaient séparées du corps; un trou à l'emplacement du cou permettait de les fixer. On pense qu'elles pouvaient être en bois ce qui expliquerait leur disparition.

Au Musée National est aussi exposé un modèle réduit montrant la façade du temple tel qu'il se présente actuellement.

Ħaġar Qim continue de poser des questions tant est complexe la multitude d'autels, de "chambres d'oracles", de ruptures dans la continuité architecturale, et la réutilisation des éléments à des époques différentes.

L'impressionnante façade et la grande entrée d'Ħaġar Qim.
The impressive facade and main entry to Ħaġar Qim.
Die eindrucksvolle Fassade und der Haupteingang von Ħaġar Qim.

Une vénus néolithique.
A neolithic Venus.
Eine neolithische Venus.

L'enfilade de seuils d'un temple tarxien.
The series of thresholds of a Tarxien templ
Schwellenreihen eines tarxischen Tempels.

Les Maltais étaient déjà des constructeurs, il n'est pour s'en convaincre que de visiter quelques uns parmi les plus importants de la trentaine de temples préhistoriques de l'archipel. Certains murs reconstitués de Ggiantija font 6 mètres de haut, des blocs de plusieurs centaines de kilos ont dû être transportés. Il a fallu disposer de techniques de levage assez élaborées. Le professeur Atkinson a calculé qu'un bloc d'une tonne posé sur des rouleaux de bois en terrain plat pouvait être transporté par deux hommes disposant de leviers. Pour une pente de 9° il fallait sept hommes supplémentaires. Pour la mise en place d'énormes pierres, constituant soit un linteau de porte soit un pilier, un plan incliné en terre était probablement construit et le matériau amené sur des rouleaux à l'emplacement prévu. Quoi qu'il en soit, la population devait être suffisamment nombreuse à l'époque pour fournir la main d'oeuvre nécessaire à ces constructions.

grand "bol".
great "bowl".
grosse "Tasse".

Tarxien

En 1914, un fermier étonné trouva dans des champs des blocs de pierre d'un volume inattendu. Grâce à cette découverte, le Docteur Zammitt mit au jour en 1915 les premières structures de l'admirable ensemble des temples Tarxiens. Les premières fouilles amenèrent presque immédiatement des résultats étonnants. En effet, durant des siècles la couche de terre qui recouvrait les ruines a protégé les sculptures de pierre et permis la conservation d'une importante quantité d'objets, tant dans la partie comprise dans les temples proprement dits que dans les sépultures.

Les temples tarxiens sont maintenant entourés d'immeubles d'habitation et font partie de la grande zone urbanisée qui ceinture La Valette.

Ici également un modèle réduit a permis de reconstituer la façade du temple. L'aspect général ne diffère guère de ce qu'on a pu voir jusqu'à présent: un couloir central joignant des absides se faisant face deux par deux. Le seuil franchi, on est par contre assez impressionné par le nombre de pierres gravées de spirales ou d'animaux formant des frises. Sur la droite, une statue géante de femme obèse habite les lieux.

Cette statue est coupée à la hauteur de la taille mais on a calculé que sa hauteur totale ne devait pas être inférieure à 2 mètres 75. Les originaux de toutes ces sculptures sont au Musée National en bon état de conservation.

Dans cette première partie se trouve sur la droite, un petit autel au soubassement décoré de spirales. Lors des fouilles, on y a découvert des ossements d'animaux, notamment de chèvre, ainsi qu'un couteau de sacrifice en silex. Les frises représentant des animaux montrent des moutons, des chèvres et des porcs.

Dans la deuxième série d'absides, un seuil sur la droite permet d'accéder à un autre temple à trois séries d'alvéoles. C'est l'un des derniers temples de cette importance. Il est daté à peu près comme le précédent de 2400 avant Jésus Christ.

Les gigantesques murs sont colorés par le feu. Au centre une grande coupe de pierre devait permettre de brûler des plantes aromatiques, plus loin, un gigantesque bol en céramique devait servir à différentes cuissons, mais on n'a pas encore pu déterminer son utilisation véritable.

Sur les blocs, on peut distinguer de grands animaux gravés, bœuf, truie et ses petits cochons.

La bonne conservation des temples tarxiens permet d'imaginer l'état des autres temples qui, au cours des âges ont subi les "visites" des conquérants successifs mais aussi la dégradation naturelle des éléments atmosphériques.

Tarxien

One day in 1914 a farmer was astounded to find huge blocks of stone in one of his fields. As a result, Dr Zammit brought to light, in 1915, the original structure of the admirable group of temples at Tarxien. The first excavations yielded amazing results almost immediately, for the layer of earth which had covered the ruins for centuries had protected the carvings on the stone and ensured the preservation of numerous objects both in the area containing the temples proper and the sepulchres.

The Tarxien temples are now surrounded by houses and form part of the suburbs of Valletta.

Here too it was possible to reconstitute the facade of the temple by means of a scale model. The general aspect differs little from others already discussed – a central aisle with apses facing each other two by two. However, once you are inside you will be impressed by the number of stones carved with spirals or animal shapes forming the frieze. On the right, there is a statue portraying a huge fat woman.

This statue is cut off at the waist, but it has been calculated that its total height cannot have been less than nine feet. The originals of all the sculptures are to be found in the National Museum in a good state of preservation.

In this first part there can be seen on the left a small altar the base of which is decorated with spirals. During the excavations, animal skeletons, including that of a goat, together with a flint sacrificial knife were found. The animals portrayed on the friezes are sheep, goats and pigs.

In the second series of apses, an opening on the right leads to another temple with three series of alveoles. It is one of the last temples of its size and, like the other one, dates back to 2400 BC.

The gigantic walls have been discoloured by fire. A large block of stone in the middle must have been used for burning aromatic plants; further on, there is a huge ceramic bowl which was possibly used for cooking, though its exact purpose has not been determined.

The blocks are covered with engravings of bulls and a sow with her piglets.

The good state of preservation of the Tarxien temples makes it possible to imagine others which, throughout the ages, were subjected to the depradations of successive conquerors and the natural erosion of the elements.

Hal Saflieni

Not far from the Tarxien temples, there is one of the most important prehistoric sites in Malta. The hypogeum of Hal Saflieni was discovered accidentally at the beginning of the century when reservoirs were being dug for new houses, and an entire system of subterranean cavities communicating with and sometimes superimposed on one another were found twenty feet below ground level.

Pottery taken from it makes it possible to date the hypogeum as originating from the Mġarr epoch and that of the first Tarxien temple; i.e. between 2900 and 3200 BC.

These pre-catacomb catacombs are carved out of the living rock. You get to them by a circular stairway in the basement of a small museum situated in Burials Street in the Pwala district. The chief caves are reached after a short descent. The original entrance is situated almost opposite what is known as the "Holy of Holies".

What first strikes the visitor is that some of the apses are almost completely covered with sculptures, as to some extent are the doors which have been restored, the walls and the well-preserved vaults near the surface. Here the lintels of the doors and there the framework of niches can be discerned. The most spectacular part, which is practically unique in the world, is the oval-shaped Holy of Holies with its semi-circular vaulted roof, entirely carved out of the rock . . . 4,500 years ago!

Other halls, however, contain no sculptures. A considerable part of the ceiling and walls is covered with designs of curves, spirals and circles linked coherently together. The red ochre colour has been very well preserved. On one of the walls the outline of a hand has been drawn in charcoal.

A bull nearly three feet high and four feet long engraved in the rock is, however, fairly difficult to distinguish.

On the floor of one of the decorated halls were found two terra cotta statuettes, one of which, the "sleeping woman", can be considered a prehistoric masterpiece.

The oracle chamber is also very peculiar. Most of the surface of the ceiling and walls is decorated with spirals of red ochre. A small niche carved in one of the walls gave this hall the name of the "Oracle Chamber", since, if you speak into this cavity in a fairly low voice, the sound becomes even lower, fills the entire hypogeum and seems to have no point of origin. This must certainly have produced a very strong impression on the people of the epoch. During excavations in this part of the hypogeum, human remains corresponding to nearly 6,000 skeletons were removed.

Non loin des temples tarxiens, se trouve l'un des plus importants sites préhistoriques de Malte. Situé aussi en pleine ville l'hypogée de Hal Saffieni a été découvert d'une manière fortuite au début du siècle lors du creusement de citernes pour les nouvelles habitations. Il s'agit d'un ensemble de cavités souterraines, à six mètres de la surface environ, reliées entre elles et se juxtaposant, ou se superposant parfois sur deux niveaux.

Les poteries qui en ont été retirées permettent de dater l'hypogée de l'époque de Mġarr et du premier temple tarxien, soit environ entre 2900 et 2300 avant J.-C.

Catacombe d'avant les catacombes, elle est entièrement creusée dans le roc. On y accède par un escalier en colimaçon au fond d'un petit musée situé rue de l'Hypogée, dans le quartier de Pawla. On aboutit à quelques mètres seulement des pièces principales. L'entrée primitive est située presque à l'opposé de ce qui a été appelé le "Saint des Saints".

Ce qui frappe en premier lieu est l'aspect entièrement sculpté de certains alvéoles, un peu comme une reconstitution des portes, des murs et des voûtes des temples bien conservés qui sont en surface. Ici, on voit la représentation des linteaux de portes, là, des encadrements de niches. Le plus spectaculaire, et pratiquement unique au monde, le Saint des Saints est de forme ovale avec une voûte semi-circulaire entièrement sculptée dans le roc . . . il y a 4500 ans de cela!

D'autres salles, au contraire, ne comportent aucune sculpture. Une importante partie du plafond et des parois est recouverte de dessins représentant des courbes, des spirales, des cercles, liés les uns aux autres de façon cohérente. La couleur de l'ocre rouge s'est très bien conservée. Sur l'un des murs on peut voir une trace de main faite au charbon de bois.

Il est par contre plus difficile de distinguer, gravé dans le roc, un grand boeuf qui fait près d'un mètre de haut sur un mètre vingt de large.

Sur le sol de l'une des salles décorées, on a trouvé deux statuettes de terre cuite, dont l'une, la "dame endormie" peut être considérée comme un chef-d'oeuvre de la préhistoire des îles maltaises.

La salle de l'Oracle est aussi très particulière, Une grande partie du plafond et des parois est décorée de spirales d'ocre rouge. Une petite niche pratiquée dans l'une des parois a fait donner à cette pièce le nom de "Salle de l'Oracle". En effet. si l'on parle dans cette cavité avec une voix assez grave, le son devient encore plus grave, emplit tout l'hypogée et semble n'avoir aucun point d'origine. Cela devait certainement produire une très forte impression sur les hommes et les femmes de cette époque. Lors des fouilles de cette partie de l'hypogée on enleva des ossements correspondant à près de 6000 squelettes humains.

Le " Saint des Saints ".
The "Holy of Holies".
Das Allerheiligste.

La chambre de l'oracle.
The oracle chamber.
Das Orakelzimmer.

Le " Saint des Saints "
The "Holy of Holies".
Das Allerheiligste.

Haches néolithiques
Neolithic axes.
Neolithische Axte.

Niche creusée dans le roc.
Niche cut into the rock.
In den Felsen gehauene Nische.

Les spirales d'ocre rouge.
Spirals of red ochre.
Ockerrote Spiralen.

Borg in-Nadur

The last prehistoric period was marked by the building of fortified villages, which may have been a sign of the insecurity of the islands.

The Borg in-Nadur site, dominating the bay of Marsaxlokk a few hundred yards from the grotto of Ghar Dalam, still retains some of the imposing protecting walls. The stones are far from being the huge blocks used for the building of the temples, and practically none of the latter appear to have been built during this epoch.

It seems that newcomers from southern Italy came to live in the islands about 1500 BC, and other villages such as that of Bahrija have been discovered.

It would appear that the deep ruts made by cart wheels in the rock, traces of which can be seen almost everywhere in the island (Borg in-Nadur, Ta' Cenc, etc.) also date from this epoch. The network of roads which probably connected the villages with one another is only partly visible, and no trace of it exists in the bottoms of the valleys or on ground subject to considerable erosion.

Borg in-Nadur, vestige d'un temple.

Borg in-Nadur, remains of a temple.

Borg in-Nadur, Tempelreste.

Les villages fortifiés

La dernière période de ces temps sans écriture est marquée par l'existence de villages fortifiés, preuves peut-être de l'insécurité qui devait exister dans les îles.

Dominant la baie de Marsaxlokk, à quelques centaines de mètres de la grotte de Ghar Dalam, le site de Borg in-Nadur présente des parties encore imposantes de murs d'enceinte. On est loin de retrouver les gigantesques blocs qui ont servi à la construction des temples. Ces derniers sont d'ailleurs quasiment absents à cette époque.

Il semble que de nouveaux arrivants, venus d'Italie du Sud, vers 1500 avant J.-C., aient alors habité les îles, où d'autres villages comme celui de Bahrija ont été découverts.

De cette époque dateraient les nombreuses traces de roues de charrettes (cart rut) qui ont creusé de profondes ornières dans le roc un peu partout dans l'île (Borg in-Nadur, Ta'Cenc, etc). Ce réseau de chemins joignait probablement les villages entre eux mais il n'est visible que par endroits, inconnu dans le fond des vallées et les parties du sol soumises à une forte érosion.

Région de Marfa.
Marfa region. ⟶
Das Gebiet von Marfa.

Borg in-Nadur, enceinte du village fortifié.
Borg in-Nadur, protective wall of fortified village.
Borg in-Nadur, Schutzmauer eines befestigten Dorfes.

The stone houses

Les maisons de pierres

A large number of stone houses, evidence of the more recent application of old techniques, are to be found in some parts of the islands (St Paul's Bay). The majority of these are former shepherds' huts situated in the midst of fields which are now neglected. Some of them are very old, while others date back little more than a century. The buildings are in the same style as those of Apulia in Italy and the Bories of Provence.

Seeing these shepherds' houses with their little stone cupolas and arches over the doors, it is difficult not to think of Agamemnon's tomb in Mycenae. True enough, there are not so many ways of building a house of stone in which each element helps to hold up the others.

It is difficult to fix an exact date for these buildings apart from their style, but it may be assumed that they existed more or less always. Such builders as the Maltese are have maintained throughout the centuries traditions which date back to the beginning of their appearance in the archipelago.

Application plus récente des techniques de constructions anciennes, de nombreuses maisons de pierres se trouvent en grand nombre dans certaines parties des îles (Baie de Saint Paul). Il s'agit pour la plupart d'anciennes habitations de bergers situées au milieu de champs maintenant abandonnés. Certaines sont anciennes, d'autres doivent dater d'un peu plus d'une centaine d'années. Ce sont des bâtiments du même style que ceux des Pouilles italiennes ou les Bories de Provence.

Comment ne pas penser, en voyant ces maisons de bergers, avec la petite coupole de pierre et le petit arc de décharge au dessus de la porte, au ''tombeau d'Agamemnon'' à Mycènes. On s'aperçoit facilement qu'il n'y a pas beaucoup de possibilités de construire une maison en pierre où chaque élément se trouve incorporé l'un dans l'autre.

Il est difficile de dater exactement ces constructions, sinon par leur style, mais on peut penser qu'elles ont toujours plus ou moins existé. Les bâtisseurs que sont les Maltais ont gardé tout au long des siècles des traditions qui prennent naissance à l'aube de leur apparition dans l'archipel.

LES PEUPLES
VENUS DE LA MER

MILLE ANS AVANT JÉSUS CHRIST DES COMMERÇANTS NAVIGATEURS VENUS DE L'EST BOULEVERSÈRENT LA CIVILISATION DES BATISSEURS DE TEMPLES.
AVEC EUX ILS APPORTAIENT L'ÉCRITURE.
MALTE ENTRAIT DANS L'HISTOIRE...

THE PEOPLE
COMING FROM THE SEA

A THOUSAND YEARS BEFORE CHRIST MERCHANT SAILORS FROM THE EAST OVERTHREW THE CIVILISATION OF THE TEMPLE BUILDERS. WITH THEM THEY BROUGHT THE ART OF WRITING.
MALTA WAS ENTERING HISTORY...

Vestige de temples néolithiques à Birzebbuga

Remains of neolithic temples at Birżebbuga　　　*Neolitische Tempelreste in Birżebbuġa*

Les Phéniciens

Avec l'arrivée des Phéniciens, Malte entre dans l'histoire. Ceux-ci abordèrent les îles à la fin de l'époque des villages fortifiés.

A partir du 10 ème siècle, ces hardis navigateurs commencèrent à parcourir la Méditerranée. Ils établirent des relais sur la route de l'Espagne d'où était rapporté le précieux cuivre. Malte et ses ports bien protégés étaient pour eux une excellente escale.

Il ne reste pas de vestiges importants de la présence phénicienne. C'est un peu normal, si l'on songe que seuls les ports intéressaient ces lointains navigateurs. L'importance stratégique de l'île croissant d'une façon continuelle, les occupants successifs n'avaient de premier souci que d'agrandir, donc de transformer, les constructions antérieures.

Les noms de Gozo et de Malte proviendraient du phénicien Gaulo (bateau) et Mala (port, refuge). A défaut de vestiges architecturaux, on a trouvé des tombes contenant des poteries et divers objets de cette période.

Le port principal établi par les phéniciens, Birgu, est à l'origine du Borgo du Moyen Age qui devint Vittoriosa, en face de La Valette. On y a trouvé deux cippes (petites bornes funéraires) dédiées au dieu Moloch, écrites en grec et phénicien. C'est grâce à ces inscriptions que cette dernière langue a pu être traduite. Lors de la querelle linguistique entre les deux guerres – les Italiens affirmant l'italianité de Malte – l'origine sémitique de la langue maltaise fut mise en avant par les Anglais.

Après une période pendant laquelle il y eut, semble-t-il, une influence grecque, les Carthaginois prirent naturellement le relais des Phéniciens.

Quelques inscriptions sont restées de l'époque carthaginoise, ainsi qu'un sarcophage d'influence manifestement égyptienne que l'on peut voir au Musée National.

Il faut croire que les Maltais ne goûtaient guère la présence de ces occupants puisqu'ils aidèrent activement le Consul Tibérius Sempronius à prendre possession de l'île en 218 avant J.-C. qui fut au centre des guerres puniques. Au cours de ces périodes troublées, Carthaginois et Romains s'étaient disputés à plusieurs reprises ce territoire. Ce dernier servit par la suite aux légions romaines de point de départ pour l'expédition de Scipion en Afrique et la destruction définitive de l'ennemi héréditaire en 146 avant J.-C.

Port de Birżebbuġa.

Birżebbuġa harbour.

Der Hafen von Birżebbuga.

The Phoenicians

Malta steps into history with the arrival of the Phoenicians, who landed in the islands towards the end of the fortified village epoch.

From the tenth century BC onwards these courageous navigators began to sweep through the Mediterranean. They established trading stations on the way to Spain, from which the precious copper was obtained. Malta, with its well-protected harbours, provided an excellent staging point.

Very few traces of the presence of the Phoenicians remain. This is not surprising when we consider that these travellers from afar were interested only in the harbours. And since the strategic importance of the island increased as time passed, successive occupants were chiefly concerned to enlarge, and therefore transform, the former installations.

The names Gozo and Malta are derived from the Phoenician Gaolo (boat) and Mala (harbour or refuge). In the absence of architectural remains, tombs containing pottery and other objects from this period remain as evidence.

The Phoenicians' chief port, Birgu, was at the origin of the mediaeval Borgo which later became Vittoriosa, opposite Valetta. Two small *cippi* (sepulchral monuments) inscribed to the god Moloch in Greek and Phoenician have been found there, and it was thanks to the inscriptions that it was possible to translate the latter. During the linguistic disputes of the period between the wars, when the Italians claimed that Malta was Italian, the Semitic origin of the Maltese language was advanced by the English.

After a period during which, it appears, the islands came under Greek influence, the Carthaginians naturally took over from the Phoenicians.

A few inscriptions remain from the Carthaginian epoch; there is also a sarcophagus of obviously Egyptian style in the National Museum.

It can only be assumed that the Maltese did not much appreciate the presence of these occupants since they actively assisted the Consul Tiberius Sempronius in taking possession of the island, which was at the centre of the Punic Wars, in 218 BC. During this troubled period, the Carthaginians and Romans disputed the territory on several occasions. The island was subsequently used by the Roman legions as a base for Scipio's expedition to Africa and the final destruction of the hereditary enemy in 146 BC.

Cippe avec inscription gréco-phénicienne, Musée National.

Cippus with Graeco-Phoenician inscription, National Museum.

Halbsäule mit griechisch-phönizischer Inschrift, Nationalmuseum.

Un Bateau phénicien, d'après gravure.

Phoenician boat, after an engraving.

Phönizisches Schiff, nach einem Kupferstich.

Poterie punique, Musée National.
Punic pottery, National Museum.
Punische Töpferwaren.

Sarcophage d'influence égyptienne, Musee National.
Sarcophagus showing Egyptian influence, National Museum.
Von der ägyptischen Kunst beeinflusster Sarkophag, National museum.

Ulysses and the Greeks

Ulysse et les Grecs

"Ulysses . . . lay in an island tortured by sickness; the nymph Calypso, in her manor, kept him there by force. He could not return to the land of his fathers, for he had neither the men nor the boats to row over the back of the seas . . ."

The Maltese say that Calypso's island was Gozo, but there are many other Mediterranean islands which claim this honour.

On the north coast of Gozo, a fault in the cliffs dominating the bay of Ramla is supposed to be the grotto where Ulysses waited seven years with the goddess before the gods ordered her to allow him to continue his voyage.

Although there is no trace of the presence of the hero of the Odyssey on the island, the presence of the Greeks in the archipelago is fully attested.

According to one version, the name Malta is derived from the Greek meli (honey) or melta (bee), but there are only a few words of Greek origin in the Maltese language. During the sixth century BC the Greeks competed with the Carthaginians for the possession of colonies, including southern Italy and Sicily. It would not appear that their presence in the Maltese islands was coloured by any form of political domination. Their coexistence with the Phoenicians was peaceful.

Greek coins and pottery have been discovered, together with the famous Graeco-Phoenician *cippi*.

"Ulysse . . . gît dans une île, où les maux le torturent, là-bas, en son manoir, la nymphe Calypso, de force le retient, il ne peut revenir au pays de ses pères, n'ayant ni les vaisseaux à rames ni les hommes pour voguer sur le dos de la plaine marine . . ."

Les Maltais appellent Gozo l'île de Calypso. Mais nombreuses sont les îles méditerranéennes qui revendiquent cet honneur.

Sur la côte nord de Gozo, une anfractuosité de rochers dominant la baie de Ramla est montrée comme étant la grotte dans laquelle Ulysse attendit sept ans auprès de la déesse que les dieux ordonnent à celle-ci de le laisser continuer sa route.

Si le passage du héros de l'Odyssée n'est pas démontré, des vestiges attestent dans l'archipel de la présence grecque.

Selon une autre version, le nom de Malte viendrait du grec meli (miel) ou de mélita (abeille), mais les mots d'origine grecque sont rares dans la langue maltaise. Au 6 ème siècle avant J.-C. les grecs, en concurrence avec les Carthaginois, possédaient des colonies dont l'Italie du Sud et la Sicile. Il ne semble pas que leur présence dans les îles maltaises ait été marquée par une domination politique. La coexistence avec les Phéniciens a été surtout pacifique.

On a retrouvé des monnaies grecques, de la céramique et les célèbres cippes gréco-phéniciens.

The Romans

For services rendered to Rome in her struggle against Carthage, the Maltese were rewarded by being considered "allies of the Roman people". So true is it that happy people have no history, that during the centuries of the Pax Romana, Malta was little renowned for feats of arms or political events.

Roman legislation was introduced, and Malta and Gozo became two municipia.

Cicero, in his famous oration against Verrus, the propraetor of Sicily, who had filched the wealth of the Maltese temples just as he had in Sicily, tells us about the life of the Maltese.

Of the many buildings of the period (theatres and baths) few remain in a good state of preservation. Among the ruins of particular interest, it is worth mentioning the Roman villa unearthed at Rabat, the catacombs and the public baths at Għajn Tuffieħa. The temple of Juno, where ivory tusks were placed by sailors as votive offerings, was built in Tas Silġ Marsaxlokk.

Above the remains of the Roman house at Rabat, was built a small museum containing mosaics, glassware, pottery and other objects of the Punic and Arab epoch. In the immediate neighbourhood is a large quantity of tombs containing what is known as funerary furniture.

Some mosaics such as that found under the impluvium and representing birds, possibly peacocks, at the edge of a pool are very well preserved. Another smaller one, very delicately worked, shows the figures of a man and a woman; unfortunately, part of it is damaged, rendering identification difficult. Suggestions have been made that they are Omphale and Hercules or Samson and Delilah, though it is by no means certain that they do not represent another famous couple from classical mythology.

At the entrance to the museum there is a large olive press. Behind the building excavations have revealed fragments of ceramics and an entire system for supplying water to the storage tanks.

Għajn Tuffieħa, the Apple Tree Spring, was used from the time of the prehistoric temples. Its present yield is more than 15,000 litres per hour. Here the Romans set up a number of baths – the caldarium for sweating (the heating was from the floor which was supported by pillars between which the hot air passed) and the frigidarium for cold baths. Most of the rooms in these bath-houses were covered in mosaics, which are fairly well preserved. The whole system was completed by a swimming pool and communal latrines, as was usual at the time.

Les Romains

Les services que les Maltais rendirent aux Romains, en leur facilitant la lutte contre Carthage, leur valurent d'être considérés comme "alliés du peuple romain". S'il est vrai que les peuples heureux n'ont pas d'histoire, la paix romaine pendant plusieurs centaines d'années rendit Malte peu prolifique en faits d'armes ou événements politiques.

Les lois romaines y furent introduites. Malte et Gozo formèrent deux municipes.

La vie des Maltais nous est relatée dans le fameux discours de Cicéron contre le propréteur de Sicile Verrès qui, de même qu'en Sicile, avait fait main basse sur les richesses des temples de Malte.

Des nombreux monuments construits à cette époque (théâtres et bains), peu ont survécu dans un état acceptable. Parmi les vestiges intéressants on peut signaler la ville romaine mise au jour à Rabat, les catacombes et les bains publics de Għajn Tuffieħa.
Le temple de Junon, où de gigantesques dents d'ivoire étaient déposées par les marins en guise d'ex-voto, était édifié à Tas-Silg Marsaxlokk.

La maison romaine de Rabat est aménagée en petit musée contenant des mosaïques, des verres, des poteries et d'autres objets d'époque punique ou arabe. En effet, on a découvert dans les environs immédiats une grande quantité de tombes contenant ce que l'on appelle du mobilier funéraire.

Certaines mosaïques sont très bien conservées comme celle qui se trouvait sous l'impluvium et qui représente deux oiseaux, peut-être des paons, au bord d'une vasque. Une autre, plus petite et très fine de travail, montre deux personnages, une femme et un homme, mais dont une partie est abîmée en sorte que l'identification en est difficile. On a suggéré Omphale et Hercule ou Samson et Dalila mais sans être bien certain qu'il ne s'agit pas d'un autre couple célèbre de la mythologie antique.

On peut voir à l'entrée du musée un ancien pressoir à olives. Derrière le musée, une partie du champ de fouilles laisse entrevoir des fragments de céramiques et tout un système d'adduction d'eau et de stockage par citernes.

Għajn Tuffieħa, la Source du Pommier, a été utilisée depuis la période des temples préhistoriques. Son débit actuel est supérieur 15.000 litres à l'heure. Les Romains y ont installé tout un ensemble de bains: le caldarium pour la sudation (le chauffage se faisait par le sol supporté par des piliers entre lesquels passait de l'air chaud) et le frigidarium pour le bain froid. La plupart des pièces de ces bains comportaient des mosaïques assez bien conservées. Une piscine et des latrines collectives, comme il était d'usage à cette époque, complétaient l'ensemble.

Mosaïque de bains romains; Għajn Tuffieħa (le frigidariu

Mosaic of Roman baths; Għajn Tuffieħa (frigidarium).

Mosaik römischer Bäder, Għajn Tuffieħa (Frigidarium).

Latrines, Għajn Tuffieħa.
Latrines, Għajn Tuffieħa.
Latrinen, Għajn Tuffieħa.

←

Villa romaine, Rabat.
Roman villa, Rabat.
Römische Villa, Rabat.

Petit masque de terre cuite, Rabat.
Small terra cotta mask, Rabat.
Kleine Terrakotta-Maske, Rabat.

Mosaïque de la villa romaine, Rabat.
Mosaic of Roman villa, Rabat.
Mosaik einer römischen Villa, Rabat.

St Paul

Les catacombes de Saint Paul.

St Paul's catacombs.

Die Katakomben von St. Paul.

La Baie de Saint Paul.

Saint Paul's Bay.

Die Bucht von Saint Paul.

⟶

"And when they were escaped, then they knew that the island was called Melita.

"The barbarous people shewed us no little kindness; for they kindled a fire, and received us everyone, because of the present rain, and because of the cold . . .

"In the same quarters were possessions of the chief man of the island, whose name was Publius; who received us and lodged us three days courteously.

"And it came to pass that the father of Publius lay sick of a fever and of a bloody flux: to whom Paul entered in, and prayed, and laid his hands on him, and healed him . . ."

Paul, who had been imprisoned in Caesarea, had appealed to Rome and, during his voyage to the Emperor, was shipwrecked in the bay which now bears his name. He was accompanied by Saint Luke and a number of other Christians. From this time, about AD 60, dates the profound Christian tradition of the island.

A vast number of catacombs have been dug in the chalky subsoil of the island. Most of them date back to the Roman period. The best known group are Saint Paul's catacombs at Rabat near Mdina. They have been restored for visits by tourists. Next to what is known as the chapel, there is a large hall which seems to be at the centre of the catacombs. Two round tables, carved out of the rock and slightly raised, were used for funeral feasts.

"Une fois sauvés, nous apprîmes que l'île s'appelait Malte. Les indigènes nous traitèrent avec une humanité peu banale. Ils nous accueillirent tous auprès d'un grand feu qu'ils avaient allumé à cause de la pluie qui était survenue et du froid . . ." "Il y avait à proximité de cet endroit un domaine appartenant au Premier de l'île nommé Publius. Celui-ci nous reçut et nous hébergea complaisamment pendant trois jours. Justement, le père de Publius, en proie aux fièvres et à la dysenterie, était alité. Paul alla le voir, pria, lui imposa les mains et le guérit . . ."

Paul qui avait été emprisonné à Césarée en avait appelé à Rome et, au cours du voyage qui devait le mener devant l'empereur avait fait naufrage dans la baie qui actuellement porte son nom. Il était accompagné par Saint Luc et d'autres chrétiens. Depuis cette époque, environ en l'an 60 de notre ère, date la profonde tradition chrétienne de l'île.

De multiples catacombes ont été creusées dans le sous-sol calcaire de l'île. Elles se rattachent pour la plupart à l'époque romaine. Le groupe le plus souvent cité est celui des Catacombes de Saint Paul à Rabat près de Mdina. Elles sont aménagées pour la visite. On peut y voir, à côté de ce que l'on a appelé "la chapelle", une grande pièce qui paraît être au centre de ces catacombes. Deux tables rondes, sculptées dans le roc, et légèrement surélevées étaient utilisées pour les agapes, festins de funérailles et dernier repas avec la mort.

Les Arabes

Un prince arabe, voulant faire plaisir à sa bien-aimée fit greffer un grenadier sur un oranger. Le résultat fut une orange sanguine et très juteuse que l'on a fort justement appelée "maltaise". C'est du moins ce que la légende affirme. Et s'il faut chercher longtemps pour trouver des champs d'orangers à Malte, car ceux-ci poussent de préférence dans les cours des maisons ou les endroits qui peuvent être facilement irrigués, n'oublions par que les "Maltaises" proviennent dans leur grande majorité de la Tunisie voisine.

Car c'est de Tunisie que vinrent les arabes en 869 quand Ahmed, fils de l'émir Aghlabide de Tunisie et de Tripolitaine, essaya de prendre pied dans l'archipel. La garnison byzantine, ayant réussi à encercler les envahisseurs, repoussa ces derniers vers la mer. Le répit fut très court. Les Byzantins, isolés et sans secours, ne purent résister aux troupes de renfort envoyées aux Arabes par le gouverneur de Sicile Mohamed Ibn Hafagab. Le 29 août 870, l'évêque de Malte fut déporté, et durant toute la domination arabe aucun évêque ne fut nommé.

Il semble que la résistance aux envahisseurs ait surtout été le fait des occupants grecs d'alors. De nombreux habitants se convertirent à l'Islam tandis que d'autres étaient soit disparus dans les combats soit emmenés captifs. De nombreux barbares s'établirent dans l'île.

On sait peu de chose de l'importance de la population de l'île à cette époque, combien il y avait d'habitants au départ des byzantins, combien restèrent et quel nombre de musulmans s'installèrent à Gozo et à Malte. On ne sait pas non plus si la totalité de la population se convertit à l'Islam. Il semble toutefois qu'un noyau important de chrétiens ait continué à vivre dans les îles.

L'archipel fut profondément bouleversé par ce renversement politique qui entraîna un profond changement culturel et économique.

Les arabes introduisirent la culture du coton, qui fut l'une des principales productions pendant plusieurs siècles celle du citronnier et surtout les techniques d'irrigation avec le système de la noria pour le puisage de l'eau. L'utilisation d'un animal pour cette tâche qui occupait habituellement les humains pour un rendement moindre permit d'augmenter les productions.

Les remparts de Mdina.
Ramparts at Mdina.
Die Wälle von Mdina.

Mais c'est au niveau de la langue que l'empreinte fut la plus forte. Et c'est l'un des grands étonnements que l'on a encore de nos jours en lisant une carte et tous les noms de lieux en particulier.

Un chroniqueur arabe parle de Malte en ces termes: "Mahlita riche en toute chose, bonne et une bénédiction de Dieu... bien peuplée, possédant villes et villages, arbres et fruits".

Cette présence de plus de deux cents ans n'a pas laissé de traces encore visibles. Il faut cependant imaginer que les monuments ont été remplacés par d'autres (lieux du culte notamment). Ainsi à Mdina, l'une des rues étroites s'appelle rue de la Mosquée. Cette ville qui durant l'époque romaine était la capitale, fut entourée de fortifications sur une circonférence plus réduite. Elle a d'ailleurs gardé son nom arabe de "médina". Elle continue à remplir son rôle de ville principale. Les murs d'enceinte que l'on peut voir actuellement sont des reconstructions plus récentes (Normands, Chevaliers de Malte) mais dont les assises sont arabes. C'est également de l'époque arabe que daterait l'installation d'une forteresse à l'emplacement de l'actuel fort Saint Ange.

Quelques poteries, de style berbère, et des pièces de monnaie ont été retrouvées.

Les fouilles de la ville romaine de Rabat ont donné des pierres tombales musulmanes car un cimetiere avait été installé à la porte de la ville. Cela permet de penser que lors de la construction de la cité arabe, la population devait être moins élevée qu'à l'époque romaine.

Le plus émouvant est certainement la découverte à Victoria d'une grande pierre tombale en marbre, recouverte de caractères arabes de style çoufique. Elle avait été utilisée comme matériau de construction. Elle était destinée à la tombe d'une petite fille musulmane morte au 12ème siècle à l'âge de 12 ans.

Il y eut une tentative de reprise de l'île par les Byzantins au cours du XIème siècle. Les musulmans se voyant perdus proposèrent aux esclaves chrétiens de les affranchir et de leur donner des terres s'ils les aidaient à résister aux Byzantins, ce qui fut fait avec succès.

C'est pendant cette période que Malte commença à devenir, pour de très nombreux siècles, un des principaux centres méditerranéens de la piraterie. De ces expéditions étaient ramenées, outre des marchandises, de nombreux captifs qui étaient par la suite utilisés soit sur les galères soit comme serviteurs de notables ou plus simplement comme travailleurs au service des administrations.

The Arabs

An Arab prince who wanted to please his beloved grafted a pomegranate tree on to an orange tree. The result was a very juicy blood orange rightly known as the "Maltese". At least, so the legend says. But while you would have to look a long time to find an orange orchard in Malta (since the trees grow best in the gardens of houses where they can be easily watered), it should not be forgotten that most "Maltese" oranges do in fact come from neighbouring Tunisia.

And it was from Tunisia that the Arabs came in 869, when Ahmed, son of Aglabide, Emir of Tunisia and Tripolitania, attempted to occupy the islands. The Byzantine garrison, however, encircled the invaders and threw them back into the sea. But the respite was a short one. The Byzantines, isolated and cut off from help, were unable to withstand the reinforcements sent by Mohamed Ibn Hafagab, the Arab governor of Sicily. On 29 August 870, the Bishop of Malta was deported, and no further bishop was appointed throughout the Arab occupation.

It would appear that resistance to the invaders was mainly provided by the Greek occupants. Numerous inhabitants were converted to Islam, while others either disappeared in the fighting or were taken away as prisoners. Numerous Berbers took up residence in the island.

Little is known concerning the population of the islands at this period, how many inhabitants there were when the Byzantines left or how many Muslims installed themselves in Gozo and Malta. Nor is it known whether the entire population was converted to Islam, though it would appear that a considerable number of Christians went on living there.

The archipelago was thrown into utter confusion by this political upheaval which involved a profound cultural and economic change.

The Arabs introduced the cultivation of cotton, which was one of the main crops for several centuries, and of lemons; they also introduced irrigation techniques, using norias to pump the water. There were driven by animals in place of the human beings formerly employed, thus increasing production.

But it was upon the language that the Arabs had the greatest impact, as can be judged today by looking at the place names on a map of the islands.

An Arab chronicler spoke of Malta in the following terms: "Malta rich in everything good . . . a blessing from God . . . well populated, with towns and villages, trees and fruit."

Although the Arabs were present for more than two centuries, very little visible trace of their stay remains. However, it may be assumed that their buildings were replaced by others (particularly in the case of places of worship). Thus, one of the narrow roads in Mdina is called Mosque Street. This town, which was the capital during the Roman period, was surrounded by fortifications on a reduced perimeter. In any case, its name is derived from the Arabic "medina". The protective walls which can be seen nowadays are of more recent date (Norman and Knights of Malta) but the foundations are Arab. The building

of a fortress where the present Fort St Angelo stands would also appear to date from the Arab epoch.

Vestiges include a few pieces of Berber-style pottery and some coins.

The excavations of the Roman town of Rabat produced Muslim tombstones, for a cemetery had been laid out at the gates of the town. It may be deduced from this that, when the Arab city was built, the population was much less than during the Roman epoch.

The most touching discovery was certainly that of a large marble tombstone at Victoria, covered with Arabic Cufic-style letters, which had been used as part of a building. It was intended for the tomb of a little Muslim girl who died in the twelfth century at the age of twelve.

During the eleventh century, the Byzantines attempted to retake the island. The Muslims, who thought they had lost, promised to free their Christian slaves and give them land if they would help them to resist the Byzantines, which they did successfully.

It was during this period that Malta began to be one of the chief Mediterranean pirate lairs, which it remained for many centuries. In addition to seizing goods, the pirates captured slaves who were used either to row the galleys of the notables or as workers in government service.

The Jewish Community   La communauté juive

One hundred and fifty years after the Arab forces left, a census carried out in Malta revealed that there were still more Muslims than Christians. There were 771 families practising the religion of the Prophet as against 250 families following the Christian religion – that of the new conquerors – the Normans. There were also thirty-three Jewish families.

At the entrance to the Rabat Museum can be seen a large tombstone engraved with Hebrew characters. St Paul's catacombs contain a number of chambers, sometimes independent of one another, on the walls of which seven-branched candlesticks are engraved. The community was expelled in 1492 by the Inquisition.

A gate in the ramparts of the fortified city of Valetta, known as the "Jews' Sally Porte", gives directly onto the cliffs.

Cent cinquante ans après le départ des occupants arabes, un recensement effectué à Malte montrait qu'il y avait encore plus de Musulmans que de Chrétiens. On dénombrait en effet sept cent soixante et onze familles pratiquant la religion du prophète contre deux cent cinquante familles le Christianisme, religion des Normands, les nouveaux conquérants. On notait en outre la présence de trente trois familles juives.

A l'entrée du musée de Rabat on peut voir une grande pierre tombale gravée de lettres hébraïques. Les catacombes de Saint Paul comportent un certain nombre d'alvéoles, parfois indépendants les uns des autres, sur le mur desquels on peut voir gravés des chandeliers à sept branches. La communauté fut expulsée en 1492.

Une porte, dite "porte de sortie des Juifs," percée dans le rempart de la ville fortifiée de La Valette donne directement sur les rochers du bord de mer.

Pierre tombale avec inscription hébraïque, Rabat.

Tombstone with Hebrew inscription, Rabat.

Grabstein mit hebräischer Inschrift, Rabat.

Danse traditionn...

Traditional danc...

Traditioneller Ta...

The Maltese Language

La langue maltaise

The lengthy controversy over the origin of the Maltese Language is still not finished, and those in favour of the "Phoenician hypothesis" oppose the partisans of the "Arabic theory".

The former point out that both the Maltese and their language are distantly related to the Phoenician sailors. For example, the adjective "barbarous" applied to the Maltese by Saint Luke in the narration of his shipwreck with St Paul shows that they spoke neither Latin nor Greek, but a Semitic tongue, at the time. The other faction retorts that "barbarous" also meant rude and uneducated and that words of Semitic origin were introduced only at the time of the Arab conquest a few centuries later.

This discussion which, after all, is purely scientific, became a first-class linguistic battle between the English and the Italians before the last war, with vested interests on each side, since the English wanted the Phoenician hypothesis to triumph, thus cutting the ground from under the feet of Mussolini, who was intent on the annexation (at least culturally) of a territory so close to Sicily and of such strategic value.

L'origine de la langue maltaise a été le sujet d'une longue controverse qui n'est pas encore close, les partisans de la "thèse phénicienne" s'opposant aux tenants de la "thèse arabe".

Les premiers font valoir que les maltais ainsi que leur langue descendent des marins phéniciens. Par exemple, la notion de "barbare" appliquée aux Maltais par Saint Luc dans la relation de son naufrage avec Saint Paul démontre que ceux-ci ne parlaient à l'époque ni grec ni latin, et par conséquent une langue sémitique. Les opposants rétorquent que "barbare" voulait aussi dire frustre ou inculte, les mots d'origine sémitique n'auraient été introduits que par la conquête arabe, quelques siècles plus tard.

Cette discussion somme toute scientifique devint entre les deux guerres une querelle linguistique de premier plan entre les Anglais et les Italiens qui avaient chacun des intérêts contradictoires à voir triompher l'une et l'autre thèse. En effet, les Anglais avaient intérêt à voir reconnue la thèse phénicienne qui enlevait à l'Italie de Mussolini des arguments tendant à annexer, au moins culturellement, un territoire si proche de la Sicile et si utile stratégiquement.

enêtre époque normande, Mdina.
Vindow from Norman epoch, Mdina.
enster der normannischen Epoche, Mdina.

Maison "normande", Mdina.
"Norman" house, Mdina.
"Normannisches" Haus, Mdina.

The Normans

Les Normands

In May 1061 Roger the Norman, who was the son of Tancrede de Hauteville, taking advantage of the weakness of the Muslim Empire, seized the island by trickery. Once again, the aim was to protect shipping in the Mediterranean on its way to the Holy Land. The Normans made a diversionary landing in St Paul's Bay, while other troops took the Arabs in the rear. Mdina was easily taken, and a few months later Roger extended his influence over the entire island.

The story goes that, during the battle for the possession of Malta, Roger tore off part of his scarlet banner and made the future flag of Malta from it.

He recognised local institutions and endowed the island with a large measure of independence. The church assumed considerable influence. A cathedral was built at Mdina, the capital, this was destroyed by an earthquake in 1693.

During the Crusades, the island acted as a staging point on the way to the Holy Land.

After a short period under the domination of Charles of Anjou, the island fell to Peter I of Aragon (1282), and the archipelago was annexed by the kingdom of Spain.

Until the arrival of the Knights in 1530, the Maltese archipelago had to defend itself against the Saracens and pirates attracted by the economic development of the islands and by numerous trading vessels, mostly Italian, which called there.

En Mai 1061 Roger le Normand, fils de Tancrède de Hauteville, profitant de la faiblesse de l'empire Musulman, s'empara de l'île par ruse. Une fois de plus, le but était de protéger les navires en Méditerranée, qui se dirigeaient vers la Terre Sainte. Les Normands débarquèrent par surprise dans la baie St Paul, pendant que les autres troupes attaquaient les Arabes par l'arrière. Mdina fut prise facilement, et quelques mois plus tard Roger étendit son influence sur l'île entière.

Selon l'histoire de la conquête de Malte, Roger déchira un morceau de son étendard écarlate pendant le combat et en fit le futur drapeau de Malte.

Il reconnut des institutions locales et donna beaucoup d'indépendance à l'île.

L'église eut une influence considérable. Une cathédrale fut construite à Mdina, la capitale, elle, fut détruite par un tremblement de terre en 1693.

Pendant les croisades, l'île servait de relais pour aller en Terre Sainte.

Pour une courte période, l'île fut la possession de Charles d'Anjou, puis appartint à Pierre 1er d'Aragon (1282) et l'archipel fut annexé par le royaume d'Espagne.

Jusqu'à l'arrivée des chevaliers en 1530, l'archipel maltais devait se défendre lui-même contre les Sarrazins et les pirates, attirés par le développement économique des îles et par les nombreux vaisseaux-marchands, la plupart italiens, qui y faisaient escale.

Les Maltais au Moyen Age

Labourage avec charrue traditionnelle.

Ploughing with traditional plough.

Ackerbestellung mit dem traditionellen

Composée surtout de marins, la population cultivait le blé, le coton et le cumin qu'ils exportaient.

Dans les villes, les artisans étaient groupés en corporations: maçons, charpentiers, cordiers, toiliers, car, outre les constructions dont l'île commençait à se couvrir, les ports étaient de plus en plus utilisés par les bateaux de la chrétienté qui pouvaient y faire relâche soit pour commercer soit pour y faire des réparations.

Une des productions artisanales qui fait encore la renommée des Maltais est la fabrication des bijoux en filigrane. Mais, apparaît à cette époque, une institution typiquement maltaise: l'Université. C'est la transformation en assemblée plus restreinte de l'ancien "Conseil Populaire" qui réunissait tous les chefs de famille libres. L'Université (universitas civium) prétendait donc représenter l'ensemble des habitants de Malte à part entière, mis à part les esclaves et autres captifs de guerre ou de razzias.

On peut encore voir à La Valette un bâtiment de construction plus récente dont le rôle était de redistribuer, sous l'égide de l'Université, le blé à la population.

Récolte des artichauts, région de Marfa.
Gathering artichokes, Marfa region.
Artischockenernte im Gebiet von Marfa.

Un lavoir à la sortie de Victoria.
Wash-house just outside Victoria.
Waschhaus ausserhalb Victorias.

The Maltese in the Middle Ages

The population, chiefly sailors, cultivated wheat, cotton and cumin, which they exported.

In the towns the artisans formed guilds (masons, carpenters, rope-makers, sailmakers, etc.) for in addition to the buildings which began to rise all over the island, the harbours were increasingly frequented by ships calling either to trade or for repairs.

One of the crafts for which Malta is still famous is the production of filigree jewels.

At this epoch there appears a typically Maltese institution, the University. This was a more select meeting of the former "People's Council", which grouped all the heads of free families. The University (universitas civium) therefore claimed to represent all full citizens of Malta, apart from slaves and others made prisoner as the result of war or raids.

There is still in Valletta a building of more recent date from which wheat was distributed to the population under the auspices of the University.

Eglise de l'Annonciation, Salina [
Church of the Annunciation, Sali
Mariä Verkündigungskirche, Salin

Eglise Sainte Marie à Gudja.
St. Mary's church at Gudja.
Die Heilige Marienkirche in Gudja.

The Parishes

Before the Knights arrived and Valetta was built, together with a number of centres all of which now constitute a vast town, the Maltese lived in small villages and the two chief towns of Mdina (Citta Vecchia) and Birgu. From this epoch date the little chapels hewn out of the rock "sheltered from the curious and the raids of pirates". The few churches which existed were merely rectangles enclosing a space.

In 1436 the island was divided up into a number of parishes. Several churches were built for this purpose, and they constitute the most interesting buildings dating from this period. Thus, the little church of St Mary near Gudja has porches in a style resembling that of the Norman houses in Mdina. Two gutters, one on each side of the facade, drain off the rainwater from the terrace. The church is surrounded by a wall which includes a large courtyard round the building. The belfry is a recent addition. The church now stands in the open country about one kilometre from the town, which was built more recently. It was used by a number of small neighbouring villages.

The inside of St Gregory's church on the way out of Żejtun has Gothic vaults. It was built in the fifteenth century. As in the case of St Mary's, there have been more recent additions, including a Renaissance-style porch.

Though less spectacular than more recent buildings, these small village churches and chapels impart a human note to the history of Malta and remind us that these peasants were at the mercy of constant insecurity.

Les Paroisses

Avant l'arrivée des Chevaliers et la construction de la Valette, accompagnée de la création des nouveaux centres qui ne forment plus maintenant qu'une immense agglomération. Les Maltais vivaient dans de petits villages et dans les deux villes principales de Mdina (Citta Vecchia) et du Bourg. C'est de cette époque que datent les petites chapelles creusées dans le roc "à l'abri des regards indiscrets et des raids de corsaires . . . Les quelques églises existantes étaient simplement un rectangle enfermant un compartiment..."

En 1436 l'île avait été divisée en une dizaine de paroisses. Plusieurs églises furent construites à cet effet. Elles comptent parmi les monuments les plus intéressants qui nous restent de cette époque. Ainsi, là petite église de Sainte Marie près de Gudja présente des porches d'un style voisin des "maisons normandes" de M'dina. Deux gouttières de chaque côté de la façade permettaient à l'eau de la terrasse de s'écouler. Elle est entourée d'un mur laissant une large cour autour de l'édifice; le clocher a été rajouté ultérieurement. L'église se trouve actuellement en rase campagne à environ un kilomètre de la ville, de construction plus récente. Elle était utilisée par plusieurs petits villages des environs.

L'intérieur de l'église Saint Grégory, à la sortie de Żejtun, a des voûtes de forme gothique. Sa construction date du 15ème siècle. Comme pour l'église précédente, des éléments nouveaux ont été ajoutés, telle une porte style renaissance.

Moins spectaculaires que les monuments qui ont été édifiés postérieurement, les petites églises et chapelles de villages marquent l'histoire de Malte d'une note humaine, à la mesure de ces paysans en proie à l'insécurité constante.

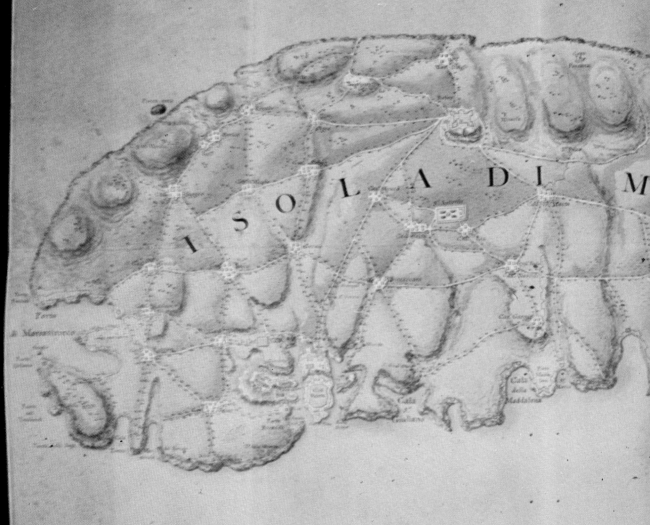

Carte de Malte et de Gozo - 1/ème.
Map of Malta and Gozo, seventeenth century.
Karte von Malta und Gozo - 17. Jahrhundert.

BARBERIA

LTA

Cala
della
Melcha

Rada delli Freghi,
ò
del Frioul

ISOLA DEL GOZO

SICILIA

LES CHEVALIERS DE MALTE

Que serait devenue Malte sans les Chevaliers? Peut-être intégrée à la Sicile comme semblait le vouloir le cours de l'histoire. Mais celle-ci en a décidé autrement. Il a suffit que la Méditerranée soit l'enjeu des puissances riveraines pour que l'une de ses îles en deviennent un bastion stratégique. Depuis, Malte n'a cessé d'être convoitée par les pays qui tour à tour voulaient s'assurer la liberté de navigation.

Les Chevaliers ont construit à Malte la plus puissante ville fortifiée de leur temps. Les palais, les églises, les batiments publics qu'ils ont fait élever, parfois avec leur propre argent, sont parmi les plus remarquables de leur époque. Ils ont fait appel aux artistes les plus renommés. Ainsi, la volonté d'un Grand Maître, le talent d'un architecte maltais comme Cassar, le travail de ces batisseurs nés que sont les habitants de l'île et la merveilleuse pierre des carrières, cela donne une église Saint Jean à La Valette.

Sans Malte, que seraient devenus les Chevaliers ?

Pendant 250 ans, l'Ordre fut souverain absolu et ses Grands maîtres régnèrent également comme des souverains, traitant d'égal à égal avec les autres pays de la chrétienté et eurent avec eux des relations diplomatiques. Ils furent victimes des séquelles de la révolution française et d'un personnage historique qui ne fut pas Suliman le Magnifique mais un petit général né sur une autre île non loin de Malte qui avait nom Bonaparte.

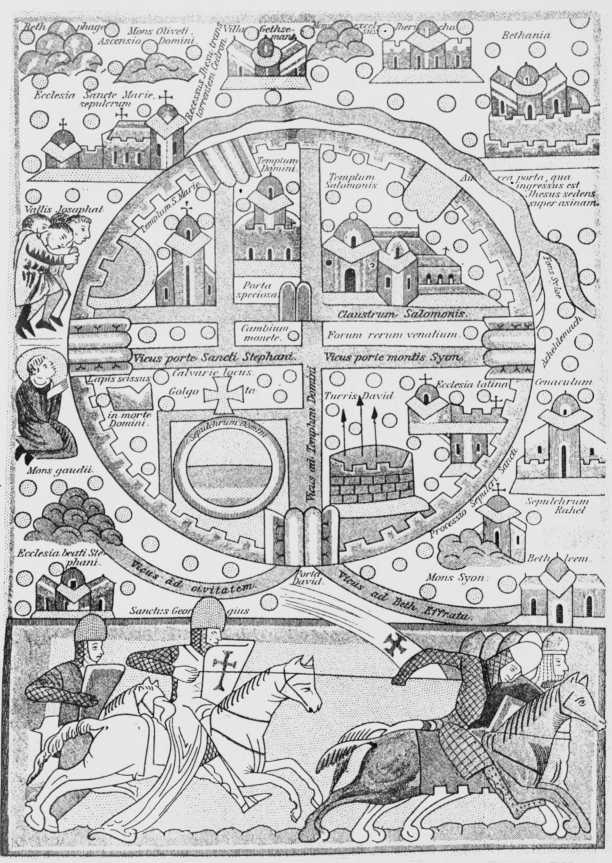

Carte de Jérusalem au Moyen Age (1170).
Map of Jerusalem in the Middle Ages (1170).
Karte von Jerusalem im Mittelalter (1170).

Représentation de Jérusalem, tapisserie de la Création de Gérone.
Gerona tapestry showing Jerusalem.
Darstellung von Jerusalem, Wandteppich von Gerona.

Le pélerinage à Jérusalem

"Jérusalem est la cité des cités, la sainte parmi les saintes, la reine des peuples, la princesse des provinces. Elle est située au centre du monde, au milieu de la terre, afin que tous les hommes puissent se diriger vers elle."

Jacques de Vitry, XIIIème siècle.

"Elle doit attirer les fidèles comme l'aimant attire le fer, comme la brebis attire l'agneau par le lait de ses mamelles, comme la mer attire les fleuves auxquels elle a donné naissance."

Poète du XIIIème siècle.

Avec la conquête de la Palestine par les Arabes au VII ème siècle, la situation des chrétiens vivant en terre sainte ou se rendant à Jérusalem commença à changer. Les restrictions imposées à l'exercice de la religion (églises transformées en mosquées, interdiction des emblèmes extérieurs du culte), les contributions frappant les populations soumises, autant de choses qui provoquèrent un sourd mécontentement dans la Chrétienté.

L'approche de l'an Mille et de la fin du monde, la résurrection du Christ en Judée, imminente, firent affluer les croyants en cette partie du monde. Ne devait-on pas y trouver le pardon des péchés? Gens de pauvre condition et grands de la terre se transformèrent en pélerins et vinrent à Jérusalem où le sultan d'Egypte, Hakem, avait ordonné la démolition de l'église du Saint Sépulcre qui ne fut reconstruite que quarante ans plus tard.

L'arrivée des Turcs et la conquête des villes de la chrétienté en Asie Mineure et en Syrie (Ephèse, Tarse, Antioche) aboutirent à des vexations et des excès pires encore. Quand les nouveaux venus commencèrent à perturber le commerce en Méditerranée, une expédition de Pisans, de Génois et d'habitants d'Arles débarqua en Syrie pour un raid punitif. Ce fut, le début de la grande idée des Croisades qui rassembla aussi bien les croyants aux pieds nus que les chevaliers en quête d'héroïques exploits, et nombres d'aventuriers de toute sorte.

"Que la croix brille sur vos armes et vos étendards! Portez la sur vos épaules et sur votre poitrine; elle deviendra pour vous l'emblème de la victoire ou la palme du martyre."

Urbain II, Première Croisade.

Saint Jean d'Acre

Rhodes

Dès 1020, des marchands d'Amalfi et de Salerne avaient obtenu du calife d'Egypte l'autorisation de construire à Jérusalem un hôpital qu'ils placèrent sous la bénédiction de Saint Jean Baptiste. Pèlerins et voyageurs en Terre Sainte y étaient soignés. L'institution prit de l'importance avec les Croisades et Pierre Gérard de Martigue, qui fut le premier chef de l'Ordre, proposa à ceux qui s'occupaient de l'hôpital de se transformer en ordre monastique: renonciation au monde et port d'un habit. Ainsi fut créé l'Ordre des Hospitaliers de Saint Jean de Jérusalem. Outre les voeux classiques d'obéissance, de chasteté et de pauvreté, ils devaient également assurer la sécurité des pèlerins voyageant en Palestine.

Ils furent les derniers à quitter Jérusalem, conquise par Saladin. Ils prirent une part très active à la prise d'Acre et s'établirent dans la ville sous le nom de "Chevaliers de Saint Jean d'Acre". C'est pendant leur séjour à Acre que l'Ordre prit toute son efficacité militaire. A la protection des voyageurs s'ajoutait la fortification de la ville. De puissants remparts furent édifiés, ainsi que des édifices religieux.

A la chute de Saint Jean d'Acre, reprise par les musulmans en 1291, les Chevaliers réussirent à se réfugier par petits groupes dans l'île de Chypre, où ils restèrent une douzaine d'années. Le Grand Maître Jean de Villiers réunit tous les Chevaliers décidés à continuer la lutte. Mais les relations avec le roi de l'île n'étant pas très bonnes, le nouveau Grand Maître, Villaret, et les Chevaliers, décidèrent de trouver une autre base.

A la suite d'une expédition en quelque sorte une petite croisade – à laquelle prirent part bon nombre de chevaliers réunis en secret dans un port du sud de l'Italie, l'Ordre s'établit dans l'île de Rhodes. Un long siège leur permit de s'emparer de la capitale (1310). Ils y restèrent deux cents ans.

Une première offensive turque fut repoussée en 1455. Mais les Hospitaliers, qui s'appelaient maintenant les Chevaliers de Rhodes. avaient fort à faire. Outre Mahomet II, qui avait conquis Constantinople, et le sultan d'Egypte, ils eurent à se défendre contre les Vénitiens qui avaient commis des ravages considérables. Le Grand Maître Raimond Zacosta mit à profit un court répit dans ces luttes continuelles pour construire le fort Saint Nicolas destiné à défendre le port et la capitale de Rhodes.

C'est au cours de leur séjour dans cette île que les Chevaliers devinrent hommes de la mer. La lutte contre les musulmans ne se faisait plus à cheval sur la terre de Palestine mais en Méditerranée, face à la puissance montante de la Turquie. En effet, la Chrétienté s'était bien rendue compte que toutes les expéditions en Orient n'avaient été possibles que par la maîtrise des routes maritimes.

En représailles contre les invasions incessantes des corsaires turcs, le Grand Maître alors en fonction envoya des galères de l'Ordre sur les côtes d'Asie Mineure. Mahomet II, furieux de cette incursion, confia une puissante flotte à son grand vizir, Misach Paléologue, un renégat grec, avec pour mission de s'emparer de Rhodes. Le 23 mai 1480, 160 bâtiments de guerre tentèrent le débarquement. La bataille fit rage et les Turcs réussirent à prendre pied sur les remparts. Ils proposèrent une capitulation au Grand Maître Pierre d'Aubusson (qu'ils avaient tenté par ailleurs de faire empoisonner). Devant le refus de ce dernier, le grand vizir fit préparer des pieux et jura de faire empaler ou passer par le fil de l'épée tous les habitants. Mais l'assaut vit le repli des Turcs qui firent une dernière tentative une vingtaine d'années plus tard.

En 1522, Soliman le Magnifique envoya près de 400 bateaux et plus de 150.000 hommes. Il avait été averti secrètement de la faiblesse relative des défenses de l'île par André Amaral, chancelier de l'Ordre et grand prieur de Castille, dépité de ne pas avoir été choisi comme grand maître.

Le Grand Maître Villiers de l'Isle Adam dirigeait la défense, avec seulement 7.000 hommes. Les assaillants réussirent à pénétrer dans la place, mais les Chevaliers les arrêtèrent et refusèrent de se rendre.

Sur l'insistance de la population et aussi selon le désir de Soliman d'en finir au plus vite, le Grand Maître consentit à traiter. Le respect du sultan pour ces combattants si valeureux fut tel qu'il permit aux Chevaliers de quitter l'île la veille de Noël en emmenant avec eux plus de quatre mille personnes conduites par Villiers de l'Isle Adam.

Les remparts de Saint Jean d'Acre.
Ramparts of St John of Acre.
Die Wälle von Akka.

Installation à Malte

Après leur départ de Rhodes, les Chevaliers cherchèrent une nouvelle base. Leur Grand Maître, Villiers de l'Isle Adam les emmena à Candie (Crète), Viterbe (Italie), Syracuse (Sicile) et à Nice. Par bonheur, le pape de l'époque avait été chevalier de Saint Jean. Il essaya de convaincre Charles-Quint de laisser les Chevaliers s'établir à Malte. Leur Grand Maître n'était d'ailleurs guère enthousiasmé par cette hypothèse. Il songeait même à reconquérir l'île de Rhodes.

Enfin, en 1529, avec l'amélioration des relations entre les états européens, Charles-Quint et le pape, la solution de Malte semble s'imposer. Le 24 mars 1530, le souverain espagnol signe à Bologne la cession de l'île aux Chevaliers. Ils y resteront plus de deux cent cinquante ans, jusqu'à ce jour de juin 1798 qui vit Bonaparte, en route pour l'Egypte, y faire débarquer ses troupes.

Par tradition, le Grand Maître était, jusqu'alors tenu d'envoyer chaque année au roi de France des oiseaux de proie. Désormais, Charles-Quint recevrait en contrepartie de son geste, le jour de la Toussaint, un faucon "chaperonné de soie, portant sonnettes d'or et bagué de vervelle aux armes impériales". Il pouvait en outre continuer à nommer les évêques de l'île comme avant l'arrivée des Chevaliers.

Et les Maltais? On ne leur avait pas tellement demandé leur avis. Des promesses leur furent faites que les institutions locales ne seraient pas changées. Ils demandèrent sans succès à pouvoir être acceptés dans l'Ordre en tant que Chevaliers: ils pourraient être chapelains mais rien de plus.

Le Grand Maître promulga des ordonnances qui remplacèrent les lois siciliennes, et l'île fut coupée en deux. Une partie relevait de l'ancienne capitale, la Citta Vecchia, et l'autre du Bourg où l'Ordre établit son quartier général et le siège de ses institutions.

Le Grand Maître promulgua des ordonnances mourut quatre ans après l'installation de l'Ordre à Malte. L'Ordre avait une terre mais n'y avait pas de Grand Maître. Le nouveau, Pietro del Monte, ne vint pas dans l'île et ne survécut que huit mois à son élection. Son successeur, Juan d'Olmedes n'y mit les pieds qu'une quinzaine de mois après sa nomination.

On était loin de la hâte qui avait présidé à l'installation à Rhodes quelques deux cents ans plus tôt. Durant ces premières années peu de batiments furent construits: un hôpital de l'Ordre rapidement achevé en 1532, un palais épiscopal et le palais du Grand Maître en 1555.

L'Ordre de Saint Jean de Jerusalem

C'est pendant son séjour à Rhodes que l'Ordre des Hospitaliers devint cette formidable institution militaire et religieuse. De protecteurs des pélerins en Terre Sainte, ils devinrent le fer de lance de la Chrétienté dans la lutte contre l'hégémonie turque en Méditerranée. Ils s'engageaient à défendre la religion du Christ et à ne jamais faire acte d'hostilité quelconque envers une nation chrétienne.

Les membres de l'Ordre étaient divisés en trois groupes: les chevaliers de justice, les chapelains et les frères servants.

Les chevaliers comprenaient les nobles des plus grandes familles catholiques européennes. Seize quartiers de noblesse étaient exigés des Allemands et huit seulement des Français. Chaque famille s'enorgueillit d'envoyer un de ses fils combattre dans les rangs de l'Ordre. Il pouvait y avoir des *Chevaliers de Grâce* bien que de condition inférieure, en raison de leur valeur militaire peu commune.

Les *chapelains* étaient les aumoniers et en règle générale ceux qui avaient des fonctions exclusivement religieuses.

Les *frères servants* devaient simplement prouver qu'ils étaient d'origine honorable et pouvaient être aussi bien combattants qu'infirmiers dans les établissements hospitaliers.

Les membres de l'Ordre portaient un habit noir et un manteau de même couleur en poil de chameau. Il rappelait celui dont était vêtu Saint Jean-Baptiste. Ce manteau n'était porté que pour les cérémonies. A la hauteur du coeur, une croix blanche à huit pointes représentait les huit obligations ou aspirations.

— Vivre dans la vérité
— Avoir la foi
— Etre repentant de ses fautes
— Faire preuve d'humilité
— Aimer la justice
— Etre miséricordieux
— Etre sincère et net de coeur
— Endurer la persécution

Ils suivaient la règle de Saint Augustin et prononçaient les trois voeux de chasteté, d'obéissance et de pauvreté. Sans trop de rigueur cependant car, à part les chapelains, c'étaient surtout des militaires à qui il était même recommandé de se bien nourrir et de se maintenir en forme afin d'être dans les meilleures conditions possibles pour combattre l'ennemi. Ils devaient avoir la barbe et les cheveux courts pour ne pas être gênés dans la bataille. Au musée d'armes de La Valette on peut voir leurs armes, sans ornements particuliers mais d'une solidité impressionnante.

Celui qui désirait se mettre au service de l'Ordre devait subir un rituel chargé du symbolisme de la religion et de la chevalerie.

Il se présentait d'abord devant l'autel avec un cierge et une longue robe sans ceinture, pour montrer qu'il était libre de tout lien. Le chevalier assesseur lui remettait une épée dorée pour lui signifier qu'il devait défendre la religion "au nom du Père, du Fils et du Saint Esprit". La ceinture qu'on lui passait alors autour de la taille signifiait qu'il était maintenant lié aux voeux de l'Ordre. L'épée était brandie au dessus de sa tête en signe de défi aux infidèles et ensuite mise dans son fourreau après avoir été comme essuyée pour montrer au candidat qu'il devait se préserver de toute souillure.

Des éperons dorés lui étaient mis pour qu'il foule aux pieds les richesses de ce monde. Un cierge allumé à la main, on lui demandait s'il était marié, s'il avait des dettes et s'il était membre d'un ordre quelconque. On le conduisait alors à l'autel où il prononçait ses voeux sur le missel. Il devait chaque jour prononcer un certain nombre de prières pour honorer Dieu et la Vierge et pour l'âme des Chevaliers trépassés.

L'Ordre était divisé en huit "langues" ayant chacune à leur tête un "pilier" ou bailli conventuel. Il y avait les "langues" de Castille, d'Angleterre, d'Italie, d'Aragon, d'Allemagne et les trois françaises de Provence, de France et d'Auvergne. N'oublions pas que le premier grand maître fut le provençal Gérard de Martigues. Quarante-quatre des soixante-huit grands maîtres furent d'origine française. La langue d'Angleterre ne fut plus représentée après la séparation de ce pays d'avec la religion catholique.

Chaque bailli avait par tradition une position bien définie. Celui d'Aragon s'occupait des habits de l'ordre, il était "drapier"; le Grand Hospitalier qui s'occupait des hospices était bailli de la langue de France; celui d'Angleterre commandait la défense côtière; le Grand Amiral était toujours de langue Italienne; le grand bailli, de langue allemande maintenait les fortifications en état.

Les "langues" prirent l'habitude de faire construire une sorte de quartier général pour chacune d'elles, des "auberges", qui bientôt rivalisèrent de beauté architecturale. Avec les cathédrales, ce sont les plus importants monuments qui soient restés. Près de la moitié des auberges de Malte ont été détruites pendant la dernière guerre.

Le grand maître était élu à vie trois jours au plus après le décès du précédent. Ainsi pensait-on éviter l'intervention du Pape et tout marchandage politique de la part des puissances européennes.

Cette "éminence", comme on l'appelait, pouvait battre monnaie. L'indépendance de l'Ordre était un fait acquis et celui-ci était représenté diplomatiquement auprès de plusieurs souverains européens.

The Knights of Malta

What would have happened to Malta without the Knights? Perhaps it would have been integrated into Sicily as the course of history seemed to indicate. However, history decided otherwise. It was sufficient that the Mediterranean should be the stake played for by the powers surrounding it for one of the islands to become a strategic bastion. Since then, Malta has never ceased to be coveted by the countries which wanted to ensure the freedom of the seas.

The Knights built on Malta the most powerful fortified city of their time. The palaces, churches and public buildings which they erected, often with their own money, are among the most remarkable of the epoch. They called upon the most renowned architects. Thus, the combined result of the determination of a Grand Master, the skill of a Maltese architect such as Cassar, the work of those great builders who inhabited the islands and the wonderful stone from the local quarries is a church such as St John's at Valetta.

And what would have happened to the Knights without Malta?

For two hundred and fifty years, the Order was supreme, and its Grand Masters reigned as sovereigns, dealing on an equal footing with the other countries of Christendom and maintaining diplomatic relations with them. And at last they fell a victim to the results of the French Revolution and to a great historic personnage who was not Suliman the Magnificent, but a little general who was born on another, not very distant, island – Bonaparte.

The Pilgrimage to Jerusalem

The Pilgrimage to Jerusalem
"Jerusalem is the city of cities, the saint of saints, the queen of peoples, the princess of provinces. It is situated at the centre of the world, in the middle of the earth, so that all men can go there."
Jacques de Vitry, thirteenth century.
"It attracts the faithful as a magnet attracts iron, as the ewe attracts the lamb with the milk of her teats, as the sea attracts the rivers to which it gave birth."
Thirteenth century poet.

With the conquest of Palestine by the Arabs in the seventh century, the situation of the Christians living in the Holy Land or going to Jerusalem began to change. The restrictions imposed on the exercise of the religion (churches turned into mosques, prohibition of external emblems of worship, and the taxes levied from the population concerned) all gave rise to veiled discontent in Christendom.

The approach of the millennium which was to herald the end of the world and the imminent resurrection of Christ in Judaea brought believers to this part of the world, for was it not here that absolution could be obtained? The great of the earth and people of low degree became pilgrims and flocked to Jerusalem, where Hakem, the Sultan of Egypt, had ordered the demolition of the church of the Holy Sepulchre, which was only to be rebuilt forty years later.

The arrival of the Turks and the conquest of the Christian towns in Asia Minor and Syria (Ephesus, Tarsus, and Antioch) gave rise to persecution and even worse excesses. When the newcomers began to interfere with trade in the Mediterranean, an expeditionary force consisting of Pisans, Genoese and Arlesians landed in Syria on a punitive raid. This was the beginning of the exalted idea of the Crusades in which joined not only barefooted believers but also Knights in search of heroic exploits and many adventurers of all sorts.

"May the Cross shine out from your arms and standards! Wear it on your shoulders and on your hearts; it will become for you the emblem of victory or the palm of the martyr."
Urban II, First Crusade.

In 1020, the merchants of Amalfi and Salerno had obtained permission from the Caliph of Egypt to build in Jerusalem a hospital the patron saint of which was St John the Baptist. Here treatment was provided for pilgrims and travellers in the Holy Land. With the crusades, the institution attained greater importance, and Pierre Gérard de Martigues, the first Head of the Order, suggested that those who ran the hospital should become monks, implying renunciation of the world and

wearing a habit. Thus was created the Order of Hospitallers of Saint John of Jerusalem. In addition to the usual vows of obedience, chastity and poverty, they also had to undertake to ensure the safety of pilgrims journeying to Palestine.

They were the last to leave Jerusalem when it was conquered by Saladin. They played a very active part in taking Acra and set up in the town as the "Knights of Saint John of Acra". It was during their stay in the town that the Order assumed full military efficiency. In addition to protecting travellers, they fortified the town. Powerful ramparts, as well as religious edifices, were built.

Upon the fall of Acre, retaken by the Muslims in 1291, the Knights succeeded in fleeing in small groups to the island of Cyprus, where they remained for a dozen years. Grand Master Jean de Villiers assembled all the Knights who were determined to continue the struggle, but relations with the king of the island were not good, and the new Grand Master, Villaret, together with the Knights, decided to find another base.

Following on an expedition – a sort of minor crusade – in which a number of Knights who had met secretly in a port of southern Italy took part, the Order set itself up in the island of Rhodes. After a long seige, they captured the capital in 1310 and remained there for two hundred years.

A first Turkish offensive was repelled in 1455, though the Hospitallers, now known as the Knights of Rhodes, had difficulty in achieving this. They had to defend themselves, not only against Mahomet II, who had conquered Constantinople, and the Sultan of Egypt, but also against the Venetians who had wrought great havoc. Grand Master Raimond Zacosta took advantage of a short respite in the continual fighting to build Fort St Nicolas with the aim of defending the harbour and the capital.

It was during their long stay on the island of Rhodes that the Knights became seamen. The struggle against the Muslims was no longer conducted on horseback on the soil of Palestine but on the Mediterranean against the mounting power of Turkey, for Christendom had learnt that expeditions to the east had been rendered possible only by the mastery of the sea routes.

By way of reprisals against the endless invasions by Turkish pirates, the Grand Master then in office sent the ships of the Order to the coasts of Asia Minor. Mahomet II, furious at this move, sent his Grand Vizier, a Greek renegade named Misach Palaeologus, in command of a fleet with the order to occupy Rhodes. The landing was attempted on 23 May 1480 with 160 warships. After fierce fighting, the Turks succeeded in gaining a footing on the ramparts. They called on the Grand Master, Pierre d'Aubusson (whom they had tried to have poisoned) to capitulate. When

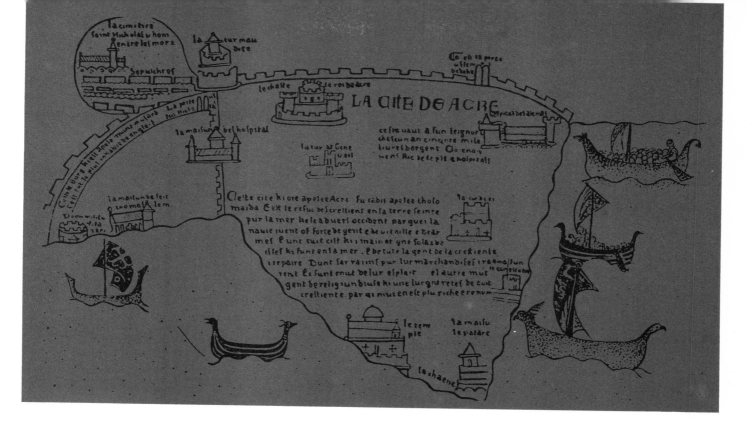

the latter refused, the Grand Vizier swore to have all the inhabitants impaled on the stake or put to the sword. But the assault was repulsed; the Turks retreated and made no further attempt for twenty years.

In 1522, Suliman the Magnificent sent nearly 400 ships and over 150,000 men. He had been secretly informed about the weak points in the island's defence by André Amaral, Chancellor of the Order and Grand Prior of Castille, who was furious at not having been chosen Grand Master.

The defence was conducted by the Grand Master, Villiers de l'Isle Adam with only 7,000 men. The invaders succeeded in penetrating into the town, but the Knights halted them and refused to surrender.

Finally, at the request of the population and upon Suliman's wish to finish things off quickly, the Grand Master agreed to parley. So great was the Sultan's respect for these courageous fighters that he allowed the Knights to leave on Christmas Eve, taking with them more than four thousand persons led by Villiers de l'Isle Adam.

After the departure from Rhodes, the Knights tried to find a new base of operations. Villiers de l'Isle Adam, the Grand Master, took them successively to Candia (Crete), Viterbo (Italy), Syracuse (Sicily) and Nice (France). Fortunately, the Pope at that time had been a Knight of St John. He tried to persuade Charles the Fifth to allow the Knights to settle in Malta. The Grand Master, by the way, was not very enthusiastic about this project. His idea was to reconquer the Island of Rhodes.

At last, in 1529, with the improvement in relations between European countries, Charles the Fifth and the Pope, Malta seemed to be the best possible choice. On 24 March 1530 the Spanish monarch signed the cession of the island to the Order, where it remained for two hundred and fifty years until one day in June 1798, when Bonaparte, on his way to Egypt, landed there with his troops.

Traditionally, the Grand Master had always sent a present of birds of prey every year to the King of France. Henceforward on All Saints Day every year, Charles the Fifth received "a falcon, hooded with silk, with golden bells and with varvels adorned with the Imperial arms". In addition, he continued to appoint bishops to the island as he did before the arrival of the Knights.

What about the Maltese? They had not really been asked for their opinion. They were promised that there would be no change in local institutions. They asked unsuccessfully to be admitted to the Order as Kinghts, but they were never allowed to be anything more than chaplains.

The Grand Master promulgated ordinances replacing the Sicilian laws and the island was partitioned. One part was dependent on Citta Vecchia, the former capital, and the other on Birgu, where the Order set up its headquarters.

Grand Master Villiers de l'Isle Adam died four years after the Knights settled in Malta. The Order now had a home but no Grand Master. The new one, Peitro del Monte, never came to the island and died only eight months after his election. His successor, Juan d'Olmedes, only set foot there fifteen months after his nomination.

This was a long way from the haste which had presided over the installation in Rhodes two hundred years before. During the first few years very little building was done. A hospital of the Order was rapidly completed in 1532, and an episcopal palace and the palace of the Grand Master in 1555.

The organization of the Order of Malta

It was during the Rhodes period that the Order of Hospitallers became the formidable military and religious institution of the Knights of Malta. From being the protectors of pilgrims in the Holy Land, they became the spearhead of Christendom in the fight against Turkish hegemony in the Mediterranean. They undertook to defend the religion of Christ and never to take any hostile action whatsoever against a Christian nation.

The members of the Order were divided into three classes — knights, chaplains and serving brothers.

The knights included nobles from the greatest European catholic families. Sixteen quarterings were required from the Germans, but only eight from the French. Every family was proud for one of its sons to be sent to fight in the ranks of the Order. "Knights of grace", though of inferior condition, were accepted providing they had outstanding military qualities.

The chaplains were the almoners and were usually the only class which had purely religious duties.

The serving brothers merely had to prove that they were of honourable origin and could be either soldiers or nurses in the hospitals of the Order.

Members wore a black habit and a camel-hair cloak of the same colour, very like that worn by St John the Baptist. The cloak was worn only for ceremonial occasions. A white eight-pointed cross covering the breast represented the eight obligations or aspirations:—

to live in truth
to have faith
to repent of sins
to give proof of humility
to love justice
to be merciful
to be sincere and whole-hearted
to endure persecution.

They followed the precepts of Saint Augustin and took the three vows of chastity, obedience and poverty, though the last was not observed over-strictly since, apart from the chaplains, they were above all soldiers who were recommended to eat well and keep in good form to fight the enemy. They were required to keep their hair and beards short so as not to be encumbered in battle. Their arms can be seen in the Museum at Valetta; they are without any special ornamentation but are impressively solid.

He who wished to enter the Order had to undergo a ritual full of the symbolism of religion and chivalry.

First he had to stand before the altar holding a candle and wearing a long robe without a belt, to show he was free of all bonds. The Knight Assessor then presented the candidate with a golden sword to show him that he had to defend religion "in the name of the Father, the Son and the Holy Ghost". A belt was then placed round his waist, signifying that he was now bound by the vows of the Order. The sword was then brandished above his head as a sign of defiance to the infidels, wiped to show the candidate he must keep himself unsullied, and returned to its sheath.

Gilt spurs were then presented to him with which to spurn the riches of this world. Holding a lighted candle in his hand, he was asked if he was married, if he had any debts and if he belonged to any other order. He was then conducted to the altar, where he made his vows upon the missal. He had to say a number of prayers each day in honour of God, the Virgin and the souls of deceased knights.

The Order was divided into eight "tongues" each of which was governed by a monastic prior. Castille, England, Italy, Aragon and Germany each constituted a "tongue", while there were three French ones — Provence, France and Auvergne (it should not be forgotten that the first Grand Master was the Provençal Gérard de Martigues). Forty-four out of the total of sixty-eight Grand Masters were of French origin. After the Reformation, England was no longer represented as a "tongue".

Traditionally, each priory had a well-defined task. That of Aragon concerned itself with the habits of the Order and was known as the "Drapier". The Grand Hospitaller who dealt with the hospitals was prior of the French "tongue". That of England was responsible for coastal defences, while the Grand Admiral was always from the Italian "tongue". The German Grand Prior kept the fortification in repair. Each of the "tongues" developed the custom of building a sort of headquarters for itself; these were the "auberges", which soon began to rival one another in architectural beauty. These, together with the cathedrals, are the most important monuments to the Order remaining. Nearly half the "auberges" in Malta were destroyed during the last war.

The Grand Master was elected for life not more than three days after the death of his predecessor. It was thus hoped to avoid intervention by the Pope and any political manoeuvring on the part of European powers.

This "Eminence", as he was known, was entitled to mint money. The independence of the Order was an accomplished fact, and it maintained diplomatic representation at a number of European courts.

Sacrements donnés à un Chevalier de Malte.

A Knight of Malta receiving the sacraments.

Die Heiligen Sakramente werden einem Ordensritter verabrei

Dragut the Pirate

In addition to Malta, the Knights were awarded the town of Tripoli, about two hundred miles south on the coast of Africa. They undertook to Charles the Fifth to defend it against Turkish invasions and the assault of the pirates based on Algiers.

Reacting to a victory by Kaireddin Barbarossa over the Christian galleys off the Greek coast, the Spanish decided to take action against Algiers. They were accompanied by about one hundred Knights, including Savignac de Balaguer, the standard-bearer of the Order.

The expedition became a catastrophe when the Algerians, taking advantage of a storm, attacked the invaders, who had not yet landed all their equipment and had to put out to sea for safety's sake. Savignac rallied a few fighters around him and, taking the offensive, repelled the enemy, taken by surprise in their turn. He pursued them to the gates of the city, which were hastily closed. Before leaving, Savignac de Balaguer planted his dagger in the wood of the Bab-Azun gate and cried: "We'll come back for it."

The Knights fought courageously to protect the army which was trying to re-embark, but nearly half of them were lost during this unfortunate expedition (1541).

The Turks had almost complete mastery of the seas, and the ships of the great trading towns such as Ragusa (now Dubrovnik), Venice and Marseilles could not venture on them without a trading or political agreement. France herself was allied to the Muslim pirates, and Barbarossa's ships even came and wintered at Toulon (1543).

Dragut, a Greek renegade who had entered the Sultan's service, launched terrible raids from the North African coast against the Spanish possessions, either by land, in which case the inhabitants were taken off and all property destroyed, or by sea, as when a ship of the Order of Malta bearing the revenues from the Italian commanderies was seized.

On 30 April 1551, Dragut landed in the Marsamxett roadsteads at the head of Suliman II's fleet. Such of the local inhabitants as were able, fled to the fortified places of Mdina, Birgu and Fort St Angelo. Dragut laid waste the deserted villages for two and a half months.

He then received reinforcements of about ten thousand men brought by a Turkish squadron. The Knights, including Sir Nicholas Upton, an Englishman who died of wounds on the same day, tried to contain them but, being outnumbered, retired to their citadel. But the Turks, finding the siege of Fort Saint Angelo too costly, left to lay siege to Mdina, laying waste a number of towns on the way.

Fearing that Christian reinforcements might arrive and deterred by the imposing fortifications of the old capital, they decided to attack Gozo and Rabat, its capital, which was less well defended. The defence lasted only a few days, and nearly the entire population was taken away into slavery. It is said that the island did not return to its former level of population for another one hundred and fifty years.

The Knights had still not had time to fortify the island properly, though it must be admitted that they were still reluctant to stay there definitely. However, the events that followed had the effect of making them stay there whether they liked it or not.

The Turks immediately turned their attention to Tripoli, which was defended by Marshal Valies of the Auvergne "tongue". Here all resistance was in vain owing to the avarice of the Grand Master, Jean d'Omedes of Aragon, which was responsible for the weakness of the fortifications. The citadel capitulated on 14 August 1551. The French Ambassador to Constantinople had conducted some of the negotiations between the opposing sides. The Knights were to be allowed to go free, but their soldiers were to man the Muslim galleys. Valies, who was considered responsible for this defeat, was thrown into prison until the death of the Grand Master, which occurred two years later, and expelled from the Order. A controversy now arose between the French and Spanish as to responsibility for the defeat.

The Turks made another attempt in 1555, but came up against the new fortifications erected by Grand Master Claude de la Sengle, who gave his name to what is now the suburb of Senglea.

Shortly after the great raid on Gozo and the landing in the bay of Marsamxett, it was decided to protect the peninsula upon which now stands the town of Valetta – Mount Sceberras. The result was a star-shaped fort with high walls – Fort Saint Elmo – which was to play such a predominant role later and provide the Knights with a respite during the great siege of 1565.

During one of their expeditions the Knights had occupied the town of Madhia in Tunisia, which had formerly been the capital of an Arab kingdom. In view of the reluctance of the Order to settle in Malta, Charles the Fifth suggested that they should retake it, particularly as they had just lost Tripoli.

The last expedition was that to Djerba (February 1560). Once the idea of Madhia had been rejected, de La Valette, who had been Grand Master for three years, came to an agreement with the Spanish on re-taking Tripoli, the fortifications of which were still deficient. Dragut, who still retained mastery over the region, had left to crush a revolt among the nomad tribes.

Fort Saint Ange.
Fort St Angelo.
Fort Saint Ange.

Instead of taking Tripoli by surprise, the ships of the Order allowed themselves to be diverted to operations of secondary importance. Dragut regained mastery of the situation, and the Christians descended on the island of Djerba, where the pirate's headquarters had been established for a long time. Djerba, with its resources of oil and wheat, had often been tackled by the forces of Christendom. But this time it was necessary to take ship again in a hurry, for Dragut and Ali Pasha, heads of the Turkish fleet, arrived in force. The citadel was guarded by a few thousand men, who were forced to yield two months later. Nearly thirty ships, representing half the naval strength of the expeditionary force, were lost during the precipitate withdrawal of the soldiers of Philip II of Spain, who had just succeeded to Charles the Fifth.

Malta remained the Order's only base; and it was urgently necessary to fortify it, for danger was threatening.

Dragut le corsaire

En plus de Malte, les Chevaliers reçurent la place de Tripoli sur la côte africaine quelques trois cents kilomètres au sud. Ils s'étaient engagés auprès de Charles-Quint à la défendre contre les entreprises turques et les assauts des pirates basés à Alger.

C'est en réponse à une victoire de Kaîreddin Barberousse sur les galères chrétiennes au large des côtes grecques, que les Espagnols se décidèrent à agir contre la ville nord africaine. Une centaine de chevaliers les accompagnaient, dont Savignac de Balaguer, porte-drapeau de l'Ordre.

L'expédition tourna à la débâcle quand, profitant de la tempête, les Algériens attaquèrent les assaillants qui n'avaient pas encore débarqué tout leur matériel et dont les bateaux avaient dû regagner le large par mesure de sécurité. Savignac réunit autour de lui quelques combattants et prenant la contre-offensive, repoussa les attaquants, surpris à leur tour. Il les poursuivit jusqu'aux portes de la ville qui se refermèrent en hâte. Avant de repartir, Savignac de Balaguer planta sa dague dans le bois de la porte Bab – Azoun et s'écria: "Nous reviendrons la chercher!".

Protègeant l'armée qui cherchait à rembarquer, les chevaliers luttèrent courageusement et près de la moitié d'entre eux restèrent dans cette malheureuse expédition (1541).

Les Turcs avaient la presque totale maîtrise de la mer. Les navires des grandes villes marchandes comme Raguse (Dubrovnik), Venise, Marseille ne pouvaient s'y aventurer sans accord commercial ou politique. La France même était alliée aux corsaires musulmans. Les navires de Barberousse ne venaient-ils pas hiverner à Toulon (1543) ?

Un renégat grec passé au service du Sultan, Dragut, lançait à partir de la côte nord africaine de terribles raids contre les possessions espagnoles, soit sur terre, avec chaque fois l'enlèvement des habitants et la destruction de tous les biens, soit sur mer, comme le détournement de ce navire de l'Ordre de Malte chargé des revenus des commanderies d'Italie.

Le 30 avril 1551 Dragut débarque dans la rade de Marsamxett à la tête d'une flotte de Soliman II. La population qui le peut se réfugie dans les lieux fortifiés, Mdina, le Bourg et le Fort Saint Ange. Pendant deux mois et demi Dragut dévaste les villages désertés.

C'est alors qu'une escadre turque lui amène un renfort d'une dizaine de milliers d'hommes. Les chevaliers, parmi lesquels se distingua un Anglais, Sir Nicolas Upton qui mourut de ses blessures le soir-même, essayèrent de les contenir. Mais inférieurs en nombre, ils se réfugièrent dans leur citadelle. Jugeant trop coûteux le siège du Fort Saint-Ange, les Turcs partirent assièger Mdina en dévastant quelques agglomérations au passage.

Craignant une arrivée de renforts chrétiens, et devant les imposantes fortifications de l'ancienne capitale, ils se décidèrent à attaquer Gozo et sa capitale moins bien défendue, Rabat. La défense dura quelques jours seulement. La quasi totalité de la population fut emmenée en esclavage. On dit que l'île n'atteignit son niveau démographique antérieur que 150 ans après.

Les chevaliers n'avaient pas encore eu le temps de fortifier Malte comme il convenait. Il faut dire qu'ils étaient encore réticents à s'y établir définitivement. La suite des événements devait, bon gré mal gré les fixer dans l'île.

Aussitôt après les Turcs se tournent vers Tripoli. La place était défendue par le maréchal Valies, de la langue d'Auvergne. Toute résistance était sans issue, car l'avarice du Grand Maître aragonnais Juan d'Omedes était, dit-on, responsable de la faiblesse des fortifications. La citadelle capitula le 14 août 1551. L'ambassadeur de France à Constantinople avait mené une partie des négociations entre les combattants. Les chevaliers auraient la vie sauve et la liberté, tandis que leurs soldats iraient garnir les galères musulmanes. Valies, reconnu responsable de cette capitulation, fut jeté en prison jusqu'à la mort du Grand Maître qui survint deux ans plus tard. On lui avait retiré son habit. Et une polémique s'engageait entre Français et Espagnols sur le partage des responsabilités.

Les Turcs firent une autre tentative en 1555, mais se heurtèrent aux nouvelles fortifications édifiées par le Grand Maître Claude de la Sengle, qui donna son nom au quartier actuel de Senglea.

Peu après le grand raid sur Gozo et le débarquement dans la baie de Marsamxett, on décida de protéger la presqu'île sur laquelle s'élève maintenant La Valette, le mont Sceberras. On contruisit ainsi un fort en forme d'étoile avec de hautes murailles, le Fort Saint-Elme, qui devait jouer par la suite un si grand rôle et donner aux Chevaliers un répit pendant le grand siège de 1565.

Au cours d'une de leurs expéditions les chevaliers avaient occupé la ville de Madhia en Tunisie qui fut dans le passé la capitale d'un royaume arabe. Charles-Quint, devant les réticences de l'Ordre à s'installer à Malte, leur proposa de la reprendre — d'autant plus qu'ils venaient de perdre Tripoli.

La dernière expédition fut celle de Djerba (février 1690). L'idée de Madhia n'ayant pas été retenue, La Valette, qui était Grand Maître depuis trois ans, décida en accord avec les Espagnols de reprendre Tripoli toujours aussi peu fortifiée. Dragut, qui régnait en maître sur la région, était parti réprimer une révolte des tribus nomades.

Au lieu de prendre Tripoli par surprise, les bateaux de l'Ordre se laissèrent entraîner à des opérations d'intérêt secondaire. Dragut se ressaisit et les Chrétiens se rabattirent sur l'île de Djerba où depuis longtemps le chef corsaire avait établi son quartier général. Riche en huile et en blé, Djerba avait souvent été abordée par les forces de la chrétienté. Cette fois, il fallut rembarquer rapidement, car Dragut et Ali Pacha, chefs de la flotte turque, arrivaient en force. Quelques milliers d'hommes gardèrent la citadelle. Ils devaient se rendre deux mois plus tard. Près d'une trentaine de galères, soit la moitié des bâtiments composant le corps expéditionnaire, furent perdus lors du repli précipité des soldats de Philippe II d'Espagne, qui venait de succéder à Charles-Quint.

Malte restait pour l'Ordre la seule base qu'il fallait fortifier d'urgence, car les périls s'annonçaient.

Attaque du Fort Saint Michel par Aleccio.
"Attack on Fort St Michael" by Aleccio.
"Angriff auf das Fort Saint Michel", von Aleccio.

Le siège de Malte en 1565 par les Turcs a été abondamment commenté par les chroniqueurs de l'époque. Il y avait bien longtemps que l'unanimité des croisades avait fait long feu, mais la résistance des Hospitaliers où chaque pays de la Chrétienté pouvait reconnaitre ses fils sous la bannière de l'Ordre, avait rempli d'admiration l'Europe entière. De plus, on y voyait un arrêt aux entreprises turques en Méditerranée. En effet, six ans plus tard c'était la victoire de Lépante sur les Musulmans, victoire à laquelle participèrent des galères de Malte.

Sur le plan local la résistance aux troupes de Soliman eut pour conséquence l'installation définitive à Malte de l'Ordre des Hospitaliers et la construction de la ville fortifiée de La Valette dont la création paraissait maintenant impérieuse. Le siège avait en effet montré le danger de laisser dégarni le Mont Scébérras en face du Bourg et de Senglea. Les opérations militaires qui se montraient d'années en années plus puissantes en matériel (canons, bateaux, machines de siège) et plus nombreuses en hommes, exigeaient une nouvelle architecture défensive.

A la fin de l'année 1564 des agents secrets de l'Ordre travaillant à Constantinople envoyèrent des rapports alarmistes annonçant la construction de galères en grand nombre.

A quelles nouvelles expéditions ces bateaux étaient-ils destinés? De toute façon il ne fallait pas compter sur une attaque en plein hiver, les galères, bateaux très bas sur l'eau, ne pouvant affronter la mer pendant la mauvaise saison. C'était d'ailleurs une constatation couramment admise, il n'y avait jamais de combats importants à cette époque. On réparait les bateaux, les charpentiers en construisaient de nouveaux; on se préparait pour les campagnes d'été.

Sans être absolument certaine d'être la raison de tous ces préparatifs, Malte s'inquiétait. Des secours furent demandés à toute la Chrétienté, en particulier au souverain le plus proche, Don Garcia de Tolède, vice-roi de Sicile. En prévision d'une attaque d'envergure, on s'était d'ailleurs préparés depuis plusieurs années. Le fort Saint-Elme était terminé sur le Mont Sceberras, les forts Saint-Michel et Saint-Ange avaient été consolidés à la Hâte au Bourg et à Senglea.

Côté défenseurs, il y avait 9000 hommes, dont 5000 Maltais et moins de 600 chevaliers. Les huit galères de la flotte ne seraient d'aucune utilité contre une armada.

Le 18 mai 1565 au matin, les deux cents vaisseaux de la flotte turque furent en vue. Après avoir passé la journée à longer la côte en quête d'un point de débarquement, ils se décidèrent pour la baie de Marsa-siroco, lieu classique de débarquement de tous les conquérants de l'île. Les paysans qui étaient aux champs et avaient connu les incursions des corsaires turcs pensaient que ceux-ci, une fois de plus, passeraient comme des sauterelles et repartiraient rapidement comme ils étaient venus. Ils se contentèrent de se cacher sur place au lieu de chercher refuge derrière les fortifications de M'dina ou du port. Au cours des trois mois que dura l'occupation des campagnes, nombre d'entre eux perdirent la liberté sinon la vie.

L'armada turque avait choisi la baie de Marsaxlokk pour aborder. Du côté des défenseurs il n'y eut pas une grande résistance sur place. Que faire contre une armée aussi nombreuse? De toute façon, il avait été décidé que la défense se

ferait derrière les murailles. La petite cavalerie maltaise pouvait bien essayer quelques coups de mains, mais les nombreux murets de pierres séparant les champs l'empêchaient de manoeuvrer. Elle se réfugia dans Mdina et fit pourtant quelques sorties.

Les forces musulmanes étaient commandées par Mustapha Pacha et la flotte par l'Amiral Piali Pacha propre gendre du Sultan. Le principal souci de ce dernier était d'amener à pied d'oeuvre ses deux cents bateaux. Pour cela, contre l'avis de Mustapha qui voulait d'abord attaquer le Bourg et Senglea, il imposa la reddition du Fort Saint-Elme avant toute autre manoeuvre. La baie de Marxamxett lui serait alors ouverte. Ce fut une erreur que les défenseurs allaient mettre à profit.

Les Turcs établirent leur camp principal à Marsa, le vieux port phénicien, au fond de la baie composant maintenant le principal ensemble portuaire de La Valette. Ils pensaient profiter des hauteurs du mont Sceberras pour bombarder à loisir le camp retranché. Mais c'était méconnaître la position stratégique du Fort Saint-Elme, construit une douzaine d'années auparavant par Pietro Prado, ingénieur espagnol. Pour l'époque,

c'était le dernier cri de l'architecture militaire de défense. Son plan en forme d'étoile et ses hauts murs devaient le rendre imprenable. Son rôle principal, sous-estimé par l'adversaire, était d'empêcher la mise en place d'artillerie sur le Mont Sceberras, en face du Bourg et de Senglea. Avec leurs trois forts, les Chevaliers pouvaient rendre impossible toute installation durable dans le périmètre du grand port.

La contre-attaque turque permit à ceux-ci de s'emparer de quelques ouvrages de défense extérieurs au fort. Enhardis par ce succès, les musulmans s'élancèrent à l'assaut des murailles mais leurs échelles souvent trop courtes et les projectiles incendiaires hautement sophistiqués et très meurtriers que les chrétiens venaient de mettre au point leur causa de lourdes pertes. On dit que les Turcs eurent près de deux mille morts ce jour-là, certains disent cinq cents seulement. Le fort Saint-Elme perdit une centaine d'hommes dont vingt chevaliers.

Des renforts de deux milliers d'hommes arrivèrent d'Afrique du Nord avec le terrible Dragut à leur tête. Pour lui le fort Saint-Elme devait être pris sans trop de difficulté. Seule la mauvaise tactique employée jusqu'à présent était la cause

de cet échec. Il installa de nouvelles batteries, dont une au point appelé maintenant "Point Dragut", sur le promontoire situé à l'extrémité de Sliema contrôlant l'entrée de la baie de Marsamxett. De ce jour, les bombardements redoublèrent.

Durant toute la durée du siège du Fort Saint-Elme, il y eut des échanges avec le quartier général des chevaliers et leur Grand Maître La Valette qui continuaient de fortifier à la hâte le Bourg et Senglea. Les Turcs n'ayant pas le contrôle de la baie, on pouvait assez facilement, la nuit venue, accéder à l'autre rive.

C'est justement en essayant de bloquer cette voie de communication que Dragut fut mortellement blessé.

Mais le fort faiblissait et les ouvrages de défense étaient sérieusement atteints au prix de pertes terribles chez les Turcs. Deux mille cinq cents hommes de renfort venus d'Afrique du Nord furent taillés en pièces peu de temps après leur arrivée. Il en fut de même pour un millier de janissaires qui essayèrent à bord d'une dizaine de navires de franchir un pont en forme de barrage reliant le Bourg et Senglea. Un seul bateau put en réchapper. Ce jour-là les pertes des assaillants furent dix fois plus élevées que celles des chevaliers.

Le 23 juin, un assaut général submergea les défenseurs. Il y eut des survivants: quelques soldats maltais qui réussirent à gagner le camp retranché à la nage. Des Chevaliers tombèrent aux mains des corsaires. Les morts furent attachés sur de grandes croix de bois et jetés dans le port. Les têtes des prisonniers servirent de boulets aux canons.

Dans cette bataille du fort Saint-Elme, les chrétiens perdirent près de 1500 soldats et 130 chevaliers, et les Turcs plus de 8000 à ce que l'on dit.

Le problème n'était pas réglé pour autant. Les musulmans, loin de leurs bases avaient remporté une victoire limitée mais s'étaient affaiblis et se rendaient compte que la partie était difficile à gagner.

L'étau se resserrait néanmoins autour des lignes fortifiées. Les brèches se faisaient de plus en plus fréquentes, difficiles à défendre, difficiles à réparer. L'une d'elles, plus importante que les autres, permit aux Turcs de pénétrer dans l'enceinte du Bourg. Ils se ruèrent en criant victoire. Ce fut pour se retrouver prisonniers d'un deuxième mur d'enceinte construit entre-temps et du haut duquel les défenseurs firent tomber divers projectiles plus meurtriers les uns que les autres: poix, pierres, etc.

Ils parvinrent néanmoins à investir le Fort Saint-Michel. Pour les Turcs, la chance était passée. Les secours promis par Don Garcia de Tolède, étaient en route. Le roi de Sicile avait en effet attendu d'avoir réuni les forces nécessaires pour ne pas encourir un échec.

Cependant, quelques troupes en provenance de Sicile avaient profité de l'abandon du camp turc (tous étaient partis à l'assaut) pour le détruire et le brûler, aidés en cela par la cavalerie retranchée à Mdina.

Le 6 septembre, 30 galères débarquèrent les renforts à Melliehá et 2 jours après Mustapha jugea préférable d'ordonner le rembarquement.

Malte était sauvée. Elle aurait pu l'être bien plus vite si les divergences politiques européennes n'avaient empêché la réunion urgente des renforts nécessaires.

DIMOSTRAZIONE DI TUTTE LE BATTERIE

Les Turcs autour du Grand Port par Aleccio.

"The Turks surrounding the Grand Harbour" by Aleccio.

"Der von den Türken umzingelte Grosse Hafen", von Aleccio.

The Siege of 1565

Much has been written by contemporary historians about the 1565 siege of Malta by the Turks. The unanimity of the Crusades had died out long before, but the resistance of the Hospitallers under whose banner every country of Christendom could recognise its sons, had filled the whole of Europe with admiration. Moreover, it was seen as a check to Turkish activities in the Mediterranean, and six years later came the defeat of the Turks at Lepanto, in which participated the ships of Malta.

Locally, the result of resistance to the troops of Suliman was the final establishment of the Hospitallers' Order in Malta and the building of the fortified town of Valletta, which now became a matter of extreme urgency. The siege had demonstrated the danger of leaving Mount Sceberras unguarded opposite Birgu and Senglea. Military operations, which made ever-increasing demands on equipment (cannon, ships, siege engines) and manpower, also required new defensive architecture.

At the end of 1564 secret Agents of the Order in Constantinople sent panic reports about the building of large numbers of ships. The question was to what use these ships were to be put. In any case there was no question of an attack in the depths of winter, since the ships, which lay very low in the water, could not take to sea in rough weather. It was in any case generally accepted that no important battles could take place at that season, during which ships were repaired, while the carpenters built new ones and the summer campaigns were prepared for.

But Malta, while not sure whether it was the target of all these preparations, was anxious. Reinforcements were requested from throughout Christendom, particularly from the neighbouring monarch, Don Garcia of Toledo, Viceroy of Sicily. Preparations had been made for a number of years against a large-scale attack. On Mount Sceberras, Fort Saint Elmo had been completed, and Forts Saint Michael and Saint Angelo had been consolidated in haste at Birgu and Senglea.

The defence forces consisted of 9,000 men, 5,000 of whom were Maltese; there were less than 600 knights, and the eight ships of the fleet would be of no use against an armada.

On the morning of 18 May 1565 the two hundred vessels of the Turkish fleet hove into sight. Having spent the day coasting in search of a landing place, they decided on the bay of Marsa-siroco, where all the conquerors of the island had always landed. The peasants who were working in the fields and had experience of the raids of Turkish pirates, thought that these too would pass through like locusts and depart as quickly as they had come. They contented themselves with hiding on the spot instead of looking for refuge behind the fortifications of Mdina or the harbour. During the three months of occupation, many of them lost their liberty if not their lives.

The Turkish armada had chosen to land in the Bay of Marsaxlokk. The defence did not put up much resistance on the spot. What, after all, could they do against such overwhelming forces? It was therefore decided that the defence should be conducted from behind the walls. The small numbers of Maltese cavalry attempted a number of sorties, but the numerous walls separating the fields from one another prevented them from manoeuvering. They therefore took refuge in Mdina, whence they did however make a number of sorties.

The Muslim forces were commanded by Mustafa Pasha and the fleet by Admiral Piali Pasha, the Sultan's son-in-law. The latter's chief concern was to bring his two hundred ships to land. He therefore decided, against the advice of Mustafa, who wanted to attack Birgu and Senglea first, that Fort Saint Elmo must be overcome before anything else, thus leaving the Bay of Marsamxett open to him. This was an error from which the defenders were to benefit.

The Turks established their main camp at Marsa, the old Phoenician port, at the back of the bay which now constitutes the harbour area of Valletta. They hoped to take advantage of the heights of Mount Sceberras to bombard the entrenched camp at their leisure. But this showed they under-estimated the strategic position of Fort Saint Elmo, built a dozen years before by Pietro Prado – a Spanish engineer. For its date this was the very last thing in military defence architecture. Its star-shaped plan and high walls rendered it impregnable. Its chief purpose, which the enemy under-estimated, was to prevent artillery from being placed in position on the hill facing Birgu and Senglea. With their three forts, the Knights could make any lasting occupation of the perimeter of the Grand Harbour impossible.

To protect their guns the Turks had built a wall of earth and rock facing the fort. The first extensive attack took place on 22 May, preceded by an artillery preparation, which lasted several hours but did not succeed in inflicting any great damage on the fortifications. By the end of a week the beleaguered forces made a sortie, which sowed disarray in the opposing camp.

The Turks counter-attacked and captured some of the exterior fortifications. Encouraged by this success, they advanced to the assault of the main walls, but owing to the fact that many of their scaling ladders were too short and that the Christians had just perfected highly sophisticated incendiary missiles, they suffered heavy losses. It is said that the Turks lost two thousand dead that day, though some say it was only five hundred. Fort Saint Elmo lost one hundred men, twenty of whom were Knights.

Reinforcements of two thousand men led by the fearsome Dragut arrived from North Africa. Dragut considered he could take Fort Saint Elmo without difficulty, and that the only reason for the setbacks thus far suffered was the poor technique used. He set up new batteries, including one at the

promontory now called Dragut Point overlooking the Bay of Marsamxett at Sliema; The bombardments now redoubled in intensity.

Throughout the siege of Fort Saint Elmo there were exchanges with the headquarters of the Knights and their Grand Master La Valette, who continued to fortify Birgu and Senglea in haste. Since the Turks did not control the bay, it was fairly easy to cross to the other bank at night.

And it was in the act of cutting off this line of communication that Dragut was mortally wounded.

On 23 June the defenders were submerged by a general assault. The survivors – a few Maltese soldiers – succeeded in gaining the entrenched camp by swimming to it. The Knights fell to the hands of the pirates. The dead were fastened to large wooden crosses and thrown into the sea. Their heads were used as cannon balls.

During this battle of Fort Saint Elmo, the Knights lost nearly 1,500 soldiers and 130 Knights. It is said that the Turks lost more than 8,000.

This, however, did not solve the problem for the Muslims, who had won a limited victory a long way from their base, but were much weakened and realised that it would be difficult to win.

Nevertheless, the grip round the fortified lines was tightening. Breaches were made with increasing frequency; they were difficult to defend and even more difficult to repair. One of these, larger than the others, enabled the Turks to penetrate inside the town of Birgu. They rushed in victoriously, only to find themselves confronted by a second defensive wall which had been built in the meantime and from the top of which the defenders threw down weights, rocks and other murderous projectiles.

Nevertheless, they succeeded in investing Fort Saint Michael. But the Turks had missed their chance. The help promised by Don Garcia of Toledo was on the way. The King of Sicily had merely been waiting to assemble the necessary forces so as not to suffer defeat.

Meanwhile, a few troops from Sicily had taken advantage of the fact that the Turkish camp was deserted (all having left for the assault) to destroy and burn it, assisted by the entrenched cavalry at Mdina.

On 6 September 30 ships landed reinforcements at Mellieha, and two days later Mustafa thought it prudent to raise the siege.

Malta was safe. This might perhaps have happened sooner had not political divergencies in Europe delayed the assembly of the necessary forces.

Porte avancée à Vittoriosa.

Forward gate at Vittoriosa.

Ein Tor im Vorgelände von Vittoriosa.

The siege of 1565 constituted not only the greatest feat of arms on the part of the Knights but also the great date in the history of the island, for the Turks were held back partly owing to the presence of thousands of Maltese soldiers, either regulars or volunteers. Popular celebrations make frequent reference to the victory, and carnival is the occasion for reconstituting scenes of the period such as that above, where girls can be seen wearing the "faldetta" – a sort of black hood, still worn by elderly women, which is held above the head by whalebone. They remind one of the skirts which some Turkish and Tunisian women throw over their heads.

Si le siège de 1565 reste le grand fait d'arme des Chevaliers il n'en est pas moins considéré comme la grande date de l'histoire de l'île. En effet, les Turcs ont pu être contenus grâce à la présence de milliers de Maltais soit engagés comme soldats réguliers soit comme volontaires. Les fêtes populaires font souvent référence à cette victoire et le carnaval est l'occasion de reconstitutions de scènes d'époque comme ci-dessus où l'on voit notamment des petites filles portant la "faldetta", sorte de cape noire, portée encore par les vieilles femmes, maintenue au dessus de la tête par des baleines. Elle rappelle la jupe que les femmes turques et certaines tunisiennes rejettent au dessus de leur tête.

Les remparts de La Valette avec l'auberge de Castille.
The ramparts of Valletta with the auberge of Castille.
Die Wälle von Valetta mit der Herberge von Kastilien.

La Valette

"Frère Jean de La Valette, Grand Maître de l'Ordre Hospitalier de Jerusalem, se souvenant du danger auquel avaient été exposés ses Chevaliers et le peuple maltais au cours du siège que leur avaient infligé les Turcs l'année précédente, après avoir consulté les responsables de l'Ordre pour la construction d'une cité nouvelle et sa fortification par des murs, des remparts et des tours qui puissent résister à toute attaque ou la repousser ou, du moins, soutenir tout assaut de l'ennemi turc, le jeudi 28 mars 1566, après l'invocation du Dieu tout-puissant, de la Sainte vierge, du patron Saint Jean Baptiste et des autres saints, pour que l'oeuvre entreprise apporte prospérité et bonheur à l'ensemble de la communauté chrétienne, et pour le plus grand bien de l'Ordre, posa la première pierre de la Cité sur la colline appelée Sceberras par les habitants de l'île, et lui ayant donné pour blason un lion d'or sur fond rouge émit le désir qu'elle prit son nom, La Valette."

Telle est l'inscription portée sur l'une des pierres de fondation de la nouvelle cité voulue par Jean de La Valette et exécutée selon les plan de Francesco Laparelli, architecte militaire italien originaire de Cortone. Le maltais Girolamo Cassar participa également à l'élaboration de la ville et dirigea la construction de monuments comme la cathédrale Saint Jean.

Autant l'Europe s'était faite un peu tirer l'oreille pour voler au secours des Chevaliers assiégés, autant les dons pour la nouvelle construction affluèrent de nombreuses cours européennes. Le roi de France donna 140.000 livres, la plus importante contribution de toutes les sommes réunies.

Le Grand Maître s'était rendu compte, tout au long du siège du Grand Port, de la position stratégique du Mont Scéberras et du rôle capital joué par le fort Saint Elme. Pourquoi ne pas construire une ville à cet emplacement même?

L'héroïque petit fort fut reconstruit. Pour la ville, on fit appel à tout ce que l'architecture militaire avait élaboré de plus nouveau. De nombreux projets de villes fortifiées existaient car plus les armes devenaient meurtrières, plus les fortifications devaient être hautes et épaisses. On fondait des canons de plus en plus gros, on construisait des navires de plus en plus grands, et

si l'Ordre de Malte se servit encore de galères pendant plus d'un siècle, les navires de haute mer, mis au point grâce aux voyages de découverte océanique, commencèrent à sillonner la Méditerranée.

De par l'Europe les villes furent entourées de nouveaux systèmes de fortifications. Un projet de l'architecte Pietro Cataneo prévoyait une ville forte en forme d'hexagone parfait, chaque angle et chaque côté comportant des fortifications qui rendaient théoriquement la ville imprenable.

Les rues de La Valette se coupant à angle droit sont comme tracées au cordeau. La construction fut rondement menée ce qui explique que l'on n'eut guère le temps d'en remodeler le relief. La ville fait comme une bosse avec ses rues qui plongent directement vers la mer, coupées par endroit d'escaliers inattendus.

Les Turcs avaient été repoussés mais il n'était pas dit qu'ils ne reviendraient pas. Un siècle plus tard leur menace sur l'Europe pesait encore. La nouvelle ville fortifiée devait être terminée rapidement. Les projets de Laparelli ne furent pas suivis à la lettre, loin de là. Les parties bordant la mer furent ceinturées d'une haute et épaisse fortification. Le système le plus complet concerne la section portant sur toute la largeur du mont Scéberras, point faible du dispositif. Une seule porte à pont levis permettait de pénétrer dans la

Saint John Street.
Saint John Street.
Die Saint John-Strasse.

Grenier de Saint Elm
St Elmo granary,
Speicher in Saint Eln

Jean de La Valette

De l'avis même de Dragut qui avait vu La Valette enchaîné sur les galères turques, celui-ci était "le plus grand homme de guerre de son temps".

Il passa plus de cinquante ans au service de l'Ordre dont onze comme Grand Maître. Grâce à lui, Malte pouvait subir les assauts répétés des musulmans. Trois ans après la chute de Tripoli il avait en vain essayé de convaincre le Grand Maître d'alors d'augmenter les défenses de l'île. Ce militaire clairvoyant avait aussi proposé de construire une forteresse sur le mont Sceberras, projet qu'il réalisera après le siège de 1565 avec la construction de La Valette.

Il était connu comme un homme de sang-froid, exhortant ses hommes au milieu du combat et se mettant réellement à leur tête pour repousser l'ennemi. Ne s'élança-t-il pas, en une sortie audacieuse qui coûta la vie à des milliers de combattants ottomans, hors du Bourg assiégé depuis des semaines! Homme de courage, c'était aussi un tacticien, qui laissait s'épuiser les Turcs à réduire le fort Saint-Elme et profitait de ce répit pour construire de nouvelles fortifications.

ville. Un profond fossé creusé dans le roc et, de chaque côté, des bastions ajoutaient au renforcement de l'ensemble.

Moins de cent ans plus tard une autre partie du mont Sceberras fut couverte par un autre système de fortifications, renforçant ainsi celles de La Valette (1657).

Les deux frères Cottoner, qui furent successivement Grands Maîtres, englobèrent dans le même ensemble fortifié les villes de Vittoriosa, Senglea et un nouveau quartier; Cospicua (Cottonera line 1680).

Chaque nouveau Grand Maître entreprenait la construction qui d'un fortin, qui d'une nouvelle fortification.

La Valette devenait la ville au monde la plus fortifiée. Mais elle se heurtait maintenant à un autre problème. Où trouver les hommes pour défendre ces ouvrages gigantesques? Une quarantaine de milliers d'hommes auraient été, dit-on, nécessaires. Comment se serait comporté ce système défensif au cours d'un siège, on ne le sut jamais.

Au grand désespoir peut-être des experts militaires. Les Turcs n'osèrent plus jamais tenter de nouvelles offensives d'envergure contre Malte. La maîtrise de la Méditerranée restait aux puissances qui contrôlaient l'île.

The building of Valletta

"Brother Jean de La Valette, Grand Master of the Order of Hospitallers of Jerusalem, remembering the danger to which the Knights and the people of Malta had been exposed during the siege laid to them by the Turks the previous year, having consulted the authorities of the Order regarding the building of a new city and its fortification by walls, ramparts and towers capable of resisting and repulsing any attack or at least withstanding attacks by the Turkish enemy, having invoked Almighty God, the Holy Virgin, the Patron Saint John the Baptist and other saints to ensure that the work undertaken should bring happiness and prosperity to the entire Christian community and the well-being of the Order, on Thursday 28 March laid the first stone of the City on the hill known locally as Sceberras and, having bestowed on it as a coat of arms a golden lion on a red field, expressed the desire that it should bear his name — Valletta".

Such is the inscription on one of the foundation stones of the new city decided upon by Jean de La Valette and built according to the plans of Francesco Laparelli, an Italian military architect from Cortona. The Maltese Girolamo Cassar also helped to design the town and directed the building of St John's cathedral and other edifices.

Reluctant though Europe had been to come to the help of the beleaguered Knights, contributions towards the building of the new city flowed from the various European courts. The King of France gave 140,000 livres, the largest contribution of all.

The Grand Master had realised, during the siege of the Grand Harbour, the strategic importance of Mount Sceberras and Fort Saint Elmo. Why not build a city on this very spot?

The heroic little fort was rebuilt. The very latest in military architecture was used for the town. There were numerous existing projects for fortified cities, for the more destructive weapons became the higher and thicker the fortifications had to be. Increasingly large cannon were cast and increasingly large ships were built, and while the Order of Malta continued to use galleys for more than another century, the round ships perfected as a result of ocean discoveries began to plough the Mediterranean.

Throughout Europe, towns were being surrounded by new systems of fortifications. A plan by the architect Pietro Cataneo provided for a fortified city in the form of a perfect hexagon, each angle and each side of which were fortified in such a way that theoretically the whole was impregnable.

The streets of Valletta run straight as arrow and cut each other at right angles. The building was done at full speed, with the result that there was scarcely any time to level the site, and the town is like a hump with streets running straight down into the sea and crossed here and there by unexpected stairways.

Fortification protégeant l'entrée de La Valette.
Fortification protecting the entry to Valletta.
Die die Einfahrt von Valetta beschützende Befestigung.

Jean de La Valette

In the opinion of Dragut himself, who once saw La Valette in chains on the Turkish ships, he was the "greatest soldier of his time".

He spent more than fifty years in the service of the Order including eleven as Grand Master. It was thanks to him that Malta was able to withstand the repeated onslaughts of the Muslims. Three years after the fall of Tripoli he had attempted in vain to persuade the then Grand Master to improve the defences of the Island. This far-seeing soldier had also suggested building a fortress on Mount Sceberras – a project he was to accomplish with the building of Valletta after the siege of 1565.

He was known for his sang froid, for rallying his men during the fighting and putting himself really at the head of them to throw back the enemy. When Birgu was beleaguered for several weeks, he personally led an audacious sortie which cost the lives of thousands of Ottoman soldiers. Not only was he a brave man but also a tactician, allowing the Turks to wear themselves out in reducing Fort Saint Elmo and taking advantage of the respite to build new fortifications.

The Turks had been repulsed, but there was nothing to say they would not return. A century later the threat still hung over Europe. The new fortified town therefore had to be completed rapidly. Laparelli's plans were not implemented literally, or anything like it. The parts on the seashore were surrounded with a high and massive fortification. The most complete system is the section covering the entire width of Mount Sceberras, the weak point of the lay-out. The only access to the town was by a gate with a drawbridge. A deep ditch was dug in the rock and on each side of it bastions added to the strength of the defence.

Less than one hundred years later another part of Mount Sceberras was covered by a further system of fortifications, strengthening those of Valletta (1657).

The two Cotoner brothers who succeeded one another as Grand Masters extended the system of fortifications to include the towns of Vittoriosa, Senglea and a new quarter: Conspicua (the Cotonera lines, 1680).

Each new Grand Master undertook the building either of a small fort or the reinforcement of an existing one.

Valetta became the most strongly fortified city in the world, but the problem which now arose was how to man this gigantic system of defence. It is said that about forty thousand men would have been necessary. How the system would have withstood a siege was never known.

Perhaps to the great disappointment of the military experts the Turks never again dared to undertake a major offensive against Malta. The powers controlling the island remained masters of the Mediterranean.

La Valette et le Grand Port, peinture anonyme, Musée de la Marine - XVIIème siècle.
Valetta and the Grand Harbour, anonymous painting, Naval Museum, Paris.
"Valetta und der Grosse Hafen", anonymes Bild - Marinemuseum, 17. Jahrhundert.

Auberges

L'auberge de Castille.
Auberge de Castille.
Die Herberge von Kastilien.

During their stay in Rhodes the Knights had adopted the custom of grouping the members of each "tongue" in their own "auberge". When Valletta was built and became the headquarters of the Order, it was necessary to build new ones. These, together with St John's Cathedral, were the jewels of the new city. Unfortunately many of the auberges, among them some of the finest, were destroyed by German bombardments during the siege of 1942.

The Maltese architect Cassar was entrusted with the plans for the seven auberges. Each was sited according to the part of the fortification which had to be defended by the "tongue" concerned.

The auberge de Castille et Léon was completely restored in the eighteenth century under the Grand Master from that "tongue", Manuel Pinto de Fonseca, who presided over the destinies of the Order from 1741 to 1773. The architect, Domenico Cachia, had passed through Lecca in Italy, and the auberge bears marks of his visit. It is the most elegant of the public buildings of this type. Particularly noteworthy are the façade and the splendid balcony over the main entrance decorated with the arms of the Grand Master.

De leur séjour à Rhodes les Chevaliers avaient pris l'habitude de regrouper tous les membres de leur langue dans de grandes auberges. Quand on construisit La Valette et que celle-ci devint le siège de l'Ordre, il fallut édifier aussi de nouveaux bâtiments. Avec la Cathédrale Saint Jean, ils furent les joyaux de la nouvelle cité. Malheureusement plusieurs auberges, souvent les plus belles, furent détruites par l'aviation allemande durant le siège de 1942.

L'architecte maltais Cassar fut chargé de construire les sept auberges. L'emplacement de chacune d'elle était fonction de la partie de fortification qui devait être défendue par une langue précise.

L'Auberge de Castille et de Leon a été complètement remaniée au 18ème siècle sous le grand maître de cette langue, Manuel Pinto de Fonseca qui assura les destinées de l'Ordre de 1741 à 1773. L'architecte, Domenico Cachia, était passé par Lecce (Italie) et l'auberge porte la marque de ce passage. C'est le plus élégant des bâtiments publics de ce genre. On remarque surtout la façade et le splendide balcon au-dessus de la grande porte d'entrée aux armes du Grand Maître.

St John of Valletta

L'Eglise Saint-Jean

Jean de La Valette had been dead for five years when the first stone of the monastic church which took the name of St John, the patron saint of the Order, was laid. The architect was Gerolamo Cassar, a Maltese.

In his haste to make the new city the headquarters of the Order, Grand Master de la Cassière dug into his own pocket so that the religious building could be completed more quickly. However the church, which was later to become a cathedral, was completed only thirty years later. It retraces a considerable part of the history of the Knights not only on account of its decoration but also the elements added to it throughout the years. A number of Grand Masters took a hand in the building and decoration of the chapels. The floor is covered with tombstones of different coloured marbles, which illustrate in a highly realistic manner the highpoints of the lives of the Knights which they commemorate.

According to Quentin Hughes, Professor of Architecture at Malta University, this is one of the strangest and most impressive churches in Christendom.

Its early Barock, in parts only just emerging from the Gothic, makes the decoration which was added later shine at the least touch of the sun's rays.

The entire length of the vault consists of a vast fresco due to Mattia Preti. A mobile scaffolding system running on rails makes it possible to check on the state of the fresco and restore it as required. This outstanding work of the Calabrian painter was carried out at the request of the Cotoner brothers. It took five years to complete.

The chapels of the various "tongues" rivalled one another in the perfection of their decoration. They contain the remains of Grand Masters. The first Grand Masters, including Jean de La Valette. are buried in the crypt.

The oratory of the cathedral contains the famous "Beheading of Saint John" by Caravaggio, who was invited to Malta by Grand Master Alof de Wignacourt in 1608. Apart from this huge picture, which covers an entire wall of the Oratory, he also painted the portrait of his host; the picture hangs in the Louvre.

Jean de La Valette était mort depuis cinq ans lorsque fut posée la première pierre de l'église conventuelle qui prit le nom de Saint Jean, patron de l'Ordre. C'est le maltais Gerolamo Cassar qui en a été l'architecte.

Le Grand Maître de la Cassière dans sa hâte de faire de la nouvelle cité le siège de l'Ordre puisa dans ses propres caisses pour que l'édifice religieux fût achevé au plus vite. Ce qui devint plus tard une cathédrale ne fut cependant terminé qu'une trentaine d'années plus tard. Tant dans la décoration que par les éléments qui ont été ajoutés au fil des années, elle retrace une partie importante de l'histoire des Chevaliers. Plusieurs Grands Maîtres ont construit et décoré des chapelles. Le sol est recouvert de plaques tombales composées de marbres de différentes couleurs et de façon très réaliste des faits marquants de la vie des chevaliers décédés.

Selon Quentin Hughes, professeur d'architecture à l'Université de Malte, c'est l'une des eglises les plus étranges et les plus impressionnantes de la chrétienté.

Ce baroque primitif, parfois tout juste sorti du gothique, fait éclater ses décors, rajoutés ultérieurement, au moindre rayon de soleil.

Dans toute sa longueur, la voûte est constituée par une immense fresque dûe à Mattia Pretti. Un système d'échafaudage mobile sur rails permet de vérifier à tout moment la bonne conservation et – si besoin est – la restauration. Le peintre calabrais dont c'est l'oeuvre principale fit ce travail à la demande des frères Cotoner. Il mit cinq ans à le réaliser.

Les chapelles des différentes langues rivalisent par le décor et le travail des monuments. Ces chapelles contiennent les corps de grands maîtres. Les premiers Grands Maîtres – dont Jean de la Valette – sont enterrés dans la crypte.

L'oratoire de la cathédrale contient la fameuse "Décollation de Saint Jean Baptiste" du Caravage. Ce dernier fut en effet invité à Malte par le Grand Maître Alof de Wignacourt en 1608. Outre l'immense tableau qui occupe tout un mur de cette grande salle, il peignit également un portrait de son hôte dont la toile est au Musée du Louvre.

Façade de l'église Saint Jean.
Facade of St John's Church.
Fassade der Sankt Johanneskirche.

Pierre tombale polychrome.
Multi-coloured tombstone.
Mehrfarbiger Grabstein.

F. CLAUDIUS. EX DUCIBUS. DE. SAINT. SIMON
MELITENSIS. CLASSIS. PRAEFECTUS
AD. UTRIUSQ. SICILIAE. REGEM. LEGATUS
CONTIACENSIS. PRINCIPIS
IN. MAGNO. GALLIAE. PRIORATU
VICE. HONORIFICENTISSIME. FUNCTUS
AD. LUDOVICUM. XVI. GALL. REGEM. CHRISTIANIS.
SUI. ORDINIS. ORATOR
QUATUOR. COMMENDIS. AUCTUS
TOTQ. CONSPICUIS. MUNERIBUS
SUMMA. CUM. LAUDE. PERFUNCTUS
PIE. DECESSIT. A. S. MDCCLXXVII.
AETATIS. LXXIII:
AMICUS. AMICI. MEMORIAM. VENERATUS
CENOTAPHIUM. PONI. CURAVIT.

Décors de stuc
Monument de Nicolas Cotoner
La nef avec l'ensemble des
dalles de marbres colorés et la
voûte peinte par Mattia Pretti

Stucco decoration
Monument to Nicolas Cotoner
The nave with the coloured marble
flagstones and the vault painted
by Mattia Preti

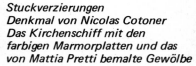

Stuckverzierungen
Denkmal von Nicolas Cotoner
Das Kirchenschiff mit den
farbigen Marmorplatten und das
von Mattia Pretti bemalte Gewölbe

Aqueduc de Wignacourt.
Wignacourt's aqueduct.
Aquädukt von Wignacourt.

Fontaine dans la cour de l'Auberge de Castille.
Well in the courtyard of the Auberge de Castille.
Fontäne im Hof der Herberge von Kastilien.

Fontaine près de l'église Saint Jean.
Fountain near Saint John's Church.
Fontäne in der Nähe der Sankt Johanneskir

Il ne suffisait pas de construire La Valette et d'en accumuler les fortifications. La stratégie traditionnelle voulait que l'on construise d'abord un bastion inexpugnable, tels les forts Saint Elme, Saint Michel ou Saint Ange. Les villes proprement dites, difficilement défendables en raison du manque d'hommes ou de la faiblesse de leurs fortifications, subissaient les assauts avec plus ou moins de bonheur.

Plus tard, les villes elles-mêmes devinrent des places-fortes entourées de hauts murs de protection et de profonds fossés. La construction de La Valette, destinée à remplacer Le Bourg comme siège de l'Ordre, n'avait pas d'autre but que la création de toutes pièces d'une ville forteresse réunissant toutes les conditions de sécurité. Au cours des années de présence des Chevaliers, de nouvelles lignes élevées en avant des bastions primitifs rendirent la cité pratiquement imprenable (construction de Floriana). Vittoriosa et Senglea furent entourées de nouvelles lignes de murs englobant de nouveaux quartiers ou créant de nouvelles aires d'urbanisation par la protection qu'elles offraient (Lignes Cotoner).

Grâce à la sécurité accrue dont bénéficiait l'archipel, la population ne tarda pas à augmenter, soit par l'arrêt des razzias traditionnelles soit par la venue de marins ou de commerçants de toute sorte. Les campagnes se développèrent et l'économie paysanne, de subsistance qu'elle était, put se tourner vers les marchés représentés par les nouvelles agglomérations. Cela devenait d'ailleurs une nécessité car l'ingratitude du sol obligeait jusqu'à présent les autorités à importer, ne serait-ce que pour la population citadine, une grande partie de ses produits. La sécurité dans les campagnes permettait, dans une moindre mesure, de réduire cette dépendance.

Des petits chateaux forts furent édifiés un peu partout dans l'île, sur les points élevés ou en bordure de mer. Strictement militaires pour certains (les tours rouges de Mellieha, fort Saint Lucien) ou mixtes (palais d'été pour le Palais Verdalla, institution pour les anciens esclaves comme le palais Selmun) ils représentent chacun un intérêt certain.

Pour prévenir une arrivée des Turcs ou des pirates, de nombreuses tours de guet ont été construites dès l'arrivée des chevaliers. Peut-être même reprenaient-elles une habitude classique dans les îles méditerranéennes exposées aux razzias. Ces tours couvraient en fait le périmètre des deux îles. Elles pouvaient communiquer entre elles par un système de signaux (fumée ou pavillons). Constituées d'un ou plusieurs étages reliés entre eux par une simple échelle que l'on pouvait retirer à la moindre alerte, elles étaient en mesure de supporter pendant quelque temps le siège d'une bande de pirates armés seulement de mousquets, en attendant des secours.

Défense des îles

Petit fortin rouge près de Marfa.
Small red fort near Marfa.
Kleines rotes Fort in der Nähe von Marfa.

Petit fortin à Sliema.
Small fort at Sliema.
Kleines Fort in Sliema.

Selmun Pala
Selmun Pala
Der Selmun

Defence of the Islands

Tour Ste Cécilie, Gozo.
St Cecilia Tower, Gozo.
Der Heilige Cäcilienturm.

It was not sufficient merely to build Valletta and the fortifications around it. In accordance with traditional strategy it was first necessary to build an impregnable bastion, such as Fort Saint Elmo, Fort Saint Michael or Fort Saint Angelo. The towns proper, which were difficult to defend owing to lack of manpower and the weakness of their fortifications, put up with assaults as best they could.

Later, the towns themselves became fortresses surrounded by high protective walls and deep moats. The only purpose in building Valletta to replace Birgu as the headquarters of the Order was the creation of a fortified town satisfying every possible security requirement. During the years when the Knights were present on the island, new elevated lines in front of the original bastions gradually rendered the city practically impregnable (Floriana). Vittoriosa and Senglea were surrounded by new lines of walls which enclosed new districts and thus created new living areas owing to the protection which they afforded (Cotoner Lines).

Thanks to the increased security which the archipelago was enjoying, the population soon increased; the traditional raids ceased, and sailors and tradesmen of all kinds arrived. The countryside developed, and the peasant economy, from being a subsistence one, began to turn to the markets provided by the towns. This, moreover, became a necessity, for the authorities had hitherto been obliged to import most of the food consumed, if only for the urban population. As the countryside became more secure, it was possible to some extent to reduce this dependence on outside resources.

Small fortified castles began to spring up all over the island, on high points or overlooking the sea. While some were purely military (such as the red towers of Mellieha and Fort St Lucien) others were summer palaces, such as the Verdala Palace and that at Selmun.

To guard against the arrival of the Turks and pirates, the Knights had undertaken the construction of a number of watch towers as soon as they arrived. To some extent these were traditional in Mediterranean islands continually exposed to raids, and in fact these towers fully covered the perimeter of the two islands. They could inter-communicate by a system of signals (smoke or flags). They consisted of one or more storeys communicating with one another by an ordinary ladder which could be withdrawn at the least sign of danger; they were able to withstand a siege by pirates armed only with muskets for some time until help arrived.

Porte des Bombes.
Bomb gate.
Das Bombentor.

Floriana

The Floriana district is named after Paolo Floriani, an architect sent by the Pope to suggest methods of improving the defences of Valletta, since the city as built after the siege of 1565 did not cover the whole of mount Sceberras owing to the lack of men to defend it. In 1634, as a result of fears of a Turkish attack, a new line of defences was built completely covering the peninsula. A new urban district grew up inside it. The church of St Publius was built, together with the huge granaries which can still be seen. Entrance is by means of a gate in the form of a triumphal arch built between 1697 and 1720; each of the pillars represents a cannon.

Le quartier de Floriana tient son nom de Paolo Floriani architecte envoyé par le pape pour proposer des solutions à une protection accrue de La Valette. En effet, la ville construite après le siège de 1565 n'avait pu être édifiée sur la totalité du mont Sceberras en raison du manque d'hommes disponibles à sa défense. En 1634, la crainte d'une attaque turque eut pour résultat la construction d'une nouvelle ligne de défenses gigantesques fermant complètement la presqu'île. Un nouveau quartier se développa à l'intérieur, on y construisit l'église Saint Publius et sur le devant de cette église d'immenses greniers que l'on peut encore voir. On y accède par une porte en forme d'arc de triomphe, la Porte de Bombes, construite entre 1697 et 1720; chacun des piliers représente un canon.

Greniers de Floriana.
Floriana granaries
Speicher in Floriana.

me fortifié.
fied system.
stigungswerk.

Le Palais
des Grands Maîtres

**RESIDENCE DU PRESIDENT
DE LA REPUBLIQUE**

The Palace
of the Grand Masters

**RESIDENCE OF THE PRESIDENT
OF THE REPUBLIC**

Palais des Grands Maîtres, le Balcon.
Palace of the Grand Masters, balcony.
Palast der Hochmeister, der Balkon.

La cathédrale de Victoria
Victoria cathedral
Die Kathedrale von Victoria

La colline de Victoria - Gozo.
Victoria hill - Gozo.
Der Hügel von Victoria, Gozo

Victoria

The chief town of Gozo has been raided and repeopled times without number. Originally named Rabat, it was renamed Victoria last century to mark the Queen's Diamond Jubilee.

During the Great Siege, the Turks went back on a promise made to a monk, brother Bartolomei Bonavia, who had negotiated an honourable surrender. The city was sacked, the archives burnt and the population deported. The Governor preferred death for himself and his wife to being sold into slavery.

Inside the fortifications rises the cathedral built in Italian Barock style by Lorenzo Cafa in 1711. There is a dome constituting an unusual optical illusion painted by the Italian artist Pozzo, and a statue of the Virgin which is brought out for the annual procession on 15 August. The extremely valuable silver pedestal was presented as a gift by two shipwrecked inhabitants of the island.

In the cathedral square is the former archbishop's palace built in 1620. This is one of the oldest buildings on Gozo.

Another old building, the Bondi Palace, now houses the museum. It provides a panorama of the prehistory and history of the island – temples of Ggantija, Roman excavations, Arab and Christian coins, the Majmuna tombstone and a fine locally made cupboard.

La ville principale de Gozo, tant de fois razziée, tant de fois repeuplée. Son premier nom de Rabat à été remplacé au siècle dernier par celui de Victoria, la grande reine.

Lors du Grand Siège, les Turcs qui assiégeaient la capitale revinrent sur leur promesse faite à un moine, Frère Bartolomé Bonavia, qui avait négocié avec eux une reddition honorable. La cité fut mise à sac, les archives brûlées et la population déportée. Le gouverneur préféra la mort pour sa femme et ses enfants plûtôt que les voir partir en esclavage.

A l'intérieur des fortifications se dresse la cathédrale construite par Lorenzo Gafa en 1711 de style baroque italien. On peut y voir un dôme en trompe l'oeil assez unique en son genre dû à l'artiste italien Pozzo, et une statue de la vierge que l'on sort pour la procession annuelle du 15 août. Le piedestal en argent d'une valeur considérable (plus de 50.000 nouveaux francs dit-on) a été donné en reconnaissance par deux habitants de l'île qui s'étaient trouvés en difficulté en mer.

Sur la place de la cathédrale se trouve l'ancien palais de l'évêque construit en 1620. C'est l'un des plus anciens monuments de Gozo.

Une autre ancienne demeure, le palais Bondi abrite maintenant le musée. Un panorama de l'histoire et de la préhistoire de l'île nous est montré: temples de Ggantija, fouilles romaines, monnaies arabes et chrétiennes, pierre tombale de Majmuna et une belle armoire locale entièrement décorée.

Mdina

Mdina, Citta Vecchia, Citta Notabile, the Silent City, was formerly the capital of Malta in the time of the Arabs, the Romans and the Normans, before the Knights came and chose first Birgu and then Valetta as the headquarters of the Order.

It is in Mdina that the most important remains from the Norman epoch can still be found. The foundations of the ramparts are of Arab origin, but were reinforced and raised by the Knights. Bastions were built at weak spots and a ditch was dug.

The main gate was built under Grand Master de Vilhena in 1724, but there is another, more discreet, gate at the bottom of the ramparts known as the Gate of the Greeks.

Mdina really is a city of silence, perhaps because the entire economic life of the island is now concentrated in Valetta and in nearby Rabat. Mdina still counts among its population the last descendants of a nobility dating back to the Norman and Spanish epoch, but it gives the impression of being a place where time has stood still. All that remains is the calm of the buildings of the past.

The cathedral is not that which was built for Count Roger in 1100 by masons from Sicily, although this was the largest in the island and was enlarged in 1419. It was destroyed by an earthquake in 1693. The new building was designed by Lorenzo Gafa (1697) who also built the church at Victoria (Rabat). Apart from the monastery church of Saint John, it is the most interesting in the archipelago. No less remarkable is the cathedral treasure house, which contains objects from the original church.

From the top of the Mdina ramparts there is a magnificent view over the entire countryside surrounding Valetta.

Mdina, Citta Vecchia, Citta Notabile, la Capitale du Silence, c'est l'ancienne capitale de Malte, celle des Arabes, des Romains et des Normands avant que les Chevaliers, marins depuis leur passage à Rhodes ne choisissent le Bourg et plus tard La Valette comme siège et port principal de l'Ordre.

C'est à Mdina que l'on trouve encore les plus importants vestiges de l'époque normande. Les remparts dont les bases sont arabes ont été consolidés et surélevés par les Chevaliers. Des bastions ont été construits aux endroits faibles, un fossé aménagé.

La porte principale a été construite sous le Grand Maître de Vilhena en 1724 mais il existe une autre porte plus discrète à la base des remparts que l'on appelle la "Porte des Grecs".

Mdina est réellement une ville du silence, peut-être parce que toute vie économique est maintenant concentrée à La Valette et plus près de là à Rabat qui est attenante. Si Mdina abrite encore les derniers descendants de la noblesse, qui remonte à l'époque normande et espagnole, elle donne l'impression d'être une cité où le temps s'est arrêté. Il n'y a plus que le calme des bâtiments et édifices publics des temps révolus.

La cathédrale n'est pas celle du comte Roger batie en 1100 par maçons venus de Sicile. Elle était pourtant la plus importante de l'île et fut agrandie en 1419. Un tremblement de terre la détruisit en 1693. Le nouvel édifice fut l'oeuvre de l'architecte de l'église de Victoria-Rabat, Lorenzo Gafa (1697). Après l'église conventuelle de Saint Jean c'est la plus intéressante de l'archipel. Non moins remarquable est le trésor de la cathédrale qui contient des objets appartenant à l'église primitive.

Du haut des remparts de Mdina on a une vue magnifique sur toute la campagne maltaise entourant La Valette.

rte principale de Mdina.
in gate of Mdina.
s Haupttor von Mdina.

hédrale de Mdina.
ina Cathedral.
 Kathedrale von Mdina.

Heurtoir de porte.
Door knocker.
Türklopfer.

Les Grands Maîtres

Les Grands Maîtres ont été les véritables souverains de l'archipel pendant plus de deux cent cinquante ans. Elus à vie par tous les chevaliers immédiatement après la mort du Précédent Grand Maître il avait tous les pouvoirs de décision. Il avait le titre d'Eminence et battait monnaie.

Bien que ne dépendant plus de leur pays d'origine, les Grands Maîtres possédaient en quelque sorte une double nationalité et les élections étaient commentées avec intérêt. La règle des trois jours maximum imposée pour l'élection du successeur empêchait ainsi toute influence extérieure. En raison de la lenteur des communications, les souverains étrangers n'étaient au courant de l'élection du nouveau responsable de l'Ordre que plusieurs jours, voire plusieurs semaines plus tard.

Chaque Grand Maître a laissé sa marque dans l'île, par la construction de nouvelles fortifications (La Valette, Cottoner, Redin), d'édifices publics, d'auberges de l'Ordre, de commandes d'oeuvres d'art (tableaux, fresques).

The Grand Masters

The Grand Masters were the absolute monarchs of the archipelago for more than two hundred and fifty years. Elected for life by the assembly of Knights immediately after the death of their predecessor, they had full powers of decision. They had the title of Emienence and minted money.

Although they no longer belonged to their country of origin, the Grand Masters had a sort of double nationality, and their election excited much comment. The rule that the new Grand Master had to be elected not more than three days after the death of his predecessor prevented any outside interference. Owing to the slowness of communications, foreign monarchs only became aware of the result of the election several days, or even weeks, after the event.

Each Grand Master left his mark on the island by the building of new fortifications (Valette, Cotoner and Redin), public buildings, auberges of the Order, or orders for works of art (pictures and frescoes).

Philippe Villiers de L'Isle Adam (France)	1530-1534
Pietro del Ponte (Italie)	1534-1535
Didier de Saint Jaille (France)	1535-1536
Juan d'Omedès (Aragon)	1536-1553
Claude de la Sengle (France)	1553-1557
Jean de la Valette (Provence)	1557-1568
Pietro del Monte San Savino (Italie)	1568-1572
Jean l'Evêque de la Cassière (Auvergne)	1572-1581
Hugues de Loubens Verdalle (Provence)	1581-1595
Martin Garzes (Aragon)	1595-1601
Alof de Wignacourt (France)	1601-1622
Louis Mendes de Vasconcellos (Castille, Leon, Portugal)	1622-1623
Antoine de Paule (Provence)	1623-1636
Jean-Paul de Lascaris Castellar (Provence)	1636-1657
Martin de Redin (Aragon)	1657-1660
Annet de Clermont de Chattes-Gessan (Auvergne)	— 1660
Rafael Cotoner (Aragon)	1660-1663
Nicolo Cotoner (Aragon)	1663-1680
Gregorio Carafa (Italie)	1680-1690
Adrien de Wignacourt (France)	1690-1697
Ramon Perellos y Rocaful (Aragon)	1697-1720
Marcantonio Zondadari (Italie)	1720-1722
Anton Manoel de Vilhena (Castille, Leon, Portugal)	1722-1736
Ramon Despuig (Aragon)	1736-1741
Manoel Pinto de Fonseca (Castille, Leon, Portugal)	1741-1773
Francisco Ximenes de Texada (Aragon)	1773-1775
Emanuel Marie de Rohan-Polduc (France)	1775-1797
Ferdinand von Hompesch (Allemagne)	1797-1798

Le Grand Maître Pinto par Antoine de Favray - 1750.

Grand Master Pinto by Antoine de Favray - 1750

"Der Hochmeister Pinto", von Antoine de Favray - 17

Departure of the Knights-Bonaparte

French influence had become preponderant. By 1789 two thirds of the six hundred knights were of French origin and more than half the ships calling at Valetta were French.

While remaining independent under the banner of the Order, Malta aroused the envy of the great powers. England, jealous of France, needed a new base in the Mediterranean since she had given up Majorca to Spain, and Russia was indulging in much intrigue for similar reasons.

The Maltese bourgeoisie, which had developed considerably owing to the island's trading situation but was nevertheless refused any major say in political matters, had held aloof from an institution which refused to accept them. The echo of liberalism found a ready hearing among them, and it is therefore not surprising that they and the remainder of the population welcomed some of the ideas of the French Revolution.

Although the majority of the Knights were in favour of the ancien régime, some had been elected, as individuals, to the States General.

On his way to Egypt, Bonaparte quite naturally found the island of Malta. Six months earlier, on his return from Italy, he had already thought of seizing the fortress and had asked the Directoire's permission to do so. Having received it, he arrived before Valetta on 9 June 1798 in command of a considerable fleet (three hundred vessels of which one third were men of war).

The fortifications served no purpose. The surrender was achieved by diplomacy, and also because Grand Master Hompesch recognized that he was on the losing side.

Three days later the Grand Master yielded to Bonaparte. The booty was considerable – 1,500 cannon, the Treasury of the Order (three millions in gold and silver) and nearly 3,500 muskets. The struggle against the Turks had long been over and "the association between the church and chivalry, between war and religion" had to suffer the repercussions of the Revolution.

The archipelago was annexed and made subject to French law and institutions. The tricolour replaced the Maltese Cross and all slaves were considered as prisoners of war.

The Maltese, who had been in favour of France in the first instance, began to show their discontent. The occupying troops had done a lot of looting and local institutions had been disparaged. The population rose in revolt.

The small French garrison at Mdina was massacred. Other troops entrenched at Valletta withstood for two years the blockade by the English fleet which prevented reinforcements from arriving. Only one ship succeeded in getting through. It had a cargo of wine and brandy!

Arc de Triomphe de Hompesch.   *Hompesch's triumphal arch.*   *Hompeschs Triumphbogen.*

Départ de l'Ordre-Bonaparte

L'influence française était devenue prépondérente. A l'aube de 1789 les deux tiers des six cents chevaliers étaient d'origine française et plus de la moitié des bateaux faisant relâche à La Valette étaient français.

Tout en restant indépendante sous la bannière de l'Ordre, Malte suscitait les convoitises des grandes puissances. L'Angleterre, jalouse de la France avait besoin d'une nouvelle base en Méditerranée depuis son abandon de Minorque à l'Espagne, et la Russie pour des préoccupations voisines intriguait beaucoup.

La bourgeoisie maltaise qui s'était considérablement développée grâce à la fonction commerciale de l'île et se voyait écartée de toute responsabilité politique majeure avait prit ses distances envers une institution qui la refusait dans ses rangs. Par conséquent il ne faut pas s'étonner de l'accueil qu'elle donna, ainsi que le reste de la population à certaines idées de la Révolution Française.

Bien que la plupart des chevaliers soient favorables à l'ancien régime, quelques uns cependant avaient été élus en France, à titre individuel, députés aux Etats Généraux.

Sur la route de l'Egypte, Bonaparte trouva tout naturellement l'île de Malte. Six mois auparavant il avait déjà songé, au retour d'Italie, à s'emparer de cette place forte et pour cela en avait demandé l'autorisation au Directoire. Ayant obtenu une réponse affirmative il arriva en vue de La Valette le 9 juin 1798. Il commandait une flotte considérable (trois cents navires dont le tiers de bâtiments de guerre).

Mais les fortifications ne servirent à rien. La reddition fut obtenue par la diplomatie, et aussi parce que le Grand Maître Hompesch vit la partie perdue.

Trois jours plus tard le Grand Maître cédait à l'Empereur. Le butin fut considérable, 1500 canons, le trésor de l'Ordre (3 millions en or et argent) et près de 3500 fusils. Il y avait bien longtemps que la lutte contre les Turcs était terminée et "l'association de l'Eglise et de la chevalerie, de la guerre avec la religion" devait subir les contre coups de la Révolution.

L'archipel fut annexé et subit la loi et les institutions françaises. La cocarde devait remplacer la croix de l'Ordre et tous les esclaves considérés comme prisonniers de guerre.

Les Maltais qui étaient favorables à la France dès le début commencèrent à faire preuve de mécontentement. Des pillages avaient été commis par les troupes d'occupation et les institutions locales battues en brèche. La population se révolta.

La petite garnison française de Mdina fut massacrée.

Les autres troupes retranchées dans La Valette subirent pendant deux ans le blocus des Maltais et des Anglais dont la flotte empêchait les secours d'arriver. Un navire pourtant réussit à passer. Il était chargé de vin et d'eau de vie ...

Valletta.

The English

Les Anglais

In accordance with the agreement reached between France and England in 1802, the island was to be returned to the Order of Malta. But the English found a number of pretexts for not complying, which caused a fresh outbreak of hostilities between the two countries.

Once England had in turn declared the annexation of the island, Malta became her military and trading base. Its importance increased with the opening of the Suez Canal in 1869 and the economic development of the British Far East Empire. All ships proceeding to or coming from India could stop at Valletta, discharge goods and above all carry out repairs. Traffic was even further increased as a result of the opening up of the Middle East oilfields. In 1888 twelve thousand ships called at Valetta.

Numerous wharves were built. These can still be seen at the foot of the now unnecessary ramparts. This was also the base of the British Fleet in the Mediterranean.

The town grew apace and swallowed up a number of surrounding villages. At present the residential area covers the two bays of the Grand Harbour and Marsamxett, together with the new town of Sliema.

The building of a gigantic arsenal was not sufficient to solve the employment problem in this island where the increase of population is so rapid that one out of every two Maltese now lives abroad. The population, which was 25,000 in 1530, rose to 100,000 by 1798, 205,000 by 1906, and was over 300,000 in 1970.

The island stirred during the European nationalist agitations of the middle of the nineteenth century. The aim of the political struggles during the British occupation was an improvement in representation of the people. They resulted in the framing of new constitutions which were constantly being called into question.

Selon les accords de paix passés entre la France et l'Angleterre en 1802 l'île devait être rendue à l'Ordre de Malte. Mais les Anglais refusèrent sous des prétextes divers, ce qui provoqua la reprise des hostilités entre les deux pays.

Ayant à son tour décrété l'annexion, l'Angleterre pouvait développer l'archipel et faire de Malte sa base militaire et commerciale. Son importance grandit encore considérablement avec l'ouverture du canal de Suez en 1869 et le développement économique de l'empire britannique d'Extrême Orient. Tous les navires venant ou allant vers les Indes pouvaient s'arrêter à La Valette, y décharger des marchandises et surtout faire effectuer des réparations diverses. L'exploitation des champs pétroliers du Proche Orient vint encore augmenter ce trafic. En 1888 douze mille navires firent escale à La Valette.

De nombreux entrepôts furent construits. On peut encore les voir aux pieds des remparts maintenant inutiles. Ce fut aussi le port d'attache de la flotte militaire britannique en Méditerranée.

La ville se développa considérablement englobant de nombreux villages. Actuellement la zone résidentielle occupe entièrement les deux baies du Grand Port et de Marsamxett avec la nouvelle ville de Sliema.

La construction d'un gigantesque arsenal ne parvint pas à régler le problème du travail dans ce petit territoire dont l'accroissement démographique est tel qu'un Maltais sur deux vit actuellement à l'étranger. De 25.000 en 1530 la population est passée à 100.000 en 1798, 205.000 en 1906 et plus de 300.000 en 1970.

L'île s'agita lors des révolutions européennes au milieu du dix neuvième siècle. Durant l'occupation anglaise les luttes politiques eurent pour but une meilleure représentation populaire. Elles débouchèrent sur l'octroi de différentes constitutions qui furent constamment remises en question.

1942

When the second World War broke out, the strategic value of Malta was questioned. Certain British strategists thought that the island, which had played a leading part in former wars (Crimea and first World War) ought to be abandoned in view of its excessive proximity to the Italian enemy, and that it would suffice if the two ends of the Mediterranean, Suez and Gibraltar, were closed.

Others, however, thought that the control of this sea ensured the safety of the British oil-producing territories in the Middle East and should be maintained at all costs, particularly in view of the length of the sea route round the Cape.

The entry of Italy into the shooting war and the operations against Rommel in North Africa decided the question. From Valletta, where airfields had been hastily constructed, the enemy convoys carrying supplies to the German forces could be harried.

But it was Malta itself which was harried, for two terrible years (10 June 1940 to 8 November 1942). Seaborne and airborne operations were numerous, and the island suffered almost continual bombardment. Supplies were cut off, and the Axis powers planned a landing in the bay of Marsaxlokk.
Bombs fell unceasingly on Valletta, the Grand Harbour and the airfields. The civilian population suffered heavy losses. A total of 14,000 tons of bombs was dropped.

Apart from the cost in human lives, 20,000 houses were destroyed and several of the Knights' auberges seriously damaged or entirely destroyed, as was the case with the Auberge de Provence.

La valeur stratégique de Malte fut remise en question au déclenchement de la Deuxième guerre mondiale. Certains stratèges britanniques pensaient que l'île qui avait joué un grand rôle dans les guerres précédentes (Crimée, 14-18) devrait être abandonnée en raison de sa trop grande proximité de l'Italie ennemie. Il suffisait de bloquer soigneusement, et ce n'était pas difficile, les deux extrémités de la Méditerranée, Suez et Gibraltar. D'autres militaires pensaient au contraire que la possession de cette mer donnait la sécurité aux territoires anglais pétroliers du Proche Orient, qu'il fallait au contraire se maintenir à tout prix, d'autant plus que la route du Cap était manifestement très longue pour acheminer l'énergie nécessaire à la conduite de la guerre.

Mais l'entrée en guerre active de l'Italie et les opérations contre Rommel en Afrique du Nord décidèrent du maintien de Malte comme citadelle. A partir de La Valette ou des terrains d'aviation que l'on avait construits à la hâte on pouvait harceler les convois ennemis qui apportaient vivres et munitions aux forces allemandes.

C'est Malte qui fut harcelée pendant deux terribles années (10 juin 1940-8 novembre 1942). Les opérations sur mer et dans les airs furent innombrables, les bombardements sur l'île continuels. Le ravitaillement ne parvenait plus et les puissances de l'Axe mettaient au point un plan de débarquement dans la baie de Marsaxlokk.

Les bombes tombaient sans discontinuer sur La Valette, le Grand Port et les aérodromes. La population civile subit de lourdes pertes. 14.000 tonnes de bombes furent larguées.

En plus du tribut en vies humaines vingt mille maisons avaient été détruites et plusieurs auberges de Chevaliers gravement atteintes ou sinon entièrement détruites, comme l'Auberge de Provence.

Reconstruction des bâtiments démolis pendant la guerre.
Reconstruction of buildings destroyed during the war.
Wiederaufbau der während des Krieges beschädigten Gebäude.

The Maltese as a builder

Since the most urgent problem in Malta today is unemployment it can be understood that the inhabitants emigrate in large numbers to bigger countries with developing economies, such as Canada and particularly Australia.

In the archipelago every possible scrap of land is cultivated, and several crops a year are not rare, but irrigation suffers from a serious shortage of water.

The gradual departure of the British armed forces has caused a reduction of employment and of the inflow of currency. The closing of the Suez Canal caused a fall-off in the amount of shipping and therefore of work in the repair yards. Resumption of traffic through the Canal is therefore awaited impatiently.

In 1965, national production covered less than half of total requirements. Agriculture accounts for 7% and industry for 17.7% of the GNP (1965 figures). The tertiary sector alone accounts for 20%.

Malta, which became a member of the Commonwealth after independence, has hitherto had the advantage of British investments and financial assistance. For some years, the island has been trying to develop her relations with other countries.

As in most islands where the sun shines throughout a good part of the year, the tourist trade has been developed, particularly for the winter months. Numerous hotels have been built, mainly on the seashore. In 1974 the island had as many visitors as it had inhabitants – more than 300,000.

Travailleur comme un maltais

Le problème actuel de Malte étant principalement le chômage, on comprend que les habitants émigrent en masse vers les pays plus vastes aux économies en plein développement, c'est-à-dire le Canada et surtout depuis quelques années l'Australie.

Dans l'archipel, tous les terrains possibles sont mis en culture et plusieurs récoltes par ans ne sont pas rares, mais on se heurte au problème de l'eau qui limite sérieusement tout développement de l'irrigation.

Le départ progressif des militaires britanniques a diminué les apports en devises et les emplois dans les bases. La fermeture du canal de Suez a fait tomber les passages de bateaux, donc le travail dans les ateliers de réparations. C'est pour cela que la réparation de cette voie d'eau est attendue avec impatience.

En 1965 la production nationale couvrait moins de un pour cent des besoins. L'agriculture représente 7 pour cent du PNB et l'industrie 17,7 pour cent (1965). Le secteur tertiaire à lui seul représente 20 pour cent du PNB.

Devenue membre du Commonwealth après l'indépendance, Malte a bénéficié jusqu'à présent des investissements et de l'aide financière de la Grande Bretagne. Elle essaie depuis quelques années de développer ses relations avec d'autres pays.

Comme pour beaucoup d'îles où le soleil brille une grande partie de l'année, on a développé le tourisme et notamment le tourisme d'hiver. De nombreux hôtels se sont construits, en bord de mer essentiellement. En 1974 on pouvait dire que l'archipel recevait par an autant de visiteurs qu'il comptait d'habitants, soit plus de trois cent mille.

P. 160-161:

*En Haut, Sliema Creek.
En Bas, quartier de Msoda.*

*Above, Sliema Creek.
Below, Msoda district.*

*Oben. Sliema Creek.
Unten, das Viertel von Msoda.*

L'église de Mosta.
Mosta church.
Die Kirche von Mosta.

Sanctuaire de Ta'Pinu.
Sanctuary of Ta'Pinu.
Das Heiligtum von Ta'Pinu.

Statue sculptée dans une carrière.
Statue carved in a quarry.
Eine in einen Steinbruch gehauene Statue.

Religion

This is perhaps the only country where the population of a small town or village decides to build a church for themselves, as with the churches and cathedrals of the Middle Ages. What does it matter how much time is spent on such collective work?

The Maltese have always been deeply religious. Were they not renowned builders of temples in prehistoric times? The struggle against the Ottomans was carried out as much for the economic and political motives of the European powers as for the mainly religious motives of the Maltese and the Knights.

Everybody is proud of St John's cathedral, built by a Maltese architect. The same applies to the more recently built church of Mosta, the dome of which is supposed to be the third largest in the world. This church was built in 1860 with contributions from Maltese emigrants. It is said that the architect was practically illiterate. During the last war a 1,000-lb bomb fell through the dome and rolled on the ground at the feet of the congregation. The defused object of this "miracle" is exhibited in the sacristy.

The sanctuary of Ta'Pinu on Gozo was built between 1920 and 1936 on the site of a former sixteenth-century chapel. This imposing building was the result of a spiritual experience undergone in 1883 by Carmella Grima, a countrywoman who heard a voice telling her to say an Ave Maria. In front of the church is a life-sized representation of the stations of the Cross entirely of marble.

In the countryside near Siggiewi a peasant has carved in the rock of a quarry huge statues of Christ, the Virgin and Saint Michael.

C'est peut-être le seul pays où la population, comme pour les églises et cathédrales du Moyen Age, décide à l'échelle de la petite ville ou du village de construire un édifice religieux. Qu'importe alors le temps consacré à cette oeuvre collective.

Les Maltais ont toujours été très religieux. N'ont-ils pas été de fameux constructeurs de temples aux époques préhistoriques? La lutte contre les Turcs musulmans se fit autant pour les motifs économiques et politiques des puissances européennes que pour des raisons en grande partie religieuses.

La cathédrale Saint Jean construite par un architecte maltais remplit tout le monde de fierté. Il en est de même pour la plus récente église de Mosta dont le dôme est paraît-il le troisième du monde. L'édifice fut construit en 1860 grâce à la contribution d'émigrants de la ville. On dit que l'architecte ne savait pratiquement ni lire ni écrire. Pendant la dernière guerre une bombe de 400 kilos traversa la coupole roula sur le sol aux pieds des fidèles apeurés. L'objet du "miracle", désamorcé, est exposé dans la sacristie.

Le sanctuaire de Ta'Pinu à Gozo a été construit entre 1920 et 1936 sur l'emplacement d'une ancienne chapelle du 16 ème siècle. Cet imposant monument fut édifié à la suite d'une expérience spirituelle vécue en 1883 par une paysanne Carmella Grima qui entendit une voix lui demander de réciter la prière de la Vierge. Sur le parvis on peut voir en grandeur nature un chemin de croix entièrement en marbre.

Dans la campagne, aux environs de Siggiewi, un paysan a sculpté dans le rocher d'une carrière de grandes statues du Christ, de la Vierge et de Saint Michel.

Emigration

Overpopulation and the lack of local resources made the Maltese emigrate during the 19th Century. 19th Century.

They went naturally to the countries of French colonisation in north Africa, Algeria and above all to Tunisia where several communities had already settled. The new emigrants, disregarding the fact that they could understand the Arab language which is similar to theirs were now under the jurisdiction of a French catholic power.

At the beginning of this century the Maltese were strongly implanted in Tunisia and the east of Algeria (Bone, Bougie, Philippeville, Constantine). Most of them were workers (stone-cutters) or merchants.

Fraternizing in the populous districts of big towns particularly in Algeria and together with other elements of a Mediterranean origin, especially Italian, they acclimatised quickly with the new French community composed of a mosaic of ethnics. of ethnics.

However, they kept, in many ways, their own personality. It is as this that the Maltese character appears in many novels written by famous French writers of North Africa during the years 1910-1930.
(Pierre Dimech)

La surpopulation et le manque de ressources locales obligèrent les Maltais à émigrer dès le 19ème siècle.

C'est tout naturellement vers les pays de colonisation française en Afrique du Nord qu'ils se tournèrent, en Algérie et surtout en Tunisie. Quelques communautés s'y trouvaient depuis fort longtemps. Les nouveaux arrivants, outre le fait qu'ils comprenaient assez bien l'arabe langue voisine de la leur, se trouvaient sous la juridiction d'une puissance catholique, la France.

Au début de ce siècle les Maltais étaient solidement implantés en Tunisie et dans l'est de l'Algérie (Bône, Bougie, Philippeville, Constantine). La plupart d'entre eux étaient ouvriers (tailleurs de pierres) ou commerçants. ''Fraternisant dans les quartiers populeux des grandes villes avec les autres éléments d'origine méditerranéenne, notamment italiens, ils s'intégrèrent rapidement à la nouvelle communauté française formée d'une mosaïque d'ethnies, surtout en Algérie. Toutefois, ils gardèrent sur beaucoup de plans une personnalité bien à eux. C'est ainsi que le personnage du Maltais figure dans maints romans écrits par les grands écrivains français d'Afrique du Nord dans les années 1910-1930''. (Pierre DIMECH).

Jeunes Maltais à Sliema
Young Maltese at Sliem
Junge Malteser in Sliem

Bibliography

Bibliographie

There are few books in French on the history of Malta, apart from the very complete work by J. Godechot (Editions "Que Sais-je?"). There is, however, an impressive number in English, though nearly all of them gloss over the important prehistoric period, even though in this respect Malta fears little competition from neighbouring countries. Books about the Knights abound in all languages. There are very old works in the major libraries.

Il existe peu de livres en français sur l'histoire de Malte, à part le très complet ouvrage de J. Godechot aux Editions Que Sais-je. En anglais par contre le nombre en est impressionnant. Cependant presque tous laissent sérieusement dans la pénombre l'importante période pré-historique alors que pour cette époque Malte a peu de choses à envier à beaucoup de ses voisins. Les livres sur les Chevaliers sont nombreux dans toutes les langues. Des ouvrages très anciens existent dans les grandes bibliothèques.

T. Zammit: Prehistoric Malta, the Tarxien Temple, Oxford 1930
J. D. Evans: Malta, London 1959
B. Blouet: The Story of Malta, Londres 1967
A. J. Agius: Guide Books, Freedom Press Valetta
J. D. Evans: The Prehistoric Culture Sequence in the Maltese Archipelago, Prehistoric Society, London 1954
The Prehistoric Antiquities of the Maltese Islands, London 1971
D. H. Trump: An Archeological Guide, London 1972
J. Godechot: Histoire de Malte, P. U. F. 1970
Quentin Hughes: Fortress, Architecture and Military History in Malta, Londres 1969
The Building of Malta, 1530-1795, London 1956
Claire-Eliane Engel: Les Chevaliers de Malte, 1961
J.-L. Miège: Histoire de Malte, 3 vol., Paris 1840
Pierre Dimech: Contribution à l'Etude de l'Histoire Constitutionelle et Politique de Malte, Eveil du Nationalisme Maltais (1800-1936)
Thêse du doctorat, Paris, 1973

Toutes les photos sont de l'auteur sauf:
M. Spinelli: page 17 (haut)
Archives: page 157
Office du Tourisme – Malte: pages 79 - 83
92 - 105 - 121 - 124 - 135 - 149 - 151 - 164

Independence

Those who conquered the island or passed through it during its history have marked it either in the form of archaeological remains or by leaving indelible traces on its culture. There has been much talk of the linguistic dispute, the political aim of which was nothing more than to determine whether Malta was culturally a part of Italy.

The fact is that, with the arrival of the Knights, the Maltese followed an independent historical road which has left its mark on them, and whereas Maltese was for a long time considered as a dialect, it is nevertheless a language which has been used for numerous works and is used in the local press. Today it is the national language, and many of the courses at the University are in Maltese.

The political struggle for autonomy was simultaneous with similar struggles in Europe during the last century. Economic and demographic problems accentuated the cleft between the local population and the tutelary power.

Once a constitution had been adopted, in 1947, a referendum was held to discover whether Malta wanted to be integrated into Great Britain. 75% of the 44.5% of the electorate which voted said Yes; the Labour Party had recommended integration and the Church had asked people to vote No. However, the poll was so slight that Great Britain decided not to take the result into account.

In 1959 a new constitution was adopted, leaving the British responsible only for Defence and Foreign Affairs. Following upon the refusal of financial assistance, a further referendum was held, and the Maltese archipelago achieved independence on 21 September 1964.

The Maltese political system is parliamentary. Power is exercised by the Prime Minister and Cabinet. The Prime Minister, Mr. Dom Mintoff, is the leader of the majority. Members of Parliament are elected by universal suffrage. The electoral system is based on the principle of proportional representation, and the island is not divided into electoral wards. There are two political parties — Conservative and Labour.

A President of the Republic was appointed in December 1974. He is Mr. Anthony Mamo.

Indépendance

Les conquérants ou "visiteurs" qui passèrent dans l'île au cours de son histoire ont laissé leurs empreintes sous forme de vestiges archéologiques. Ils ont aussi marqué la culture locale de façon indélébile. On a beaucoup parlé de la querelle linguistique. Il s'agissait en fin de compte de savoir si Malte faisait culturellement partie de l'Italie.

Le fait est que depuis l'arrivée des Chevaliers, les Maltais ont suivi un cheminement historique tout à fait original qui les a profondément marqués. Le maltais a longtemps été considéré comme un dialecte qui jusqu'à la fin du 18ème siècle n'a pas été écrit. Ce n'en est pas moins une langue, dans laquelle de nombreux ouvrages ont été imprimés. Plusieurs journaux locaux étaient édités. C'est maintenant la langue nationale. Plusieurs cours à l'Université sont donnés en maltais.

La lutte politique pour l'autonomie est apparue dès l'aube des combats similaires en Europe au siècle dernier. Les problèmes économiques et démographiques accentuèrent le divorce entre la population locale et la puissance tutélaire.

Après l'adoption d'une constitution en 1947 un référendum eut lieu pour savoir si Malte voulait s'intégrer à la Grande Bretagne. Soixante quinze pour cent des votants qui représentaient en fait moins de la moitié de la population en âge de voter se prononcèrent pour le oui. Le parti travailliste avait recommandé l'intégration et l'église avait demandé de voter non. En raison de la faible participation au vote la Grande Bretagne ne prit pas les résultats obtenus en considération.

En 1959 une nouvelle Constitution laissait seulement aux Anglais les responsabilités de la Défense et des Affaires Etrangères. A la suite d'un refus d'aide financière, un référendum fut organisé et l'archipel maltais accéda à l'Indépendance le 21 septembre 1964.

Le système politique maltais est parlementaire. Le pouvoir est exercé par le Premier Ministre et les autres membres de Cabinet. Le Premier Ministre est le chef de la majorité. Les députés sont élus par l'ensemble de la population. Il n'y a pas de découpage de l'île en circonscription. Les électeurs doivent se prononcer sur la totalité des candidats. Il y a deux partis politiques se divisant en conservateur et travailliste.

Le Premier Ministre est M. Dom Mintoff. M. Anthony Mamo a été nomine Président de la Republique en décembre 1974.

Un chapitre important de l'histoire de l'île a été écrit depuis 1974: la Naissance de la République.

Des élections au suffrage universel ont eu lieu les 17 et 18 septembre 1976 et ont reconduit au poste de Premier Ministre Monsieur Dom MINTOFF.

An important chapter in the history of the Island has been written since 1974: the Birth of the Republic.

Elections by universal suffrage took place in 17 and 18 September 1976, as a result of which Mr. Dom MINTOFF was confirmed in the office of Prime Minister.

Ein bedeutendes Kapitel der Geschichte der Insel wurde erst ab 1974 geschrieben: die Entstehung der Republik.

Wahlen mit allgemeinem Stimmrecht fanden am 17. und 18. September 1976 statt. Herr Dom MINTOFF wurde in seiner Funktion als Ministerpräsident bekräftigt.

THE REPUBLIC OF MALTA

On the 13th December, 1974, by an act of Parliament, Malta was declared a republic, founded on work and on respect for the fundamental rights and freedoms of the individuals. Several changes were made in the new Constitution, making it more liberal and truly democratic. The office of President of Malta was established to replace that of the Governor-General and thus the monarchical system of Government under the Independence Constitution was abolished. Malta remained a member of the Commonwealth.

The Constitution

The Constitution provides that the national language and the language of the Courts is Maltese, but both Maltese and English are official languages.

An independent Public Service Commission consisting of three to five members is appointed by the President on the advice of the Prime Minister to make recommendations to the Prime Minister concerning appointments to public office and the dismissal and disciplinary control of persons holding public office. An Employment Commission consisting of a chairman and four other members to ensure that in respect of employment no distinction, exclusion or preference that is not justifiable is made or given in favour of or against any person by reason of his political opinion, is also provided for.

The Judicature is independent.

Radio and television broadcasting is controlled by an independent authority.

Declaration of Principles

The Constitution upholds the right to work and to reasonable hours of work, the safe-guarding of rights of women workers, the encouragement of private economic enterprise, the encouragement of co-operatives, the provision of free and compulsory primary education, and the provision of social assistance and insurance.

Fundamental Rights and Freedoms of the Individual

The Constitution provides for the protection of the right to life, freedom from arbitrary arrest or detention, protection of freedom of conscience and protection from discrimination on the grounds of race.

The President of the Republic

The first Maltese-born Governor-General appointed by the present Labour Government in July 1971 was nominated President of Malta on 13th December, 1974.

Under the Constitution the office of President becomes vacant after five years from the date of appointment made by Resolution of the House of Representatives. He appoints the Prime Minister, choosing the Member of the House of Representatives whom he judges to be ablest to command the confidence of a majority of the Members, and on the advice of the Prime Minister he appoints the other Ministers, the Chief Justice, the Judges and the Attorney General.

The Cabinet

The Cabinet consists of the Prime Minister and such number of other Ministers as are recommended by the Prime Minister.

Parliament

The House of Representatives consists of such number of members, being an odd number and divisible by the number of divisions, as Parliament by law determines from time to time. At the moment this number of members is 55 and the number of divisions 10. In future the electoral divisions are to be not less than 9 and not more than 15 as Parliament may from time to time determine. The normal life of the House of Representatives is five years, after which a general election is held.

Election is by universal adult suffrage on the principle of proportional representation. The age of majority is eighteen years.

LA REPUBLIQUE DE MALTE

Le 13 décembre 1974, par un acte du Parlement, Malte a été instituée République, celle-ci est basée sur le travail, le respect des droits fondamentaux et des libertés individuelles. Plusieurs modifications ont été apportées à la Constitution la faisant plus libérale et réellement démocratique. La fonction du Président de la République Maltaise a été créée afin de remplacer celle du Gouverneur Général et des séquelles de la fonction. Le système monarchique avait déjà été aboli par la Constitution publiée lors de l'accession de Malte à l'Indépendance. Malte demeure membre du Commonwealth.

La Constitution

La Constitution stipule que la langue maltaise est la langue nationale, et qu'elle l'est pour des lois, mais l'anglais et le maltais sont indifféremment usités comme langue officielle.

Une commission officielle mais totalement indépendante, de 3 à 5 membres est nommée par le Président après avis du Premier Ministre, pour faire les recommandations à celui-ci quant aux manquements à la discipline dans l'administration. Une commission composée d'un Président et de quatre membres s'assure que les employés de l'administration sont bien engagés sans aucun ostracisme ni favoritisme en raison de leurs opinions politiques.

La justice est indépendante. Une autorité indépendante contrôle la Radio et la Télévision.

Déclaration de Principe

La Constitution se porte garant des droits des travailleurs (respect des horaires), respect également des droits de la femme qui travaille, encourage la libre entreprise, ainsi que les coopératives, prévoit l'enseignement obligatoire, celui-ci est gratuit, prévoit également la Sécurité Sociale.

Les droits fondamentaux et les libertés individuelles

La Constitution veille à la protection au droit à la vie, à ce que les arrestations ou les détentions arbitraires n'existent pas, protège la liberté de conscience et ne tolère pas le racisme.

Le Président de la République

Le premier Gouverneur Général maltais, mis en place par l'actuel Gouvernement travailliste, en juillet 1971, a été nommé Président de Malte le 13 décembre 1974.

Après 5 ans d'exercice (nomination qui est faite par le Parlement) le poste de Président devient vacant.

Il nomme le Premier Ministre en le choisissant parmi ceux qu'il juge le plus capable de recevoir le vote de confiance du Parlement et sur avis du Premier Ministre il nomme les autres membres, le Chef de la Cour Suprême, les Juges et le Procureur Général.

Le Cabinet

Le Cabinet Ministériel est composé du Premier Ministre et par les autres Ministres choisis par celui-ci.

Le Parlement

Le Parlement est constitué par un nombre impair de membres, et celui-ci est divisible par le nombre de circonscriptions déterminé par les votes du Parlement. Actuellement le nombre de Députés est de 55 et les circonscriptions de 10. A l'avenir les circonscriptions ne seront pas moins de 9 et pas plus de 15. Le chiffre exact est fixé par différents votes du Parlement. La durée du mandat électoral est de 5 ans.

Les élections sont faites au suffrage universel sur le principe de la représentation proportionnelle. L'âge légal de la majorité est de 18 ans.

DIE REPUBLIK MALTA

Am 13. Dezember 1974 wurde Malta durch einen Parlamentsakt zur Republik erklärt. Diese beruht auf der Arbeit, dem Respekt der Grundrechte und der individuellen Freiheiten. Die Verfassung wurde mehreren Änderungen unterworfen, die sie liberaler und wirklich demokratisch gestalteten. Die Funktion des Präsidenten der maltesischen Republik wurde geschaffen, um die des General- gouverneurs und die mit dieser verbundenen Unannehmlichkeiten aus der Welt zu schaffen. Das monarchische System war schon von der Verfassung abgeschafft worden, die nach der Unabhängigkeits- erklärung Maltas in Kraft trat. Malta ist Mitglied des " Commonwealth " geblieben.

Die Verfassung

Die Verfassung setzt fest, dass die maltesische Sprache die Nationalsprache sei und dass alle Gesetze in ihr abgefasst sein müssen, aber maltesisch und englisch werden gleicherweise als offizielle Sprachen benutzt.

Eine offizielle, aber vollkommen unabhängige, aus 3 bis 5 Mitgliedern bestehende Kommission, wird vom Präsidenten, nach Vortrag des Ministerpräsidenten, ernannt, um diesem, bei Disziplinar- verstössen in der Verwaltung, zur Seite zu stehen. Eine aus einem Präsidenten und vier Mitgliedern bestehende Kommission wacht darüber, dass alle Verwaltungsangestellten ohne jeglichen Ostrazismus und Favoritentum, was ihre politischen Meinungen anbetrifft, eingestellt werden.

Die Justiz ist unabhängig. Eine unabhängige Behörde kontrolliert Radio und Fernsehen.

Grundsätzliche Erklärung

Die Verfassung garantiert die Rechte der Arbeiter (Einhalten der Arbeitszeiten), den Respekt der Rechte der arbeitenden Frauen; sie fördert die freien Unternehmen, sowie die Konsumgenossen- schaften; es besteht Schulpflicht; der Schulbesuch erfolgt gratis: das Recht auf Sozialversicherung ist ebenfalls in der Verfassung verankert.

Grundrechte und individuelle Freiheiten

Die Verfassung schützt das Recht zu leben; sie wacht darüber, dass keine illegalen Verhaftungen oder Einkerkerungen erfolgen; sie schützt die Gedankenfreiheit und toleriert keine Rassenhetze.

Der Präsident der Republik

Der erste, von der augenblicklichen Labourregierung im Juli 1971 eingesetzte General- gouverneur, war am 13. Dezember 1974 zum Präsidenten von Malta ernannt worden.

Nach fünfjähriger Amtsausübung (die Ernennung wird vom Parlament vorgenommen), muss das Präsidentenamt neu besetzt werden. Der Präsident ernennt den Ministerpräsidenten. Seine Wahl trifft den Politiker, den er am geeignetsten glaubt, ein Vertrauensvotum des Parlaments erhalten zu können. Die anderen Regierungsmitglieder, sowie den Präsidenten des Obersten Gerichtshofes, die Richter und den Oberstaatsanwalt ernennt er auf Vorschlag des Ministerpräsidenten.

Das Kabinett

Das Regierungskabinett wird vom Ministerpräsidenten und den von ihm ernannten Ministern gebildet.

Das Parlament

Das Parlament setzt sich aus einer ungeraden Anzahl von Mitgliedern zusammen. Diese ist teilbar durch die Anzahl der Wahlbezirke, die durch Abstimmung im Parlament festgesetzt werden. Die Zahl der Abgeordneten ist augenblicklich 55 und es bestehen 10 Wahlbezirke. In Zukunft soll es nicht weniger als 9 und nicht mehr als 15 Wahlbezirke geben. Die genaue Anzahl wird durch die verschiedenen Parlamentsabstimmungen bestimmt. Das Abgeordnetenmandat beträgt 5 Jahre.

Die Wahlen gehen nach allgemeinem Wahlrecht und dem Proportionalsystem vor sich. Jeder volljährige Bürger kann mit 18 Jahren an den Wahlen teilnehmen.

UN PAYS POUR QUATRE SAISONS

par Victor Lewis

A chaque coucher de soleil flamboyant, aussi prodigieux une veille de Noël qu'en plein été, Malte et sa petite sœur Gozo, déploient tous leurs charmes. Chaque saison a ses propres attraits. Qui ne connait de Malte ses journées inondées de soleil, ses douces nuits d'été et la mer d'un bleu limpide qui l'étreint tendrement! Cependant, à la différence de la plupart des stations balnéaires, Malte ne se contente pas d'un ou de deux rubans de sable doré disparaissant sous un triple bataillon de matelas rembourrés, "tous alignés vers la droite", comme des troupes passant la revue de sorte que, ayant payé, vous risquez de vous retrouver au troisième rang, étroitement serré à droite et à gauche, ne voyant pas grand chose sinon rien de la mer qui s'étend aux pieds du premier rang.

A Malte, on ne paie pas pour accéder à la plage. Et les marchands itinérants ne viennent pas constamment vous harceler, bardés de lunettes de soleil ou encombrés de sacs de pêches peu séduisants ; tous ces gens agressifs surgissent toujours au moment où vous sombrez dans un délicieux sommeil sous la chaleur du soleil.

Rien de tout cela. A Malte, vous trouverez la liberté de la plage. Elle est toute à vous. Jetez-vous sur le sable où bon vous semble. Et si vous avez des enfants, installez-vous tout au bord de l'eau; ils pourront construire des châteaux de sable à satiété sans craindre que les vagues les emportent. Vous ne devrez pas non plus renoncer à vous assoupir ou à faire un saut au café de la plage pour vous rafraichir à cause de la marée montante. Cette utopie méditerranéenne ne connait pas de marée.

Il y a là des plages pour tous les goûts. Peut-être aimez-vous patauger dans l'eau et sentir le sable chaud effleurer vos pieds, ou vous lancer à corps perdu du haut des rochers pour plonger dans l'eau profonde. Certains préfèrent peut-être un bord de mer où, équipés de pied en cap, ils pourront plonger et nager pour voir un monde aux couleurs fabuleuses, qui vit sous la surface de cette Mer du Milieu d'une faune si particulière et qui abrite des habitants bien spécifiques.

Pour le vacancier, Malte est beaucoup plus grande que ses apparentes frontières terrestres. On peut disposer de yachts, de bateaux à voiles, de "dghajes" et de "Luzzijiet" pittoresques, de bateaux à moteur, de vedettes ou de simples bateaux à rames, permettant ainsi des distractions bien au delà des limites de la terre ferme.

Mais Malte n'est pas tout entière sur le rivage.

Dans cette île, qui est en elle même une manière de vivre, le plus doux des hivers cède le pas au printemps précoce qui chasse vite du calendrier les mois rigoureux, entrainant dans son sillage les jours dorés de l'été qui s'attardent jusqu'à ce que les douceurs de l'automne apaisent les plaisirs du grand large qui se succèdent au fil de l'an. Le printemps même ne connait pas de mesure. Dès le mois de mars il y a sept heures d'ensoleillement et une température moyenne de 20°. En avril, ces statistiques d'une importance primordiale atteignent huit heures et demi de soleil dans un ciel sans nuage et une température moyenne de 22°5. En mai ce sont dix heures de soleil et 25°5 de température ambiante. Puis, c'est l'été!

Dans la journée ou même la nuit, on peut tout faire, ou regarder faire. Le printemps est étonnant. C'est l'époque du Carnaval. Au mois de mai, pendant quatre jours, Malte devient un peu folle. A Malte, le Carnaval est un formidable amalgame strident et technicolor de l' "Oktoberfest" allemand, du "Mardi Gras" français, de la "Bataille des fleurs" de Jersey, des fameuses festivités de Hong Kong; il est aussi enrichi du folklore et de la tradition des îles maltaises. Cette fête gigantesque se concentre autour de l'ancienne ville de la Valette, dont les rues retentissent de rires, de musique et de tous les bruits de la procession du carnaval qui s'étend sur un kilomètre et demi, suivie d'une foule qui danse sur les places. Celui qui visite Malte au temps du carnaval et qui ne brûle pas de se joindre à la fête n'est assurément qu'un triste sire. Pâques aussi amène ses processions à travers les rues de nombreuses villes et villages, en dehors des manifestations à caractère spirituel, elles sont solennelles, imposantes et splendides pour s'achever sur une note de grand bonheur le dimanche de Pâques.

Lorsque le printemps cède la place à l'été, nul ne résiste à l'appel du grand large. Sous l'égide du Royal Malta Yacht Club s'organisent des régates de voiliers d'un bout à l'autre de l'île, ainsi qu'une course qui s'est gagnée une réputation internationale, les "600 miles Middle Sea Race" qui attire les yachts et les yachtmen de nombreux pays et forment un spectacle digne d'émouvoir les marins d'eau douce les plus obstinés.

A quelques encablures à l'intérieur de l'île se trouve un remarquable centre sportif situé à proximité d'un terrain de course. Le visiteur peut devenir membre à titre temporaire, ce qui lui permet de jouer et de regarder jouer au tennis, au cricket ou au squash; il peut aussi nager dans la piscine du club, regarder le tir à l'arc ou le polo, jouer au billard, déjeuner ou dîner d'un repas

typiquement maltais ou d'un barbecue à la clarté de la lune, sous les arbres. Tout à côté se trouve le Royal Malta Golf Club où l'indulgence du parcours à 18 trous et la vitesse des parcours normaux, que le soit-disant hiver maltais n'éprouve pas beaucoup, donnera au plus modeste joueur de golf l'impression que somme toute, il est bien meilleur qu'il ne le croyait. Point n'est besoin d'ailleurs que vous preniez vos clubs avec vous-ce qui ne manquerait probablement pas d'entraîner un excédent de bagages. On peut louer des clubs et le golf qui est prêt à souhaiter la bienvenue au nouveau visiteur.
nouveau visiteur.

Lorsque les mois les plus chauds de l'été se terminent on peut voir des courses tous les dimanches sur ce parcours. Ces courses n'ont en fait pas leur pareil, car dans ces courses de trot, se mêlent les poneys trépidants, les roues tourbillonnantes des sulkies et les soies joyeuses de leurs conducteurs qui se rejoignent au paroxisme à l'arrivée, en un spectacle digne de Ben Hur. De temps à autre, ont lieu des courses de vitesse avec de jolis coursiers arabes. Les courses maltaises n'ont rien d'Ascot ou de Longchamps; tout se concentre sur les chevaux et les paris. Mais, si par hasard, vous avez joué de malchance avec les chevaux, vous pouvez toujours vous rendre dans la soirée au casino de Dragonara, au bord de l'eau et vous rattraper par quelques mises modestes dans la salle de jeu.

Mais, le grand large n'implique pas nécessairement le sport. Des circuits touristiques permettent une approche passionnante de l'histoire de ces îles anciennes sur le rivage desquelles Saint Paul a fait naufrage. Des bateaux à moteur conduisent le touriste émerveillé autour du Grand Port majestueux de La Valette, qui vit tant de batailles au cours des siècles. Il faut quinze minutes en ferry boat pour se rendre du petit port de Marfa situé au Nord de cette île bijou qui fut baptisée Gozo mais qui est en vérité l'île de Calypso, aussi belle et romantique que la nymphe.

Pendant tout l'été, les "festi" se succèdent à travers l'île, de joyeux festins, d'origine religieuse pour la plupart, avec processions et feux d'artifice. Se mêler aux foules en de telles occasions, regarder passer les processions, visiter les églises gaîment caparaçonnées, dont chacun révèle son trésor; applaudir les feux d'artifice et répondre aux saluts qui fusent de toute part autour de vous. Voilà ce qu'est *connaître* Malte et les Maltais.

Ceux qui ont des aspirations plus sérieuses trouveront les joies de l'exploration au plus fort de l'été ou dans les ruissellements du printemps, ou dans la douceur et le calme de l'automne. Les journées sont souvent idéales pour la promenade et la découverte des délices de la campagne: errer à travers un paysage sauvage et fascinant, vagabonder par les sentiers qui serpentent, flâner dans les villages accueillants, rechercher les lieux historiques, les joyaux de l'architecture, les splendeurs archéologiques. Pour ceux qui savent le voir, Malte a un tapis enchanté. Il se déroule pour le visiteur qui s'éloigne des plages et des villes. Cette île, dont le centre apparaît comme un rocher volcanique privé de sol, ne possède pas moins de 600 espèces de fleurs sauvages. Si vous vous égarez par les sentiers, le long des anciennes pistes, à travers les champs, il vous faudra marcher avec précaution si vous ne voulez pas écraser quelques fleurs sauvages.

Certains paysages sont d'une beauté saisissante, notamment dans les vallées, sur la crête ou au sommet des falaises escarpées qui dominent la mer. Certains sites historiques impressionnants datent d'environ 3 800 ans avant J.C. Des églises et des chapelles qui bordent le chemin abritent maints trésors et maintes légendes; de petits joyaux d'architecture et des merveilles archéologiques, des fouilles, des villas romaines, des temples anciens, musées, catacombes, palais et grottes, villages débordant de charme et de caractère, fermiers aux champs se servant d'outils qui ont peu varié depuis les temps bibliques.

On peut dire, à tout prendre, que ce lieu d'évasion en pleine Méditerranée, bercé par le printemps et l'été, baigne dans l'insouciance, et tandis que l'accent porte sur le grand large et la bonté de la nature, il subsiste toujours dans la vie nocturne faite par l'homme et joue un rôle essentiel dans toute station balnéaire. Les hôtels, les nights clubs, les restaurants de nuit sont ouverts à tous. Les talents abondent dans ce domaine et les Maltais n'y sont pas moins nombreux. On peut entendre de la musique folklorique maltaise et admirer les danses traditionnelles de l'île. Vous pouvez dîner maltais, chinois, anglais ou italien en arrosant votre repas de vins du pays.

Par contre, si après une journée bien remplie, vous désirez prendre tranquillement votre dîner avant de vous coucher, l'on veillera à ce que vous soyiez satisfaits. Car Malte ne s'adresse pas seulement à ceux qui sont jeunes d'âge mais aussi à ceux qui sont jeunes de coeur et pour lesquels une journée riche en divertissements de toutes sortes doit être suivie d'une soirée paisible.

LAND FOR ALL SEASONS 4349

by Victor Lewis

Each side of flamboyant sunsets - and they can be as spectacular on Christmas Eve as on Midsummer's Day - Malta, and its little brother Gozo, unfold their many charms. Each season offers its own lures. The world knows of Malta's sun-drenched days and balmy summer nights; of the deep blue sea that laps around its shores. But, unlike most holiday resorts, Malta does not just offer a strip of golden sand filled with triple ranked battalions of cushioned daybeds, all accurately 'dressed from the right' like troops before a reviewing monarch so that, having paid for one, you are liable to find yourself in the third row, tightly packed on the left and right and with little or no glimpse of the sea which lies before the front rank.

In Malta there are no areas of beach for which you have to pay to enter. And there are no ceaseless visits from aggressive itinerant sellers of everything from sun glasses to bags of second rate peaches who always arrive just as you are dozing off under a beautiful sun.

No. In Malta you have the freedom of the beach. It's all yours. Sit yourself down wherever you fancy. And if you have youngsters you can pick a spot at the very water's edge, where they can build sand castles to their heart's content without having to fear that at any moment the tide will sweep it all away, or you having to feel that you just must not drop off to sleep, or pop into the beach café for a cooling drink, for fear they will be swept away by the incoming tide. There is no tide in this Mediterranean haven.

And there is a beach to suit everybody, whether it is your pleasure to wade in slowly with the warm sand under your feet, or to hurl yourself with abandon off the rocks and into deep water. Others will want and can get, the sort of shore which will allow them, properly equipped, to dive and swim below to see the fantastic colour and life below the surface of this Middle Sea which has fish peculiarly its own and seabed denizens not seen elsewhere.

Malta, for the holidaymaker, is far bigger than its actual landspace. The availability of yachts, sailing boats, colourful 'dgtrajjes' and 'luzzijiet', speed boats, cruisers and just plain rowboats extends this playground far beyond landfall.

But all Malta is not on the beach. In this island which is a way of life, the mildest of Winters gives way to early Springs which quickly nudge the harsher months off the calendar and, in turn, usher in the golden days of Summer which linger on until a benign Autumn rounds off the year-long pleasures of the Great Outdoors. Spring itself is no timid thing. March brings seven hours of sun and an average temperature of 67°F (20°C). By April those vital statistics have risen to eight and a half hours of cloudless sunshine and an average temperature of 72°F. And by May it is ten hours of sun and 78 degrees of warmth. Then comes the Summer!

By sunshine or moonlight there is everything to do – or to watch other people doing. Spring is spectacular. It is the time of Carnival. For four days each Maytime Malta goes a little mad. Carnival time in Malta is a great, strident, 'technicolor' amalgam of Germany's 'oktoberfest', France's 'Mardi Gras', Jersey's 'Battle of Flowers', Hong Kong's 'Double Tenth', plus much that is best in folklore and tradition in the Maltese islands. The focal point of this gigantic spree is the ancient city of Valletta, whose streets ring with laughter and music and all the sounds of a mile-long carnival procession with its attendant dancing in the squares. The visitor to Malta at Carnival Time who does not itch to join in the fun is a dull fellow indeed. And Eastertide, too, brings its processions through the streets of many towns and villages, outward manifestations of a devout people's spiritual character; solemn, inspiring, beautiful, ending on a note of great happiness on Easter Sunday.

The Great Outdoors calls to everybody as Spring turns to Summer. Under the aegis of the Royal Malta Yacht Club there are sailing races and regattas from one end of the island to the other and, above all, there is the now world-famed 600-mile Middle Sea Race which draws the yachts and the yachtsmen of many countries and presents a spectacle which can move the most stubborn landlubber.

Only a few cable lengths inland is a remarkable sports complex which stands within the perimeter of a race track. And here the visitor may take out temporary membership which entitles him to play or watch tennis, cricket, or squash; to swim in the club's pool, watch archery or polo, play billiards, take lunch or a typical Maltese supper, or a barbecue under the moon and the trees. Cheek by jowl is the Royal Malta Golf Club where the unpunishing nature of the 18-hole, par 67, course and the speed of the fairways, not much tempered by Malta's so-called Winter, will leave the most modest golfer that, after all, he is much better than he thought. And there is no need to lug your clubs all the way to Malta – and probably pay excess baggage on them. Clubs can be hired and the visitor is welcome to what must surely be the cheapest golf in the world.

And when the hottest months of Summer are finally over, there are, on that enfolding track, race meetings every Sunday – race meetings the like of which one rarely sees elsewhere in the world, for there are trotting races in which the combination of high-stepping ponies, the spinning wheels of the sulkys, and the gay silks of the drivers come dramatically together at the winning post to present a spectacle reminiscent of Ben Hur. And in between there are flat races, with fine Arab steeds to see. Racing in Malta is no Ascot or Longchamps; the focus is actually on the horses – and the 'tote'. And if, maybe, you have a bad day on the horses you can always retire in the evening to the Dragonara casino on the water's edge and for modest stakes recoup your losses in the gaming room.

But everything in the Great Outdoors is not necessarily sport. There are conducted coach tours into the dramatic history of these ancient islands on whose shores St Paul was wrecked. They are spectacular steamer trips around the majestic Grand Harbour of Valletta, the scene of many battles throughout the centuries; or there is a fifteen minute ferry trip from the little northern harbour of Marfa to that jewel of an island they call Gozo but which is really the isle of Calypso and as beautiful and romantic as was that nymph herself.

All through the Summer months there are innumerable 'festi' all over the island, gay junkettings, mostly religious in origin, with processions and fireworks displays. To mix in with the crowds on these occasions; to watch the processions; to visit the churches gaily caparisoned each with its own treasures on display; to applaud the fireworks and to acknowledge the greetings which come from all around you . . . this is to *know* Malta and the Maltese.

For the earnest minded there can be wonderful days of exploration, whether it be in high Summer or scintallating Spring or the calm and warm Autumn. So many of its days are made for walking, for seeking out the delights of the countryside; for tramping across the wild and fascinating landscape; wandering through the winding lanes; strolling through the friendly villages; seeking out the historical spots, the architectural gems, the archaeological splendours. Malta has a magic carpet for those who would see it. Away from the beaches and the towns this carpet is spread out for the visitor. On an island where so much of the surface at its centre appears to be volcanic rock bereft of soil there flourish no fewer than 600 species of wildflower. Wander through the lanes, along ancient tracks, across fields, and you will need to walk with caution for fear of crushing some wild flower.

There are striking beauty spots in the valleys, on the ridges and along the high cliffs above the sea. There are dramatic historic sites going back to something like 3,800 years before Christ; there are wayside churches and chapels containing many a treasure and legend; little architectural gems and archaeological excitements; excavations, Roman villas, ancient temples, museums, catacombs, palaces and grottos; villages dripping with charm and character; farmers in the fields using implements little changed from those of Biblical days.

All in all, this Mediterranean playground in the Spring and the Summer is at its most carefree, and while the accent is on the Great Outdoors and the bounty of nature, there still remains the man-made night life which is an essential part of any play resort. The hotels, the night clubs, the late night restaurants are there for all. These is plenty of entertainment talent (not a little of which is Maltese); there is the chance to hear Maltese folk music and see the traditional dances of the island. You can eat Maltese, or Chinese, or English, or Italian and you can savour the wines of the country.

And if, after a full day, you want a quiet meal and so to bed, a most understanding people will see you get them. For Malta cares not just for the young in years, but also for the young in heart who may have reached the stage in life when a full day's enjoyment demands a restful evening.

EIN LAND FÜR JEDE SAISON

von Victor Lewis

Zu beiden Seiten flammender Sonnenuntergänge - und sie können am Weihnachtsabend ebenso eindrucksvoll sein wie am Johannistag - breiten Malta und ihr kleiner Bruder Gozo ihre Reize aus. Jede Saison hat ihre besonderen Attraktionen. Die Welt kennt die sonnenüberströmten Tage Maltas und seine lauen parfümierten Sommernächte; das tiefblaue Meer, das die Inseln wie verspielt umspült. Doch Malta bietet nicht nur einen Streifen oder zwei goldenen Sandes, wie die meisten Ferienbadeorte, die vollbesetzt sind mit ihren Bataillonen von mit Kissen versehen Tagebetten, die sich in drei langen Reihen ausbreiten und sich alle nach rechts ausrichten, wie Truppen vor einem Monarchen, der die Parade abnimmt; wenn man nun eines dieser Betten bezahlt hat, so kann es vorkommen, dass man sich gerade in der dritten Reihe befindet, rechts und links festgepackt, sodass man schon den Kopf recken muss, wenn es einem gelingen soll, einen Blick auf das Meer zu werfen, das sich vor der ersten Reihe ausbreitet.

In Malta braucht man nicht dafür zu bezahlen, um sich am Strand in den Sand zu legen. Und man wird nicht endlos von Kolporteuren behelligt, die einem alles mögliche verkaufen wollen, angefangen mit Sonnenbrillen bis zum Karton von leichtzerquetschten Pfirsichen; und diese agressiven Leute kommen gerade immer dann an, wenn man gerade dabei ist, so angenehm vor sich hinzudösen. Nein . . . In Malta herrscht Strandfreiheit. Alles gehört Ihnen. Legen Sie sich hin, wo Sie wollen. Und wenn man mit Kindern kommt, so kann man sich einen angenehmen Flecken direkt am Wasser aussuchen, wo Ihr Junge oder Ihre Tochter Sandburgen bauen können, nach Herzenslust, ohne befürchten zu müssen, dass die Flut im nächsten Moment ihre stolzen Burgen hinwegspült. Auch Sie selbst brauchen nicht das Gefühl zu haben, dass Sie nur ja nicht einschlafen oder einen Fuss in das Strandcafé setzen dürfen, um dort ein kühles Getränk zu schlürfen, ohne befürchten zu müssen, dass Ihre reizenden Kinder von der steigenden Flut hinweggeschwemmt werden. Denn es gibt keine Flut in diesem mittelländischen Zufluchtsort.

Für jeden gibt es einen Strand, der ihm zusagt; möge man sein Vergnügen darin finden, langsam ins Wasser zu waten, mit dem Gefühl des warmen Sandes unter den Füssen, oder es vorziehen, sich direkt von den Felsen in das tiefe Wasser zu stürzen. Andere wieder können einen Strand suchen - und finden - wo sie, fachmännisch ausgerüstet, sich der Unterwasserjagd hingeben und unter der Wasseroberfläche die phantastischen Farben und das Leben im Mittelmeer beobachten können, das Bewohner aufweist, die man sonst nirgendwo zu sehen bekommt.

Malta erscheint den Feriengästen viel grösser als nur quadratkilometrisch gesehen. Jachten, Segelschiffe, bunte 'Dghajsas' und 'Luzzijets'. Motorboote und Ruderboote in Hülle und Fülle müssen den Quadratmetern Land noch hinzugefügt werden. Doch der Strand ist nicht alles in Malta. Auf dieser Insel, die eine ganze Lebensart darstellt, macht ein milder Winter einem frühen Frühling Platz, der dann schnell wieder die goldenen Sommertage zurückbringt, die dann die schönen Herbsttage zu verlängern scheinen. Und der Frühling bekennt gleich Farbe. März bringt sieben Stunden Sonne mit sich und eine durchschnittliche Temperatur von 20° C. Im April kann man schon auf achteinhalb Stunden wolkenlosen Sonnenschein rechnen und auf eine durchschnittliche Temperatur von 23°. Im Mai haben wir zehn Stunden Sonnenschein und 25° C. Und dann erst kommt der Sommer !

Bei Sonnen- oder Mondschein gibt es allerhand zu tun. Wenn man will, kann man sogar einfach zusehen bei dem, was die andern tun. Im Frühling ist allerhand los. Das ist die Zeit des Karnevals. Vier Tage lang ist alles in Malta ausser Rand und Band. Den der maltesische Karneval ist so ein Amalgam aus deutschem Oktoberfest, französischem 'mardi gras', Jerseys Blumenschlachten, Hongkongs 'Doppelter Zehn'. Den Höhepunkt erreicht dieses Treiben in der altehrwürdigen Stadt Valetta, in deren Strassen Gelächter, Musik und die Geräuschen einer meilenlangen Karnevalprozession ertönen; und dann wird auf den Plätzen der Stadt getanzt. Wer Malta zur Karnevalszeit besucht und keine Lust verspürt, sich in das lustige Treiben zu stürzen, an dem ist Hopfen und Malz verloren. Auch zur Osterzeit ziehen Prozessionen durch die Strassen vieler Städte und Dörfer, denn so manifestiert sich der spirituelle Charakter eines tiefreligiösen Volkes. Ostersonntag setzt dann dem Ganzen die Krone auf.

Im Sommer zieht das grosse blaue Meer die Menschen an. Der 'Royal Malta Yacht Club' veranstaltet dann Segelwettbewerbe und Regatten von einem Ende der Insel zum andern und, als Höhepunkt, der berühmte 600-Meilen Segelwettbewerb, der die Jachtbesiter zahlreicher Länder anzieht; es ist das ein Schauspiel, das den eingefleischtesten Landbewohner zum Seewolf machen kann.

Einige Kabellängen weiter im Innern befindet sich ein bemerkenswerter Sportkomplex mit einer wundervollen Aschenbahn. Hier kann der Besucher vorübergehend Mitglied werden und Tennis, Cricket oder 'Sqash' spielen. Er kann das Schwimmbad benutzen, beim Bogenschiessen oder Polo zuschauen, Billard spielen, zu Mittag oder zu Abend essen oder auch einem typisch maltesischen 'Barbecue' im

Mondschein beiwohnen. Gleich nebenan liegt der 'Royal Malta Golf Club', wo der Golfplatz mit seinen 18 Löchern und seiner Strecke, die man auch während des temperierten sogenannten maltesischen Winters schnell durcheilt, bei dem bescheidensten Golfspieler das Gefühl erweckt, dass er schliesslich besser spiele als er dachte. Man braucht nicht einmal seine Golfschläger nach Malta mitzuschleppen - und dafür noch unnötige Transportkosten zahlen - da man in Malta Golfschläger mieten und so seinem Lieblingssport frönen kann, ohne sein Portemonnaie zu sehr zu strapazieren.

Und wenn die heissesten Sommermonate endlich vorüber sind, dann finden noch jeden Sonntag Pferderennen statt. Auch diese bieten gerade in Malta etwas ganz besonderes: Trabrennen, in denen die trabenden Ponys, die sausenden Räder der Einspänner und die seidenen Blusen der Fahrer sich am Ziel in dramatischer Steigerung zu einer Symphonie vereinen, die das Schauspiel von Ben Hur in Erinnerung bringt. Es gibt aber auch Flachrennen mit rassigen Araberpferden. Die Rennen in Malta haben nichts mit Askot oder Longchamp zu tun. Hier stehen die Pferde im Mittelpunkt des Geschehens . . . und auch die Wetten. Und sollte man bei den Wetten Pech gehabt haben, dann kann man das im Dragonara-Kasino, am Meeresufer, wieder wettmachen und beim Spiel - auch mit bescheidenen Einsätzen - das Geld wieder zurückgewinnen, das einem mit den Pferden davongetrabt ist.

Doch wird im Freien nicht nur Sport getrieben. Es werden auch Führungen veranstaltet durch die dramatische Geschichte dieser altehrwürdigen Inseln, an deren Küste St. Paulus Schiffbruch erlitt. Eindrucksvolle Dampferfahrten rund um den Grossen Hafen von Valetta, durch Jahrhunderte hindurch ein Schlachtfeld; in einer Viertelstunde erreicht man mit der Fähre den kleinen nördlich gelegenen Hafen von Marfa, auf der schönen Insel Gozo, die eigentlich die 'Insel der Kalypso' ist und die so schön und romantisch ist wie es die Nymphe selbst war.

Den ganzen Sommer hindurch finden auf der ganzen Insel unzählige 'festi' statt; es sind das fröhliche Feste, die meist religiösen Ursprungs sind, mit Prozessionen und Feuerwerk. Sich bei dieser Gelegenheit den Einwohnern zuzugesellen, ihren Prozessionen zuzuschauen, die fröhlich ausstaffierten Kirchen zu besuchen, von denen jede ihre eigenen Schätze ausstellt, den schönsten Raketen beim Feuerwerk Beifall zu klatschen und von der Menge ringsumher begrüsst zu werden . . . das heisst Malta und die Malteser kennenlernen.

Für Ernstgesinnte gibt es wundervolle Tage, an denen man der Forschung obliegen kann; sei es im Hochsommer, im schillernden Frühling oder auch im stillen warmen Herbst. Diese Tage sind wie zur Promenade gemacht; zur Suche nach den Freuden, die man auf dem Lande findet; zum Vagabundieren in der wilden faszinierenden Landschaft; zur Wanderung auf den gewundenen Wegen; zum Herumstrolchen durch die freundlichen Dörfer; zur Entdeckung historischer Stätten, der architektonischen Kleinodien, der archäologischen Schönheiten. Malta bietet denen, die es sehen wollen, einen magischen Teppich dar. Vor Stränden und Städten rollt sich dieser Teppich vor dem Besucher ab. Auf einer Insel, wo ein so grosser Teil der Oberfläche ihres Innern aus vulkanischem, jeder Erde baren Gesteins besteht, wachsen und gedeihen nicht weniger als 600 Arten Pflanzen. Wer auf den Wegen, den vor langer Zeit erschlossenen Pfaden, durch die Felder wandert, muss sich davor hüten, die wild blühenden Pflanzen zu zertreten.

In den Tälern gibt es Stellen von frappierender Schönheit, auf den Felsen und den steilen Klippen über dem Meer. Und die historischen Stätten dramatischen Geschehens, die bis auf 3.800 Jahre v. Chr. zurückgehen. An den Wegen gelegene Kirchen und Kapellen enthalten manche Schätze und Legenden; kleine architektonische Kleinodien und archäologische, den Geist anregende Besonderheiten; Ausgrabungen, römische Villen, antike Tempel, Museen, Katakomben, Paläste und Grotten; reizvolle Dörfer voller Charakter; Bauern auf den Feldern, die noch Geräte gebrauchen, die sich seit biblischen Zeiten kaum geändert haben.

Alles in allem geht es auf diesem mittelländischen Spielplatz im Frühling und im Sommer am sorglosesten zu, denn alle Festlichkeiten finden im Freien statt, angefeuert von der Grosszügigkeit der Natur.Doch auch das Nachtleben kommt dabei nicht zu kurz. Hotels, Nachtklubs und Abendrestaurants empfangen den Kunden mit offenen Armen. Es treten dort hervorragende Künstler auf (viele von ihnen sind Malteser). Man kann dort maltesische 'folk-songs' hören und traditionelle maltesische Volkstänze sehen. Zu maltesischer, chinesischer, englischer oder italienischer Küche kann man die Weine des Landes trinken.

Doch wenn man, nach einem gut verbrachten Tag, in Ruhe essen und dann zu Bett gehen will, kann man das auch. Denn Malta denkt auch an die im Herzen Junggebliebenen.

MALTA

SEIT 5.000 JAHREN, EINE INSEL...

Vom Flugzeug aus gesehen ähnelt der maltesische Archipel einem zusammengestürzten Kontinent, der vom Meer überflutet worden wäre; dieses Bild wird von den enormen Klüften vermittelt, die dem Ganzen ihr geologisches Gepräge geben.

Aus dem Wasser hervorragende Blöcke, wo man nur mit Mühe bebaubare Felder von einigem Ausmass entdeckt; die Inseln bestehen im Wesentlichen aus Kalksteinfelsen. Fast die ganze Oberfläche ist in Parzellen von nur geringen Dimensionen aufgeteilt. Es sind das die Felder, die die Bauern im Laufe der Jahrhunderte angelegt haben; dazu mussten sie erst das Gestein entfernen, das die Erde, aus der sie um jeden Preis ihre Nahrung ziehen mussten, unbenutzbar machte. So hat sich wohl die Gesamtanlage der ländlichen Zonen seit Jahrhunderten nicht geändert. Einige verlassene Felder sind von Kräutern wie Thymian überwuchert, die ein starkes, pikantes Parfum verbreiten. Die Felder werden intensiv kultiviert und geben manchmal drei Ernten im Jahr ab. Man baut vor allem Kartoffeln an. In dem sehr stark abgerundeten Relief, das von der Erosion stark angegriffen wurde, findet man kaum einen Flecken, der noch nie von Menschenhand bearbeitet wurde.

Der höchste Punkt Maltas geht nicht über 258 m hinaus (198 m auf Gozo). Die Flüsse sind eher "Wadis" in deren Becken, wie in Nord-Afrika, nur nach Regen ein paar Stunden lang Wasser fliesst. Der kalksteinhaltige Boden absorbiert dieses Wasser, das jahraus, jahrein, mit Mühe und Not einige Quellen speist. Da das Trinkwasserproblem für die Einwohner lebenswichtig ist, ist das Auffangen des Regen- und Quellwassers, sowie seine Verteilung, ein Staatsmonopol. Fabriken für Meerwasserentsalzung verschaffen dem Land die zusätzlichen Wassermengen, die es unbedingt braucht. Der Wassermangel machte sich schon zur Zeit der Ordensritter bemerkbar; denn einer der Hochmeister, Alof de Wignacourt, liess im 17. Jahrhundert einen Aquädukt konstruieren, der Valetta mit Trinkwasser versorgen sollte.

Der Norden Maltas besteht aus einer Reihe von Klüften, die diesem Teil der Insel das Aussehen von ungeheuren Berg- und Talbahnen geben. In den so geschaffenen Tälern gedeihen die Kulturen gut; die Höhen dagegen sind vollkommen unfruchtbar. Man versucht, dort Aufforstungen vorzunehmen.

Malta wurde von den ersten Seefahrern "die Insel der Häfen" genannt. Während seiner ganzen Geschichte wurde es vom Schicksal ausersehen, wegen seiner strategischen Lage im Mittelmeer allen Schiffen, die es anliefen, Zuflucht zu bieten.

Seine Südwestküste mit ihren steilen einige zehn Meter hohen Klippen, ist ungastlich und macht jeden Landungsversuch sehr gefährlich; dagegen sind seine Ost- und Nordostküsten mit breiten Meerbusen und geschützten Buchten versehen. Die Phönizier haben sich darin nicht getäuscht. Zahlreich sind die Buchten auf dieser Seite der Insel, deren Name die semitische Wurzel "marsa" enthält, was Hafen oder Zufluchtsort bedeutet. So findet man Marsaxlokk, Marsaskala, Marsamxett und in Gozo Marsalforn. Die Entwicklung der Küsten ist natürlich um diese Anziehungspole herum vor sich gegangen und das um so mehr, da der Boden, der sich in langsamem Abfall dem Meer zusenkt, eine bessere Lage für die Ortschaften abgab, als die Sicherheitsprobleme die Menschen nicht mehr zwangen, im Innern des Landes zu leben.

Die touristische Auswertung der Inseln verstärkt diese Tendenzen noch. Luxushotels und Ferienclubs wurden in der Nähe der kleinen Sandstrände errichtet, die in geringer Entfernung von Valetta liegen. Doch neue Urbanisationsregeln kanalisieren zum Glück diesen Prozess.

Es gibt nur wenige Stellen, wo man nicht von der Küste aus die Wehrtürme erblickt, die von den Malteserrittern errichtet wurden und die dazu dienten, jede Attacke gleich zu melden. Fast alle nach dem gleichen Modell konstruiert (eine einzige Tür, viereckige Form mit verstärkten Grundmauern), war jeder für die anderen sichtbar und konnte mit ihnen durch optische Zeichen in Verbindung treten.

Von einigen Einbuchtungen abgesehen, die wie Axtschläge in eine Klippe sind, zu deren Füssen das Meer unaufhörlich weitergräbt, zieht die Südküste keineswegs Menschen an, die vorhätten, ihre Nahrung im Meer zu finden. Es gibt dort grandiose Landschaften mit tiefen Grotten, und für die Besucher, die es nicht befürchten, sich in den Dgħajsas (maltesische Boote), an den Fuss der Mauerwände zu begeben, die sich zum Himmel türmen, bleibt die Visite der Blauen Grotte ein unvergessliches Ereignis. Man kann so die ausserordentliche Stabilität dieser Boote feststellen, die manchmal von imposanter Grösse sind. Mit hellen Farben bemalt, enthalten sie immer eine blaue oder grüne Nuance. Zu beiden Seiten des Bugs befindet sich ein feingezeichnetes Auge.

Wenn Malta und Gozo die beiden bedeutenden Inseln sind, so existiert doch noch eine kleinere, Comino (Kemmuna). Ihre Schwester, Cominotto (Kemmunett), hat sich vor nicht allzulanger Zeit von den beiden Inseln geschieden. Der Meerarm, der sie trennt, hat den Namen "Blaue Lagune" erhalten, wegen der extraordinären türkisblauen Farbe ihres Wassers und des Schutzes, den sie gegen die Wellen bietet.

Stellenweise fallen die Klippen von Comino steil ins Meer, und man hat den Eindruck, dass es ein ganz glatter Schnitt ist, dass die Erosion sich ständig und regelmässig vollzieht. Die Menschen, die dort ständig wohnen, kann man an den Fingern einer Hand abzählen. Ein kürzlich dort erbautes Hotel bringt etwas Leben auf die Insel, die nur eineinhalb km lang ist.

Den prähistorischen Tempeln von Mnajdra und Ħaġar Qim auf der Südküste gegenüber gelegen ist die Insel Filfla, von Mysterien eingehüllt, von Legenden umwoben. Fast undurchdringlich, wurde sie immer als unheilbringend betrachtet. Sie ist der einzige Boden des Archipels, der unbewohnt ist.

Das Wasserproblem

Das Wasserproblem stellte sich in den maltesischen Inseln schon zur Zeit der Ordensritter. Da der Boden des Archipels zum grössten Teil aus Kalkstein besteht, können sich keine grossen natürlichen Wasserreserven bilden, weder an der Oberfläche noch im Untergrund. Deshalb braucht man sich auch nicht darüber zu wundern, dass heutzutage alles Trinkwasser Staatsmonopol ist. Die Fabriken für Meerwasserentsalzung bringen da nur ein geringes Plus. Während des Hochsommers werden die Inselbewohner aufgefordert, Leitungswasser nur möglichst spärlich zu benutzen.

Vierzig Jahre später als der Baubeginn von Valetta war die Wasserversorgung dieser in voller Entwicklung begriffenen Stadt schon zu einem Problem geworden. Der Hochmeister Alof de Wignacourt liess damals einen sehr langen Aquädukt bauen, um Trinkwasser vom Zentrum der Insel zur Hauptstadt zu leiten.

MALTA
Das Relief

Oberfläche 246 qkm - Länge 27 km - Breite 14 km - Küstenbereich 137 km

GOZO Oberfläche 67 qkm - Länge 14 km - Breite 7km - Küsten bereich 43 km

Regen: nur 220 mm pro Jahr - Temperaturen: im Winter 13.7°C, im Sommer 22.6°C

Gesamtbevölkerung: 320.000 Einwohner (fast genausoviel leben ausserhalb der Insel)

Hauptstadt: Valetta.

DER ARCHIPEL DER RIESEN

Der Reisende, der in Malta, der Ritter und ihrer Geschichte wegen, haltmacht, wird erstaunt sein, dort auf Reste von gigantischen Konstruktionen zu stossen. Hier blühte tatsächlich einige Jahrtausende lang eine erstaunliche mittelländische Zivilisation.

Der Legende nach wurde der Archipel in einer fernen Vergangenheit von Riesen bewohnt. Man ist fast geneigt, daran zu glauben, wenn man unter seinem, mehrere Tonnen wiegendem, Türsturz den Tempel von Ħaġar Qim betritt oder zu den Opferaltären von Mnajdra durch die aussergewöhnlichen monolithischen Steintore Zutritt erhält. Um sich vollkommen davon zu überzeugen, braucht man nur die hohen Mauern von Ġgantija zu messen, dessen Name allein ein Programm ist.

Schliesslich liessen die Tempelerbauer das maltesische Volk, das die enormen Befestigungen von Valetta, seinem Vorposten Floriana und die zahlreichen flammenden Barokkirchen erbaute, vorausahnen.

ALLES BEGINNT IN GHAR DALAM

Während mehrerer Generationen hatten Schäfer eine Grotte als Tierpark benutzt; diese war nicht weit entfernt von der jetzigen Kleinstadt Birzebbuga, am Ufer der Bucht von Marsaxlokk. Sie ahnten nicht einmal, dass in der Streu ihrer Tiere einige Meter Erde die sehr alte Geschichte ihrer Insel verbargen. Bis eines Tages, im Jahr 1865, Arthur Issel, ein englischer Wissenschaftler, dem Archipel einen Besuch abstattete, auf der Suche nach Fossilien . . .

Ausser einer Bestätigung der geologischen Kenntnisse offenbarte die Grotte von Ghar Dalam noch die ältesten Spuren menschlicher Gegenwart auf der Insel.

Das Felsgestein der maltesischen Inseln wurde vor ungefähr fünfzig Millionen Jahren von Anschwemmungen der Tertiärzeit gebildet. Diese Ablagerungen verhärteten sich, wobei sie eine Menge Muscheltiere einschlossen, was man feststellen kann, wenn man am Meeresufer, vor allem an der Küstenstrasse in Siema spaziert geht. Vor einer Million Jahren, am Anfang der grossen Vereisung, wusch eine riesige Erosion, die sintfluthaften Regenniederschlägen zuzuschreiben war, den Erdboden aus und begann ein Relief zu zeichnen.

Wissenschaftler behaupten, dass zu dieser Epoche - im Pleistozän (Eiszeitalter) - die maltesischen Inseln mit Sizilien und Afrika verbunden waren, und dass die Trennung von Afrika zuerst erfolgte. Es ist noch zu bemerken, dass die Meerestiefen zwischen dem Archipel und dem afrikanischen Kontinent manchmal 2500 m Tiefe erreichen, während sie Sizilien zu 200 m nicht überschreiten.

Das Mittelmeer war damals ein "weites Weideland mit grossen Bäumen, Gebüschen und grossen Sumpfpflanzen, zwischen denen Vögel und sonstige Flügeltiere, Süsswasserschildkröten, Elefanten, Nilpferde und zahlreiche Wirbeltiere kamen und gingen, auf der Suche nach Nahrung."

In der ungefähr 90 m langen Grotte von Ghar Dalam haben Ausgrabungen zu Entdeckungen von einer beeindruckenden Menge von Tierknochen aller Art geführt: Pflanzenfresser, wie Antilopen; Fleischfresser, wie Bären, Wölfe und Hyänen, aber vor allem Nilpferde, deren besonderes Merkmal war, dass es sich um eine Zwergrasse handelte. Das kleinste von ihnen ist nicht grösser als ein Bernhardinerhund. Dagegen hat man einen Schwan von riesenhafter Grösse gefunden.

Diese erstaunlichen Entdeckungen, die typisch für die Insel Malta sind, haben den Beweis erbracht, dass vor 250.000 Jahren die Insel noch mit Sizilien verbunden war, aber schon von Nordafrika abgetrennt war. Das übrige Europa war von Gletschern bedeckt, und die Tiere, auf ihrem Rückzug in wärmere Gebiete, fanden sich in diese Sackgasse eingeschlossen. Da sie keine anderen Ufer erreichen

konnten, nahmen sie den Aspekt einer residualen Fauna an, und da während einer grossen Anzahl von Generationen, bis sie schliesslich erloschen. Man möge sich nur an die Existenz von Elefanten in Nordafrika zur römischen Epoche, oder noch näher bei uns, an die Löwen im Atlas am Ende des letzten Jahrhunderts erinnern.

Eine Zeitlang glaubte man sogar, den Beweis zu besitzen von der Gegenwart des Neandertalmenschen auf der Insel, der vor ungefähr 100.000 Jahren lebte. Man hatte nämlich in der Grotte zwei charakteristische Zähne des prähistorischen Menschen entdeckt.

Doch leider zog eines Tages ein Zahnarzt aus dem Backenknochen eines Einwohners der Insel einen Zahn, der den beiden absolut ähnlich sah! Später bestätigten neue Analysiermethoden die Zweifel, die dieses zu günstige Zusammentreffen von Umständen hatte aufkommen lassen.

Es ist nichtsdestoweniger die Grotte von Ghar Dalam, die die ersten unwiderlegbaren Beweise für die Gegenwart menschlicher Überreste lieferte. 3.800 Jahre v. Chr. wären Tierzüchter aus Sizilien gekommen. Die Tongefässe weisen tatsächlich starke Analogien mit den Keramiken auf, die man in Stentinello in der Nähe von Syrakus gefunden hat.

Die Motive stehen aber auch denen sehr nahe, die Tongefässe aus Dalmatien und dem orientalischen Mittelmeer verzieren. Man ist der Meinung, dass diese ersten Einwohner auch Fischerleute waren. Ihre ersten Behausungen wären natürliche Grotten gewesen, die in diesem Kalksteinland zahlreich vorkamen. *(photos p.28)*

DIE UREINWOHNER

Ein neuer Bevölkerungstyp wäre im Jahre 3600 v. Chr. aus Sizilien kommend aufgetaucht. In Skorba, am Rand des Dorfes Żebbiegħ, hat man die ersten maltesischen Behausungen entdeckt. Diese Rundhütten, von denen nur noch die kaum wahrnehmbaren Steinfundamente bestehen, waren wohl die herkömmliche Form der Behausung während dieser ganzen prähistorischen Epoche, mit einigen unbedeutenden Evolutionen. Zweihundert Jahre lang haben die Einwohner graue Töpferwaren produziert (die sogenannte graue Skorba-Periode), die sie dann später mit einem roten Firnis - Farberde - überstrichen.

In Żebbuġ, nicht weit von Mdina, hat man vor ungefähr dreissig Jahren eine Reihe Gräber entdeckt - die ältesten der Insel - deren Inhalt nützliche Auskünfte gegeben hat über den Übergang von der neolithischen Epoche zur Kupfer- und Bronzeepoche (Bau der Tempel). Die geringfügigen Metallmengen, die man auf den Inseln gefunden hat, haben zur Hypothese geführt, dass der Archipel einen strengreligiösen Charakter hatte. War er nicht vielleicht ein grosses Pilgerzentrum gewesen, wo der Gebrauch von Metall verpönt war

War es nicht im Innern der Tempel so gut wie abwesend? Der undankbare Boden von Malta hat wohl nicht sehr an ziehend auf die Beutelust der Eroberer gewirkt, da diese in einer Zeit, wo die Landwirtschaft in vollem Aufschwung war, nach fruchtbarer Erde suchten.

Die Gräber von Zebbug enthielten ausser den originalen Tongefässen sehr stilisierte menschliche Figuren, darunter eine kleine Steinsäule, die unsere grössten zeitgenössichen Bildhauer nicht abgeleugnet hätten.

Mit der Periode von Mgarr (auf der Insel Malta) beginnt die der Tempel. Der Transport der enormen Steinblöcke, die für Tempel bestimmt waren, bis zu ihrem Standort, war erleichtert worden durch die Herstellung von winzigen Modellen, nach denen man sich richtete, und die dann später auf den Baustätten entdeckt wurden.

Bei den ersten Ausgrabungen, zu denen man 1925 schritt, glaubte man zuerst, dass die rohe Form der Tongefässe von Mgarr eine Ausartungserscheinung wäre, und demnach aus einer späteren Epoche stammten; doch 1953 mit den neuen Analysierungsmethoden unternommene Datierungen ermöglichten es, die Periode von Mgarr im Gegenteil vorzuverlegen, das heisst, zu Beginn der Tempelbauten. Mehrere Tempel bilden ein Ensemble. Das bedeutendste von ihnen gehört der Ggantija-Epoche (Insel von Gozo) an. *(photos p.40)*

GGANTIJA

Man erzählt auf der Insel von Gozo, dass eine riesengrosse Frau die Steine für die Tempel, die sich an der Nordküste der Insel befinden, auf ihrem Kopf transportiert hätte. Gleichzeitig trug sie ihr Kind auf dem Arm, das sie noch nährte.

Zweitausendfünfhundert Jahre v. Chr. errichteten die Malteser die ersten Monumente des Archipels, sowohl in Malta selbst (Hagar Qim, Mnajdra) wie auch in Gozo (Ggantija). Diese letztere Stätte hat der ganzen Periode ihren Namen gegeben, doch die anderen sind genauso grosse Sehenswürdigkeiten wie diese.

Man kannte schon seit langer Zeit, in der Nähe des Dorfes von Saghra, die Existenz der Ruinen eines riesigen Gebäudes. Man nannte die grossen Steine die "Türme der Riesen".

Es gibt zwei Tempel in Ggantija, die von einer Umfassungsmauer umgeben sind, deren eine Ecke, vollkommen restauriert, sechs Meter hoch ist. Am frappierendsten ist bei dem grössten Teil der maltesischen Tempel der zentrale Gang, ein langer Korridor, der auf jeder Seite zu mehreren grossen Kammern führt - Apsiden - die sich gegenüberliegen; das äusserste Ende des Korridors selbst ist von einer Kammer gebildet, die im allgemeinen einen Altar enthält. Ein im Umriss gesehener Tempel lässt an Göttinnen der Fruchtbarkeit denken, die nicht mit ihren Formen geizen.

Man glaubt, dass das Ganze von einem Dach (Holzdach ?) bedeckt war und den Aspekt einer Höhle, die man in einen Kultraum umgewandelt hatte, darstellen sollte. Nach den Gegenständen, die in den Tempeln dieser Art gefunden wurden, scheint man in ihnen einen Ahnenkult betrieben und den Göttinnen der Fruchtbarkeit Opfer dargebracht zu haben.

An den Innenfugen der Steine soll man Gipsspuren festgestellt haben, und Gips hätte die Mauern bedecken können so wie ein Gipsputz. Der Tempel links ist der grösste und der älteste. Einige fast ausgewischte Spiralen sind auf den Blöcken eingraviert. Die Gesamtoberfläche beträgt 85 qm, die Länge des Korridors 27 m.
(photos p.42)

HAGAR QIM

Der vielseitigste und am meisten ausgearbeitete Tempel der Epoche von Ggantija ist nur aus Kalkstein zusammengesetzt. Es wäre vielleicht richtiger von einem Ensemble von Tempeln zu sprechen; ihre Überprüfung lässt tiefe Veränderungen erscheinen, in einem Plan, der von Anfang an tiefgehende Analogien mit den Monumenten des gleichen Typs aufzuweisen hatte. Man hat den Eindruck, als hätte man benachbarte Tempel miteinander in Verbindung gebracht durch das Weglassen anstossender Apsiden oder das einfache Durchbrechen der Schwellen. Ein so geschaffener zentraler Korridor erlaubt den Zugang zu den verschiedenen Teilen des Monuments. Man findet dort ebenfalls innere Türen aus einem einzigen behauenen Steinblock bestehend, sowie die klassische Abzäunung an den Wänden.

Eine der Originalitäten von Hagar Qim ist das Vorhandensein von kleinen Altaren aus behauenen Steinen. Einer von ihnen, der sich im Nationalmuseum befindet, stellt den Lebensbaum dar, auf dem sich eine fast flache Schale befindet. Er war von den zahlreichen Besuchern beschädigt worden, die ihre Initialen in ihn einschnitzten, als er sich noch auf der Tempelstätte befand.

Statuetten von fettleibigen Frauen, wie die, die nebenstehend gezeigt wird (45 Zentimeter hoch), wurden dort ebenfalls gefunden. Die Köpfe sind alle verschwunden. Sie waren vom Körper getrennt; ein Loch dort, wo sich der Hals befindet, ermöglichte es, sie auf den Körper aufzustecken. Man nimmt an, dass sie aus Holz waren, was ihr Verschwinden erklären würde.

Im Nationalmuseum ist ebenfalls ein reduziertes Modell ausgestellt, das Fassade des Tempels zeigt, so wie sie heute noch zu sehen ist.

Hagar Qim wirft auch heute noch die verschiedensten Fragen auf: seine zahlreichen Altare, "die Orakelkammern", die Unterbrechungen in der baukünstlerischen Kontinuität, sowie die Wiederbenutzung der Elemente in verschiedenen Epochen. *(photos p.48)*

MNAJDRA

Nur einige hundert Meter unterhalb von Hagar Qim, nicht weit von Qrendi gelegen, weist der Komplex von Mnajdra drei Tempel auf, davon einen kleinen mit nur zwei Zellen, der die Besonderheit hat, drei Schwellen zu haben. Es scheint der älteste von ihnen zu sein.

Der links gelegene weist vier Apsiden auf, die sich je zwei zu zwei gegenüberliegen; sie enthalten zahlreiche Nischen, von denen einige verziert sind und andere sich wieder über zwei Etagen erstrecken, von denen die oberste durch einen Zentralpfeiler gestützt wird. Türen aus einem einzigen Block führen zu den "Orakelkammern", die hinter den Zellen gelegen sind. Die monolithischen Türpfosten des zentralen Durchgangs stützen Türstürze von eindrucksvollen Dimensionen. Das Eingangstor ist ungefähr drei Meter hoch.

Der zentralgelegene, zuletzt erbaute Tempel, besitzt eine künstliche Terrasse. Die Steinblöcke der Innenmauern haben praktisch alle die gleichen Dimensionen, und man hat den Eindruck, es mit grossen aufrechtgestellten Platten zu tun zu haben, mit einem gigantischen Konstruktionsspiel, dessen Elemente Hunderte von Kilo wiegen. Er enthält zweimal zwei Apsiden und ist wohl der Tempel, bei dessen Bau und Auswahl der Materialien man besonders sorgsam vorgegangen ist. *(photos p.44)*

TARXIEN

Im Jahre 1914 fand ein Landwirt in einem seiner Felder grosse Steinblöcke von gewaltigen Ausmassen; er war darüber sehr erstaunt. Dank dieser Entdeckung brachte der Doktor Zammit 1915 die ersten Strukturen der bewundernswerten Gruppe der tarxienischen Tempel ans Licht. Gleich bei den ersten Ausgrabungen kam man zu erstaunlichen Resultaten. Hatte doch die Erdschicht, die jahrhundertelang die Ruinen bedeckte, die Steinskulpturen geschützt und eine bedeutende Anzahl von Gegenständen vor der Vernichtung bewahrt, und das sowohl in dem Teil, der zu den eigentlichen Tempeln gehörte, wie auch in den Grabstätten.

Die tarxienischen Tempel sind jetzt von Wohnhäusern umgeben und gehören zu den Vorstädten, die Valetta umgeben.

Hier war es ebenfalls möglich gewesen, mittels eines reduzierten Modells die Fassade des Tempels zu rekonstruieren. Der Gesamtaspekt unterscheidet sich kaum von dem, was man bisher hat sehen können: ein zentraler Gang verbindet Apsiden, die sich je zwei zu zwei gegenüberliegen. Sobald man die Schwelle überschritten hat, ist man sehr beeindruckt von der grossen Anzahl von Spiralen und Tierbildern in Friesenform, die in die Steine eingraviert sind. Rechts befindet sich die Riesenstatue einer fettleibigen Frau.

Diese Statue ist in Höhe der Taille abgebrochen, doch nach den angestellten Berechnungen soll ihre Totalhöhe mindestens 2 Meter 75 betragen haben. Die gut erhaltenen Originale all dieser Skulpturen befinden sich im Nationalmuseum.

In diesem ersten Teil befindet sich rechts ein kleiner Altar, dessen Grundmauer mit Spiralen verziert ist. Während der Ausgrabungen hat man dort Tierknochen entdeckt, vor allem solche von Ziegen, sowie auch ein Opfermesser aus Feuerstein. Die Tierfriesen stellen Schafe, Ziegen und Schweine dar.

In der zweiten Serie der Apsiden gestattet es eine rechtsliegende Schwelle zu einem Tempel zu gelangen, in dem sich drei Zellenflüchte befinden. Es ist einer der letzten Tempel von diesem Ausmass. Wie der Vorhergehende ist er um das Jahr 2400 v. Chr. erbaut.

Die riesigen Mauern wurden vom Feuer geschwärzt. Im Zentrum konnte man wohl in einer grossen Steinschale aromatische Pflanzen verbrennen, und etwas weiter diente eine riesige Keramikschale zu verschiedenen Kochvorgängen, doch hat man ihre genaue Benutzung bisher nicht feststellen können.

Auf den Blöcken sind grosse Tiere eingraviert: Ochsen und Säue mit ihren Kleinen.

Der guten Erhaltung der tarxienischen Tempel nach kann man sich den Zustand der anderen Tempel vorstellen, die im Laufe der Zeiten die "Besuche" der verschiedenen Eroberer erhalten hatten und die ebenfalls der natürlichen Verwitterung durch die atmosphärischen Elemente ausgesetzt gewesen waren. *(photos p.50)*

DAS HYPOGÄUM VON HAL SAFLIENI

Unweit der tarxienischen Tempel befindet sich einer der bedeutendsten prähistorischen Orte Maltas. Ebenfalls inmitten einer Stadt gelegen, wurde das Hypogäum von Hal Saflieni entdeckt, und zwar ganz zufällig am Anfang des Jahrhunderts, als man Ziternen für die neuen Behausungen anlegte. Es handelt sich um eine Folge unterirdischer Gewölbe ungefähr sechs Meter unter der Erdoberfläche, die nebeneinander liegen und miteinander verbunden sind; manchmal sogar liegen sie in zwei Stockwerken übereinander.

Die Tongefässe, die man dort gefunden hat, ermöglichen es, das Hypogäum aus der Epoche von Mġarr und des ersten tarxienischen Tempels zu datieren, das heisst, ungefähr zwischen den Jahren 2900 und 2300 v. Chr.

Katakombe, die schon vor den eigentlichen Katakomben bestand, ist sie vollkommen in den Felsen gehauen. Man hat zu ihr über eine spiralenförmige Treppe Zugang, die sich am äussersten Ende eines kleinen Museums befindet, das in der "Rue de l'Hypogée" (Totengruftstrasse) gelegen ist, im Viertel von Pawla.

Die Treppe führt bis auf einige Meter zu den hauptsächlichen Höhlen. Der Haupteingang befindet sich fast an der entgegengesetzten Seite der Stelle, die "das Allerheiligste" genannt wurde.

Besonders frappierend ist die Tatsache, dass manche Kammern vollkommen ausgehauen sind, als hätte man in ihnen die Mauern und die Gewölbe der guterhaltenen an der Oberfläche gelegenen Tempel nachahmen wollen. Hier erblickt man die Wiedergabe der Türstürze; dort die der Nischeneinfassungen. Am verblüffendsten ist das Allerheiligste, das wahrscheinlich einzig in der Welt dasteht; es ist von ovaler Form mit einer halbrunden Ausbuchtung, die vollständig in den Felsen gehauen ist . . . und das vor 4500 Jahren!

In anderen Sälen dagegen findet man nicht die geringste Bildhauerarbeit. Ein bedeutender Teil der Decke und der Wände sind mit Zeichnungen bedeckt, die gebogene Linien, Spiralen und Kreise darstellen, die alle miteinander verbunden sind. Die ockerrote Farbe ist sehr gut erhalten geblieben. Auf einer der Mauern findet man eine mit Holzkohle gezeichnete Hand.

Schwieriger ist es schon, einen in den Felsen gehauenen grossen Ochsen zu entdecken, der fast ein Meter hoch ist und ein Meter zwanzig breit.

Auf dem Boden eines dieser verzierten Säle hat man zwei Terrakottastatuetten entdeckt, von denen eine, 'Schlafende Frau', als ein Kunstwerk der Vorgeschichte der maltesischen Inseln angesehen werden kann.

Der Orakelsaal ist auch sehr eigenartig. Ein grosser Teil der Decke und der Wände ist mit ockerroten Spiralen verziert. Eine kleine, in eine der Wände gehauene Nische, hat dem Saal seinen Namen "Orakelsaal" gegeben. Wenn man in diese Aushöhlung mit leiser Stimme spricht, erklingt ein tiefer Ton, der die ganze Totengruft erfüllt, ohne dass man eigentlich weiss, wo er herkommt. Dieser dumpfe Ton musste wahrscheinlich die Männer und die Frauen dieses Zeitalters tief beeindrucken. Bei den Ausgrabungen, die in diesem Teil der Totengruft vorgenommen wurden, wurden Knochenteile ans Licht gebracht, die ungefähr 6000 Skeletten entsprechen. *(photos p.54)*

DIE BEFESTIGTEN DÖRFER

Die letzte Periode dieser Zeiten, in der die Schrift noch u bekannt war, wird durch die Existenz von befestigten Dörfe gekennzeichnet, was wohl auf die damals auf den Inseln herrschen Unsicherheit hinweist.

In Borg in-Nadur, Ort, der die Bucht von Marsaxlokk beherrsc findet man einige hundert Meter von der Grotte von Ghar Dala entfernt die noch imposanten Teile einer Umfassungsmauer. Man tr aber nicht mehr auf die riesigen Blöcke, die zur Erbauung der Temp dienten.

Neuankömmlinge, die wohl um 1500 v. Chr. aus Süditali kamen, haben zu dieser Epoche wohl die Inseln bewohnt, wo no andere Dörfer wie das von Bahrija entdeckt wurden.

Aus dieser Epoche datieren wahrscheinlich die zahlreichen tief den Felsen gegrabenen Doppelgleise (cart rut), die man an viel Stellen der Insel antrifft (Borg in-Nadur, Ta' Cenc, und so weite Dieses Gleisnetz verband wahrscheinlich die Dörfer untereinand doch ist es nur noch stellenweise sichtbar; tief unten in den Tälern u den Teilen des Erdbodens, der einer starken Erosion ausgesetzt wa existiert es nicht mehr. *(photos p.5)*

DIE STEINHÄUSER

Zahlreiche Steinhäuser - neuere Anwendung älterer Bautechniken - findet man in grosser Anzahl in gewissen Teilen d Inseln (St. Paul's Bay - Sankt Pauls Bucht). Es sind das meistens al Schäferhäuser inmitten von jetzt verlassenen Feldern gelege Manche sind schon sehr alt, andere wurden vor ungefä hundert Jahren gebaut. Diese Behausungen sind im gleichen S gebaut wie die in Apulien (Italien) oder die "Bories de Provence".

Wenn man diese Schäferhäuser sieht, mit ihren kleine Steinkuppeln und den kleinen Abflussbögen oberhalb der Tür, w sollte da nicht an "Agamemnons Grab", in Mykenä denken.

Es ist schwierig, diese Bauten genau zu datieren; es ist höchste nach ihrem Stil möglich. Doch kann man annehmen, dass sie sch immer mehr oder weniger existiert haben. Die Malteser sind st Erbauer gewesen; und sie haben im Laufe der Jahrhunder Traditionen bewahrt, die bis auf ihr frühestes Erscheinen im Archip zurückgehen. *(photos p.6)*

Die Malteser waren immer schon Konstrukteure gewesen. U sich davon zu überzeugen, braucht man nur die wichtigsten d dreissig prähistorischen Tempel des Archipels zu besuchen. Einig wiedererbaute Mauern von Ġgantija sind sechs Meter hoch; zu ihre Bau haben Blöcke von mehreren hundert Kilo transportiert werde müssen. Es bedurfte dazu sehr ausgearbeiteter Hebevorrichtunge Der Professor Atkinson hat ausgerechnet, dass ein Block von ein Tonne, auf glattem Boden auf Holzrollen gelegt, von zwei Männer die über Hebel verfügten, transportiert werden konnte. Für ei Neigungsebene von 9° bedurfte es sieben zusätzlicher Männer. U enorme Steinblöcke in die für sie bestimmte Lage zu bringen, wo si als Torstürze oder als Pfosten dienten, wurde wahrscheinlich eine geneigte Fläche aus Erde konstruiert; das Baumaterial wurde dan auf Rollen zu dem vorgesehenen Platz transportiert. Wie dem auc immer sei, die Bevölkerung musste für diese Epoche zahlreich genu sein, um die für diese Konstruktionen nötigen Arbeitskräfte zu stelle

DIE SEEVOELKER

Im Jahre 1000 v. Chr. erschütterten seefahrende Händler, die aus dem Osten kamen, die Zivilisation der Tempelerbauer.
Sie brachten die Schrift mit sich.
Malta ging in die Geschichte ein.

DIE PHÖNIZIER

Mit dem Eintreffen der Phönizier geht Malta in die Geschichte ein. Diese landen auf den Inseln am Ende der Epoche der befestigten Dörfer.

Vom 10. Jahrhundert an begannen diese kühnen Seefahrer das Mittelmeer zu durchstreifen. Sie legten Relais auf der Route nach Spanien an, von wo sie das wertvolle Kupfer mitbrachten. Malta und seine gutgeschützten Häfen waren für sie ein vorzüglicher Anlegeplatz.

Es bestehen keine bedeutenden Überreste von der phönizischen Gegenwart. Das ist eigentlich ganz normal, wenn man bedenkt, dass eigentlich nur die Häfen diese fernhergekommenen Seefahrer interessierten. Da die strategische Bedeutung der Insel ständig wuchs, hatten die aufeinanderfolgenden Besatzungsmächte nur ein Ziel im Auge: die bestehenden Konstruktionen zu vergrössern und weiter auszubauen.

Die Namen "Gozo" und "Malta" kämen aus dem phönizischen "Gaulo" (Schiff) und "Mala" (Hafen, Zufluchtsstätte). Man fand zwar keine architektonischen Überreste, aber doch Gräber, die Tongefässe und verschiedene Gegenstände aus dieser Epoche enthielten.

Von dem hauptsächlichen Hafen, den die Phönizier anlegten, Birgu, stammt das mittelalterliche "Borgo" her, aus dem dann das Valetta gegenüberliegende Vittoriosa wurde. Man hat dort zwei Halbsäulen gefunden (kleine Grabmäler), die dem Gott Moloch geweiht waren, und die auf griechisch und phönizisch beschrieben waren. Dank dieser Inschriften konnte diese letztere Sprache übersetzt werden. Im Laufe der sprachwissenschaftlichen Strittigkeiten, die während der Vorkriegszeit stattfanden - wobei die Italiener auf den italianischen Ursprung Maltas pochten - behaupteten die Engländer, dass die maltesische Sprache semitischer Herkunft sei.

Nach einer Periode, während der, wie es schien, sich griechische Einflüsse bemerkbar machten, übernahmen die Karthager ganz natürlich den Relais der Phönizier.

Es bleiben aus dieser Zeit einige Inschriften karthagischen Ursprungs, sowie ein sichtlich unter ägyptischen Einflüssen entstandener Sarkophag, der im Nationalmuseum zu sehen ist.

Es ist wohl anzunehmen, dass die Besatzungsmächte nicht gerade nach dem Geschmack der Malteser waren, da diese eifrigst den Konsul Tiberius Sempronius unterstützten, als dieser im Jahre 218 v. Chr. von der Insel Besitz nahm, die dann auch im Zentrum der Punischen Kriege lag. Im Verlauf dieser verworrenen Epochen hatten sich Karthager und Römer mehrfach um dieses Territorium gestritten. Dieses diente dann später den römischen Legionen als Ausgangspunkt für die Expedition Scipions des Afrikaners und die endgültige Vernichtung des Erbfeindes im Jahre 146 v. Chr.

(photos p.65)

DIE KALYPSOGROTTE

"Odysseus . . . liegt auf einer Insel, wo ihn Schmerzen martern; dort hält ihn, in ihrem Schloss, die Nymphe Kalypso mit Gewalt zurück. Er kann nicht mehr in das Land seiner Väter zurückkehren, denn er hat weder Schiffe mit Rudern, noch Männer, um auf dem Rücken der Meeresebene dahinzugleiten . . ."

Die Malteser nennen Gozo die Insel der Kalypso. Doch zahlreich sind die Inseln des Mittelmeeres, die diese Ehre in Anspruch nehmen.

An der Nordküste von Gozo beherrschen Felshöhlen die Bucht von Ramla, und man zeigt dort die Grotte, in der Odysseus sieben Jahre lang bei der Göttin den Moment erwartete, als die Götter ihr den Befehl gaben, ihn endlich ziehen zu lassen.

Wenn auch die Durchfahrt des Helden der Odyssee nicht bewiesen ist, so zeugen doch Überreste in der Inselwelt von griechischer Gegenwart.

Einer anderen Fassung nach käme der Name Malta vom griechischen "meli" (Honig) oder von "melita" (Biene), aber die Worte griechischer Herkunft sind in der maltesischen Sprache selten. Im 6. Jahrhundert v. Chr. besassen die Griechen, im Wettbewerb mit den Karthargern, Kolonien, worunter sich Italien und Sizilien befanden. Es scheint nicht der Fall zu sein, dass ihre Gegenwart in den maltesischen Inseln Spuren einer politischen Herrschaft hinterlassen hätte. Die Coexistenz mit den Phöniziern ging vor allem friedlich vonstatten.

Man hat griechische Geldstücke vorgefunden, Keramiken und die berühmten griechisch-phönizischen Halbsäulen.

(photos p.70)

DIE RÖMER

Die Dienste, die die Malteser den Römern erwiesen, indem sie ihnen den Kampf gegen Karthago erleichterten, brachten ihnen ein, von den Römern als "Verbündete des römischen Volkes" angesehen zu werden. Wenn es wahr ist, dass die glücklichen Völker keine Geschichte haben, so kann man sagen, dass der römische Frieden mehrere Jahrhunderte lang Malta keine Waffentaten vollbringen liess und es auch sonst nicht in politische Ereignisse stürzte.

Das römische Gesetz wurde in Malta eingeführt. Malta und Gozo bildeten zwei "municipes".

Das Leben der Malteser wird uns dargestellt in der berühmten Rede Ciceros gegen Verres, den Konsul von Sizilien, der, wie er es von Sizilien her gewöhnt war, sich die Tempelschätze Maltas angeeignet hatte.

Der Junotempel, wo die Seeleute als Exvotos riesige Elfenbeinzähne niedergelegt hatten, war in Tas-Silġ, Marsaxlokk, errichtet worden.

Von den zahlreichen Gebäuden, die zu dieser Epoche erbaut wurden (Theater und Bäder), sind nur wenige in akzeptablem Zustand bis auf uns gekommen. Von den interessanten Trümmern kann man die römische Stadt angeben, die in Rabat ans Tageslicht gefördert wurde, die Katakomben und die öffentlichen Bäder von Ghajn Tuffieha.

Das römische Haus von Rabat ist zu einem kleinen Museum eingerichtet worden; es enthält Mosaiken, Gläser, Tongefässe und sonstige Objekte der punischen oder arabischen Epoche. Man hat nämlich in der unmittelbaren Umgebung eine grosse Anzahl Gräber entdeckt, die Grabbeigaben enthielten.

Mehrere Mosaiken sind vortrefflich erhalten, wie das, das sich unter dem "impluvium" befand und das zwei Vögel darstellt, vielleicht Pfauen, am Rand eines Brunnenbeckens. Ein anderes, kleineres, von sehr feiner Arbeit, stellt zwei Personen dar, eine Frau und einen Mann; ihre Identifizierung ist aber schwierig, da ein Teil des Mosaiks beschädigt ist. Man hat Omphale und Herkules oder Samson und Dalila vorgeschlagen, wobei es aber nicht sicher ist, dass es sich nicht doch vielleicht um ein anderes berühmtes Paar der antiken Mythologie handelt.

Am Eingang des Museums ist eine alte Olivenpresse zu sehen. Hinter dem Museum kann man in einem Teil des Ausgrabungsfelds Fragmente von Keramiken erblicken und ein ganzes System einer Wasserleitung und Wasseraufsparung mit Ziternen.

Ghajn Tuffieha, die "Quelle des Apfelbaums", wurde seit der Epoche der prähistorischen Tempel benutzt. Ihre augenblickliche Ausflussmenge ist über 15.000 Liter pro Stunde. Die Römer hatten dort ein Ensemble von Bädern installiert: ein "caldarium" (Schwitzbad - es wurde vom Boden aus geheizt, der auf Pfeilern ruhte, zwischen denen heisse Luft zirkulierte) sowie ein "frigidarium" für kalte Bäder. Die meisten Zimmer dieser Bäder enthielten Mosaiken, die ziemlich gut erhalten sind. Ein Schwimmbad und gemeinsame Latrinen, wie zu dieser Zeit üblich war, vervollständigten das Ensemble.

(photos p.72)

DER HEILIGE PAULUS

"Endlich gerettet erfuhren wir, dass die Insel Malta hiess. Die Eingeborenen behandelten uns mit einer ungemeinen Menschlichkeit. Sie empfingen uns alle an einem grossen Feuer, das sie angezündet hatten wegen des Regens, der plötzlich fiel, und wegen der Kälte . . ."

"In der Nähe dieses Ortes befand sich ein Landsitz, der dem Ersten der Insel, einem gewissen Publius gehörte. Dieser empfing uns und beherbergte uns netterweise drei Tage lang. Der Vater des Publius, der von Fieber und Ruhr heimgesucht war, lag zu Bett. Paulus ging zu ihm, betete, legte ihm die Hände auf und heilte ihn . . ."

Paulus, der in Cäsarea ins Gefängnis geworfen worden war, hatte in Rom Berufung eingelegt; im Laufe der Reise, die ihn zum Kaiser führen sollte, erlitt er Schiffbruch in Begleitung des Evangelisten Lukas und mehrerer anderer Christen. Seit dieser Epoche - dem Jahre 60 ungefähr - datiert die tiefe christliche Tradition der Insel.

Paulus heilte Publius und seinen Vater. Der römische Prokurator bekehrte sich. Der drei Monate währende Aufenthalt Pauli auf der Insel und seine Heilungen führten zu einer grossen Anzahl Bekehrungen.

Zahlreiche Katakomben sind in den Kalksteinuntergrund der Insel gegraben worden. Sie datieren zum grössten Teil aus der römischen Epoche. Die meistzitierten sind die Katakomben Sankt Pauls in Rabat nahe Mdina. Man kann dort ausser dem, was man eine Kapelle genannt hat, auch einen grossen Raum sehen, der im Zentrum dieser Katakomben gelegen zu sein scheint. Zwei runde, in den Felsen gehauene Tische, die leicht überhöht sind, wurden bei den Agapen, den Totenfestmählern benutzt.

(photos p.75)

DIE ARABER

Ein arabischer Prinz, der seiner Geliebten eine Freude machen wollte, liess einen Granatapfelbaum auf einen Orangenbaum pfropfen. Das Resultat davon war eine sehr saftige blutfarbene Orange, die man seitdem "Malteser Orange" nannte. Das behauptet zum mindesten die Legende. Und da man viel Zeit verliert, wenn man Orangenhaine in Malta finden will - denn die Orangen wachsen meistens in den Höfen der Häuser oder an leicht zu bewässernden Stellen - so kann man sagen, dass die "Malteser Orangen" zum grössten Teil aus dem benachbarten Tunesien kommen.

Denn aus Tunesien kamen die Araber im Jahr 869, als Ahmed, der Sohn des Emirs von Tunesien und Tripolitanien, versuchte, im Archipel Fuss zu fassen. Die byzantinische Garnison, der es gelungen war, die Angreifer zu umzingeln, warf sie ans Meer zurück. Der Aufschub war nur von kurzer Dauer. Die Byzantiner, die isoliert waren und auf keine Verstärkung zu rechnen hatten, konnten den Truppen nicht widerstehen, die den Arabern als Nachschub von Mohamed Ibn Hafagab, Gouverneur von Sizilien, geschickt wurden. Am 29. August 870 wurde der Bischof von Malta deportiert, und während der ganzen Dauer der arabischen Herrschaft wurde kein Bischof ernannt.

Der Widerstand gegen die Eindringlinge schien damals hauptsächlich von den Griechen auszugehen, die die Insel besetzt hatten. Zahlreiche Einwohner bekehrten sich zum Islam, während andere in den Kämpfen fielen oder gefangen abgeführt wurden. Zahlreiche Barbaren liessen sich auf der Insel nieder.

Man weiss nichts Genaues über die Stärke der Bevölkerung der Insel zu dieser Epoche; wieviel Einwohner nach dem Abzug der Byzantiner übriglieben, wieviel an Ort und Stelle blieben und welche Anzahl Muselmänner sich in Gozo und Malta niederliessen. Man weiss nicht einmal, ob sich die gesamte Bevölkerung zum Islam bekehrte. Ein bedeutender Teil der Christen scheint jedoch weiter auf den Inseln gelebt zu haben.

Der Archipel wurde durch diesen radikalen politischen Wechsel aufs tiefste umgewälzt; er zog entscheidende kulturelle und wirtschaftlich Veränderungen nach sich.

Die Araber führten den Anbau von Baumwolle ein, die mehrere Jahrhunderte lang eines der Haupterzeugnisse war; ebenfalls den Anbau des Zitronenbaums und vor allem neue Bewässerungstechniken mit dem System der Schöpfräder. Die Benutzung von Tieren statt Menschen für diese Aufgabe machte eine Erhöhung der Produktion möglich.

Doch die Araber beeinflussten ganz besonders die Domäne der Sprache. Und noch heutzutage ist man erstaunt, wenn man eine Karte mit den Ortsnamen liest.

Ein arabischer Chronist spricht von Malta mit folgender Ausdrücken: "Mahlita, reich an allen Dingen, gut und ein Segen Gottes . . . stark bevölkert, besitzt sie Städte und Dörfer, Bäume und Früchte".

Diese Besetzung, die über zweihundert Jahre dauerte, hat keine sichtbaren Spuren hinterlassen. Man kann sich jedoch vorstellen, dass die Monumente durch andere ersetzt wurden (besonders die Kultstätten). So heisst zum Beispiel eine der engen Strassen in Mdina "Moscheestrasse". Diese Stadt, die während der römischen Epoche die Hauptstadt war, war von Befestigungen geringeren Ausmasses umgeben. Sie hat übrigens ihren arabischen Namen "Mdina" bewahrt. Sie spielt immer noch die Rolle einer Hauptstadt. Die Stadtmauern, die man heute noch sehen kann, sind erst späteren Datums (Normannen, Malteserritter), aber die Grundmauern sind arabisch. Aus der arabischen Epoche soll auch die Errichtung einer Festung an der Stelle des augenblicklichen Forts Saint Ange herrühren.

Einige irdene Gefässe berberischen Stils und Geldstücke wurden wiederaufgefunden.

Die Ausgrabungen in der römischen Stadt von Rabat haben moslemische Grabsteine ans Licht gefördert, denn ein Friedhof war vor dem Tor der Stadt errichtet worden. Das lässt darauf schliessen, dass zur Zeit der Erbauung der arabischen Stadt die Bevölkerung weniger zahlreich war als während der römischen Epoche.

Die ergreifendste Entdeckung ist sicher die eines grossen Grabsteins, die in Victoria gemacht wurde; dieser ist mit arabischen Buchstaben bedeckt. Er war als Baumaterial benutzt worden. Ursprünglich war er für das Grab eines kleinen moslemischen Mädchens bestimmt, die im 12. Jahrhundert im Alter von 12 Jahren gestorben war.

Im 11. Jahrhundert versuchten die Byzantiner die Insel wieder zurückzuerobern. Die Muselmänner, die sich schon verloren glaubten, schlugen ihren christlichen Sklaven vor, sie zu befreien und ihnen Land zu geben, wenn sie ihnen helfen würden, den Byzantinern zu widerstehen; das geschah dann auch mit Erfolg.

Während dieser Periode wurde Malta auch - mehrere Jahrhunderte lang - zu einem der hauptsächlichen mittelländischen Zentren der Piraterie. Von ihren Expeditionen brachten die Seeräuber entweder Waren, aber auch zahlreiche Gefangene mit, die dann, sei es auf den Galeeren, sei es als Diener hochgestellter Persönlichkeiten benutzt wurden oder auch einfach als Verwaltungsangestellte.

(photos p.78)

DIE JÜDISCHE GEMEINDE

Hundertfünfzig Jahre nach dem Abzug der arabischen Besatzungen zeigte eine in Malta vorgenommene Volkszählung, dass es dort noch mehr Muselmänner als Christen gab. Zählte man doch siebenhunderteinundsiebzig Familien, deren Religion die des Propheten war, gegen zweihundertfünfzig christliche Familien, deren Religion die der Normannen, der neuen Eroberer, war. Ausserdem gab es noch dreiunddreissig jüdische Familien.

Am Eingang des Museums von Rabat kann man einen grossen Grabstein sehen, auf dem hebräische Lettern eingraviert sind. In den Sankt Pauls-Katakomben trifft man auf eine gewisse Anzahl von Kammern, die manchmal unabhängig voneinander sind und auf deren Mauern man siebenarmige Armleuchter eingraviert sehen kann. Die jüdische Gemeinschaft wurde im Jahre 1492 vom König von Spanien vertrieben.

Ein Tor, das 'die jüdische Ausfallpforte' genannt wird, das in der Befestigungsmauer von Valetta angebracht ist, geht direkt auf die Felsen des Meeresufers.

(photo p.82)

DIE MALTESISCHE SPRACHE

Der Ursprung der maltesischen Sprache ist lange strittig geblieben und ist auch jetzt noch nicht entschieden. Die Befürworter der "phönizischen These" stehen den Verteidigern der "arabischen These" gegenüber.

Die ersteren machen geltend, dass sowohl die Malteser als auch ihre Sprache von phönizischen Seeleuten abstammen. Zum Beispiel, der Begriff "Barbar", den Sankt Lukas auf die Malteser anwandte bei der Erzählung seines Schiffbruchs mit Sankt Paulus, beweist, dass jene zu dieser Zeit weder griechisch noch lateinisch sprachen, sondern eine semitische Sprache. Die Gegenpartei behauptet, dass das Wort "Barbar" nur besagen wollte, dass es sich um einfache und ungebildete Menschen handelte, und dass die Worte semitischen Ursprungs erst von den arabischen Eroberern einige Jahrhunderte später eingeführt wurden.

Diese eigentlich rein wissenschaftliche Diskussion wurde in den Vorkriegsjahren zu einem Sprachenstreit ersten Ranges, den die Engländer und Italiener untereinander ausfochten; beide waren daran interessiert, ihre eigene These den Sieg davontragen zu sehen. Den Engländern lag daran, die phönizische These durchzusetzen, die das Italien Mussolinis der Argumente beraubte, die es dazu trieben, zum mindesten auf kulturellem Gebiet ein Territorium zu annektieren, das Sizilien so nahe lag und strategisch so nützlich war.

(photos p.83)

Iva: ja
Le: nein
Grazzi: danke
Bonswa: Guten Abend
Bonġu: Guten Tag
Sahha: Seit gegrüsst
Xellug: links
Lemin: rechts
Triq: Strasse
Għajn: Quelle
Knisja: Kirche
Marsa: Hafen
Ramla: Landung
Ras: Kopf
Wied: Tal
Ghar: Grotte
Baħar: Pfuhl
Gebel: felsiger Hügel
Nadur: Höhe
Xaghra: Felsplateau
Kbir: breit

(photo p.83)

DIE NORMANNEN

Im Monat Mai 1061 nutzte Roger der Normanne, der Sohn Tancreds de Hauteville, die Schwäche des moslemischen Reiches aus und bemächtigte sich der Insel durch Anwendung von List. Sein Ziel war, den Schiffsverkehr im Mittelmeer mit dem Heiligen Land zu sichern. Die Normannen unternahmen ein Ablenkungsmanöver, indem sie in der St. Paul's Bay landeten, während andere Truppen den Arabern in den Rücken fielen. Mdina wurde schnell genommen, und einige Monate später erstreckte Roger seinen Einfluss über die ganze Insel. Man erzählt, dass Roger während der Schlacht um den Besitz von Malta, einen Fetzen seines scharlachroten Banner abriss und daraus die zukünftige Flagge Maltas machte.

Er erkannte die lokalen Institutionen an und liess der Insel eine gewisse Autonomie. Die Kirche gewann einen bedeutenden Einfluss. Eine Kathedrale wurde in Mdina, der Hauptstadt, erbaut; diese wurde 1693 durch ein Erdbeben zerstört.

Während der Kreuzzüge spielte die Insel die Rolle einer Zwischenlandungsstelle auf dem Weg nach dem Heiligen Land.

Nach einer kurzen Periode unter der Herrschaft Charles' d'Anjou, fiel die Insel Peter I. von Aragon zu (1282), und der Archipel wurde vom Königreich Spanien annektiert.

Bis zur Ankunft der Ordensritter im Jahre 1530 musste sich der maltesische Archipel gegen die Sarazenen und die Piraten verteidigen, die die wirtschaftliche Entwicklung der Inseln anzog, sowie auch die zahlreichen Handelsschiffe (meistens italienische), die dort anlegten.

(photos p.84)

DIE MALTESER IM MITTELALTER

Die vor allem aus Seeleuten bestehende Bevölkerung baute Getreide, Baumwolle und Kümmel an, Waren, die sie exportierte.

In den Städten waren die Handwerker in Korporationen gruppiert: Maurer, Zimmerleute, Seiler, Leinwandzubereiter. Denn die Insel begann nicht nur sich mit Bauten zu bedecken, auch die Häfen wurden immer mehr von den Schiffen der ganzen Christenheit angelaufen, sei es, um ihren Kommerz auszuüben, sei es, um dort Reparaturen vornehmen zu lassen.

Eines der handwerklichen Erzeugnisse, die heute noch das Renommee der Malteser ausmachen, ist die Drahtarbeit von Schmucksachen. Zu dieser Zeit erscheint auch eine typisch maltesische Institution: die Universität. Es war das die Umwandlung des früheren "Volksrates", der alle freien Familienväter umfasste, in eine weniger umfangreiche Versammlung. Die Universität (universitas civium) erhebt Anspruch darauf, die Vertretung sämtlicher vollberechtigter Einwohner Maltas zu sein, abgesehen von den Sklaven und sonstigen Kriegsgefangenen.

Man sieht heute noch in Valetta ein Gebäude von früherer Bauart, dessen Rolle es war, im Namen der Universität das Getreide an die Bevölkerung neu zu verteilen.

(photos p.86)

DIE PFARRGEMEINDEN

Vor der Ankunft der Ordensritter und der Erbauung von Valetta, die die Schöpfung neuer Zentren nach sich zog, die dann nur noch eine einzige sehr ausgedehnte Siedlung bildeten, lebten die Malteser in kleinen Dörfern und den beiden hauptsächlichen Städten: Mdina (Citta Vecchia) und Le Bourg. Aus dieser Epoche datieren auch die kleinen in die Felsen gehauenen Kapellen "vor indiskreten Blicken und den Raids der Piraten versteckt . . . Die wenigen existierenden Kirchen bildeten ein einfaches Rechteck, das nur einen Raum einschloss . . ."

1436 war die Insel in ungefähr zehn Pfarrgemeinden geteilt worden. Daraufhin wurden mehrere Kirchen gebaut. Sie gehören zu den interessantesten Monumenten dieser Zeit. Die kleine Muttergotteskirche (Sainte Marie) in der Nähe von Gudja gelegen, besitzt ein Vorhalle, die im Stil den "normannischen Häusern" von Mdina ähnelt. Zwei Regentraufen, an den beiden Seiten der Fassade angebracht, führten das Wasser ab, das sich auf der Terrasse ansammelte. Die Kirche ist von einer Mauer umgeben, die einen weiten Vorhof umrahmt. Der Kirchturm wurde erst später hinzugefügt. Die Kirche befindet sich jetzt mitten auf dem Land, ungefähr einen Kilometer von der Stadt entfernt; diese ist erst später erbaut worden. Die Kirche diente mehreren kleinen Dörfern der Umgebung.

Die Sankt-Gregory-Kirche, am Ausgang von Żejtun gelegen, besitzt im gotischen Stil geformte Gewölbe. Sie wurde im 15. Jahrhundert erbaut. Auch bei dieser Kirche wurden neue Elemente hinzugefügt, so zum Beispiel ein Tor im Renaissancestil.

Weniger eindrucksvoll als die später erbauten Monumente fügen die kleinen Kirchen und Dorfkapellen der Geschichte Maltas eine menschliche Note hinzu, die sehr wohl diesen Bauern entspricht, die ständig unter der herrschenden Unsicherheit zu leiden hatten.

(photos p.90)

DIE MALTESERRITTER

Was wäre Malta ohne die Malteserritter geworden? Es wäre vielleicht Sizilien einverleibt worden, doch die Geschichte hat anders entschieden. Sobald das Mittelmeer zum Einsatz der anliegenden Mächte wurde, war es nur natürlich, dass eine seiner Inseln zur strategischen Bastion wurde. Seitdem erschien Malta all den Ländern begehrenswert, die, der Reihe nach, die Freiheit ihrer Seeschiffahrt sicherstellen wollten.

Die Ordensritter erbauten in Malta die am stärksten befestigte Stadt ihrer Zeit. Die Paläste, die Kirchen, die öffentlichen Gebäude, die sie errichten liessen - manchmal mit ihren eigenen Finanzen - gehören zu den bemerkenswertesten ihrer Zeit. Sie wandten sich an die berühmtesten Künstler. So entsteht, dank dem Willen eines Hochmeisters, dem Talent eines maltesischen Architekten wie Cassar, der Arbeit dieser geborenen Erbauer, wie es nun einmal die Einwohner der Insel sind, und den wundervollen Steinen der Steinbrüche, die Johanneskirche in Valetta.

Die Ritter, was wären sie ohne Malta geworden ?

250 Jahre lang haben der Orden und seine Hochmeister wie Monarchen regiert. Sie standen auf gleichem Fuss mit den anderen Ländern der Christenheit und waren dort diplomatisch vertreten. Dann wurde der Orden ein Opfer der französischen Revolution und eines Eroberers, der nicht Soliman der Prächtige war, sondern ein kleiner General, der in einer nicht entfernt liegenden Insel geboren war: Bonaparte.

DIE PILGERFAHRT NACH JERUSALEM

"Jerusalem ist die Stadt der Städte, die heiligste von allen heiligen, die Königin der Völker, die Prinzessin der Provinzen. Es ist im Zentrum der Welt gelegen, in der Mitte der Erde, damit alle Menschen ihre Schritte zu ihm hinlenken können."
Jacques de Vitry, 13. Jahrhundert

"Es zieht die Gläubigen an, wie der Magnet Eisen anzieht, wie das Schaf das Lamm anzieht mit der Milch seiner Zitzen, wie das Meer die Ströme anzieht, denen sie das Leben gegeben hatte." Dichter des 13. Jahrhunderts

Mit der Eroberung Palästinas durch die Araber im 7. Jahrhundert veränderte sich die Lage der Christen, die im Heiligen Land lebten oder die sich nach Jerusalem begaben. Die der Ausübung der Religion auferlegten Restriktionen (in Moscheen verwandelte Kirchen, Verbot des äusseren Anbringens jeglicher Kultuszeichen), die der unterworfenen Bevölkerung auferlegten Steuern: all diese Dinge riefen eine dumpfe Unzufriedenheit in der Christenheit hervor.

Das Herannahen des Jahres 1000 und mit ihm des Endes der Welt, die bevorstehende Auferstehung von Christus in Juda liessen die Gläubigen in diesem Teil der Welt zusammenströmen. Konnte man dort nicht Verzeihung für seine Sünden finden? Arme Leute und die Grossen dieser Erde verwandelten sich in Pilger und kamen nach Jerusalem, wo Hakem, der Sultan von Ägypten, das Niederreissen der Heiligen Grabeskirche (l'église du Saint Sépulcre) angeordnet hatte; diese wurde erst vierzig Jahre später wieder aufgebaut.

Die Ankunft der Türken und die Eroberung der Städte, die die Christenheit in Kleinasien und Syrien besass (Ephesus, Tarsus, Antiochia), gaben zu Verärgerungen und schlimmen Ausschreitungen Anlass. Als die Neuankömmlinge begannen, den Handel im Mittelmeer zu stören, landeten Pisaner, Genuesen und Einwohner von Arles in Syrien zu einer Strafexpedition. So nahm die grosse Idee der Kreuzzüge ihren Anfang, die sowohl die Gläubigen mit nackten Füssen, wie auch die Ritter, die auf Heldentaten auswaren, und eine grosse Anzahl Abenteurer aller Art versammelten.

"Möge das Kreuz auf euren Waffen und auf euren Bannern glänzen! Tragt es auf eurer Schulter und auf eurer Brust; möge es euch zum Abzeichen des Sieges oder zur Palme des Märtyrers werden."
Urban II. , Erster Kreuzzug   *(photos p.96)*

186

AKKA

Im Jahre 1020 hatten Kaufleute von Amalfi und Salerno vom Kalifen von Ägypten die Erlaubnis erhalten, in Jerusalem ein Hospital zu erbauen, zu dessen Schutzpatron sie Johannes den Täufer auserkoren. Dort wurden Pilger und Reisende, die ins Heilige Land kamen, gepflegt. Mit den Kreuzzügen wuchs die Bedeutung dieser Institution, und Pierre Gérard de Martigue, der erste Hochmeister des Ordens, schlug den Besorgern des Hospitals vor, sich in einen Mönchsorden umzuwandeln, auf die Welt zu verzichten und ein Gewand zu tragen. So wurde der Johanniterorden von Jerusalem gegründet. Ausser den herkömmlichen Gelübden von Gehorsam, Keuschheit und Armut mussten die Mitglieder dieses Ordens über die Sicherheit der Pilger wachen, die in Palästina reisten.

Sie verliessen als letzte das von Saladin eroberte Jerusalem. Sie nahmen sehr aktiv an der Eroberung von Akka teil und liessen sich in der Stadt nieder, unter der Bezeichnung "Chevaliers de Saint Jean d'Acre" (die Ritter von Akka). Während seines Aufenthalts in Akka war der Orden militärisch besonders rege. Zum Schutz der Reisenden kam noch die Befestigung der Stadt hinzu. Mächtige Wälle wurden errichtet und religiöse Gebäude erbaut.

Beim Fall von Akka, das die Muselmänner 1291 zurückeroberten, gelang es den Rittern, sich in kleinen Gruppen auf die Insel von Zypern zu flüchten, wo sie ungefähr zwölf Jahre lang blieben. Der Hochmeister Jean de Villiers versammelte alle Ritter, die entschlossen waren, den Kampf fortzuführen. Doch da die Beziehungen zum König der Insel nicht besonders gut waren, beschlossen der neue Hochmeister Villaret und die Ritter, sich anderswo niederzulassen.

Infolge einer Expedition, die sozusagen ein kleiner Kreuzzug war - und an der eine grosse Anzahl von Rittern, die sich heimlich in einem Hafen in Süditalien versammelt hatten, teilnahmen - liess sich der Orden auf der Insel Rhodos nieder. Nach einer langen Belagerung glückte es ihnen, sich der Hauptstadt zu bemächtigen (1310). Sie blieben dort zwei Jahrhunderte lang.

Eine erste türkische Offensive wurde 1455 zurückgeschlagen. Doch die Johanniter, die sich jetzt Rhodosritter nannten, waren stark beschäftigt. Ausser gegen Mahomet II., der Konstantinopel erobert hatte, und den Sultan von Ägypten, mussten sich auch gegen die Venezianer verteidigen, die das Land verwüsteten. Der Hochmeister Raimond Zacosta benutzte eine kurze Ruhepause, die ihm die ständigen Kämpfe liessen, um das Fort Saint Nicolas zu erbauen, das dazu bestimmt war, den Hafen und die Hauptstadt von Rhodos zu verteidigen.

Während ihres Aufenthaltes auf dieser Insel wurden die Ritter zu Seefahrern. Der Kampf gegen die Muselmänner ging nicht mehr auf palästinischem Boden zu Pferd, sondern im Mittelmeer vor sich, gegen eine aufsteigende Macht: die Türkei. Denn die Christenheit war sich bewusst geworden, dass alle Orientexpeditionen nur durch die Herrschaft über die Seewege möglich gewesen waren.

(photos p.98)

RHODOS

Als Vergeltungsmassnahmen gegen die ständigen Einfälle der türkischen Seeräuber schickte der damals regierende Hochmeister die Galeeren des Ordens an die Küsten Kleinasiens. Mahomet II., den dieser Streifzug mit Zorn erfüllte, vertraute seinem Grossvizir, Misach Paleologue, einem griechischen Renegaten, eine mächtige Flotte an, mit der Mission, sich Rhodos' zu bemächtigen. Am 23. Mai 1480 machten 160 Kriegsschiffe einen Landungsversuch. Im Schlachtgetobe gelang es den Türken, an den Wällen Fuss zu fassen. Sie schlugen dem Hochmeister Pierre d'Aubusson (den sie übrigens versucht hatten zu vergiften) vor zu kapitulieren. Auf seine Weigerung liess der Grossvizir Pfähle zuspitzen und schwor, dass er sämtliche

Einwohner aufspiessen oder köpfen lassen würde. Doch die Türken mussten einem Gegenangriff weichen. Zwanzig Jahre später machten sie dann noch einen letzten Versuch.

1522 schickte Soliman der Prächtige fast an die 400 Schiffe und über 150.000 Mann. Er war im geheimen von der relativen Schwäche der Inselbefestigungen unterrichtet worden, und zwar durch André Amaral, Ordenskanzler und Prior von Kastilien, der erbittert darüber war, dass er nicht zum Hochmeister gewählt worden war.

Der Hochmeister Villiers de l'Isle Adam leitete die Verteidigung mit nur 7000 Mann. Es gelang den Angreifern, in den Platz einzudringen, aber die Ritter hielten sie auf und weigerten sich, sich zu ergeben.

Der Hochmeister willigte ein zu verhandeln, da die Bevölkerung darauf bestand, und auch Soliman wollte aufs schnellste dem Kampf ein Ende machen. Die Ehrfurcht des Sultans vor diesen wackeren Kämpfern war so gross, dass er den Rittern gestattete, die Insel am Weihnachtsabend zu verlassen und über 4000 Personen mit sich zu führen unter der Leitung von Villiers de l'Isle Adam.

NIEDERLASSUNG IN MALTA

Nachdem sie Rhodos verlassen hatten, suchten die Ordensritter eine neue Basis. Ihr Hochmeister, Villiers de l'Isle Adam, führte sie nach Candie (Kreta), Viterbe (Italien), Syrakus (Sizilien) und nach Nizza. Zum Glück war der damalige Papst Ritter des Johanniterordens. Er versuchte, Karl V. zu überreden, es zuzulassen, dass die Ordensritter sich in Malta niederliessen. Ihr Hochmeister war übrigens gar nicht von dieser Aussicht entzückt. Er dachte eher daran, die Insel Rhodos wiederzuerobern.

Schliesslich, im Jahr 1529, als sich die Beziehungen zwischen den europäischen Staaten und zwischen Karl V. und dem Papst verbesserten, machte die Lösung Malta Fortschritte. Am 24. März 1530 unterzeichnete der spanische Souverän in Bologna die Abtretung der Insel an die Ordensritter. Sie verweilten dort über zweihundertfünfzig Jahre, bis zu dem Tag im Juni 1798, als Bonaparte, auf dem Wege nach Ägypten, dort seine Truppen landen liess.

Traditionsgemäss musste der Hochmeister dem König von Frankreich jedes Jahr Raubvögel schicken. Von nun ab erhielt Karl V. - als Gegenleistung für sein Verhalten - an Allerheiligen einen Falken "mit einem Seidenkäppchen, goldenen Glöckchen und einem Ring mit dem kaiserlichen Wappen um den Fang". Er konnte ausserdem, wie vor der Ankunft der Ordensritter, die Bischöfe der Insel bestimmen.

Und die Malteser? Die hatte man eigentlich gar nicht um ihre Meinung gefragt. Es wurde ihnen versprochen, dass die lokalen Institutionen nicht berührt würden. Sie verlangten vergeblich, im Orden als Ritter aufgenommen werden zu können; sie konnten es aber höchstens bis zum Kaplan bringen.

Der Hochmeister gab Vorschriften heraus, die an die Stelle der sizilischen Gesetze traten, und die Insel wurde in zwei Teile geteilt. Ein Teil hing von der ehemaligen Hauptstadt Citta Vecchia ab und der andere von Le Bourg, wo der Orden sein Hauptquartier aufschlug und wo sich von nun ab der Sitz seiner Institutionen befand.

Der Hochmeister Villiers de l'Isle Adam verstarb vier Jahre nach der Installierung des Ordens in Malta. Jetzt hatte der Orden zwar Land aber keinen Hochmeister mehr. Der neue, Pietro del Monte, begab sich nicht nach der Insel; er überlebte nur acht Monate seine Wahl. Sein Nachfolger, Juan d'Homedes, betrat die Insel erst fünfzehn Monate nach seiner Ernennung.

Vor zweihundert Jahren, als sich der Orden in Rhodos niedergelassen hatte, war alles viel schneller vor sich gegangen. In den ersten Jahren wurden nur wenige Gebäude erbaut: ein Hospital des Ordens, das ziemlich schnell im Jahre 1532 vollendet wurde, ein Bischofspalast und der Palast des Hochmeisters im Jahre 1555.

(photo p.105)

DRAGUT DER PIRAT

Ausser Malta erhielten die Ordensritter noch den Platz von Tripolis an der afrikanischen Küste einige dreihundert Kilometer weiter im Süden. Sie hatten sich Karl V. gegenüber verpflichtet, es gegen die türkischen Unternehmungen und die Angriffe der Piraten, die in Algier ihr Hauptquartier aufgeschlagen hatten, zu verteidigen.

Als Gegenmassnahme zu dem Sieg von Kaîreddin Barbarossa über die christlichen Galeeren vor der griechischen Küste, beschlossen die Spanier gegen die nordafrikanische Stadt vorzugehen. Sie wurden von ungefähr hundert Ordensrittern begleitet, unter ihnen Savignac de Balaguer, der Fahnenträger des Ordens.

Die Expedition wurde zu einem Debakel, als die Algerier, sich einen Sturm zunutze machend, die Angreifer überfielen, die noch nicht ihr ganzes Material ausgeschifft hatten und deren Schiffe, als Sicherheitsmassnahme, aufs weite Meer zurücksegeln mussten. Savignac versammelte einige Kämpfer um sich, ergriff die Gegenoffensive und schlug nun die überraschten Angreifer seinerseits zurück. Er verfolgte sie bis zu den Stadttoren, die in aller Eile geschlossen wurden. Savignac de Balaguer stiess seinen Dolch in das Holz des Tores von Bab-Azoun, wobei er ausrief: "Wir werden wiederkommen und ihn zurückholen!"

Die Armee bei ihrem Versuch sich wieder einzuschiffen schützend, kämpften die Ritter mutig weiter, und fast die Hälfte von ihnen verlor das Leben bei dieser unglücklichen Expedition (1541).

Die Türken besassen nun fast die totale Seeherrschaft. Die Schiffe der grossen Handelsstädte wie Ragusa (Dubrovnik), Venedig, Marseille konnten sich nicht ohne ein vorheriges Handels- oder politisches Abkommen dort hinwagen. Frankreich war sogar mit den moslemischen Seeräubern verbündet. Kamen doch die Schiffe Barbarossas bis nach Toulon, um dort zu überwintern(1543).

Dragut, ein griechischer Renegat, der in die Dienste des Sultans getreten war, unternahm, von der nordafrikanischen Küste aus, vernichtende Raids gegen die spanischen Besitzungen, sei es zu Lande, wobei die Bewohner geraubt und alle ihre Güter zerstört wurden, sei es zu Wasser, wie das Abfangen des Ordensschiffes von Malta, das die Einkommen der Komtureien Italiens transportierte.

Am 30. April! 1551 landete Dragut in der Reede von Marsamxett an der Spitze einer Flotte Solimans II. Die Bevölkerung flüchtete sich, soweit sie es vermochte, in die Befestigungen von Mdina, Le Bourg und das Fort Saint Ange. Zweieinhalb Monate lang verwüstete Dragut die verlassenen Dörfer.

Ein türkisches Geschwader brachte ihm Verstärkung von ungefähr zehntausend Mann. Die Ordensritter, unter denen sich ein Engländer, Sir Nicolas Upton, besonders auszeichnete - er starb noch am selben Abend an seinen Wunden - versuchten sie aufzuhalten. Sie konnten aber der Übermacht nicht standhalten und zogen sich in ihre Zitadelle zurück. Da sie glaubten, dass ihnen die Belagerung des Forts Saint-Ange zu teuer zu stehenkommen würde, machten sich die Türken an die Belagerung von Mdina, wobei sie die umliegenden Ortschaften verwüsteten.

Da sie die Ankunft christlicher Verstärkungen befürchteten und da ihnen die imposanten Befestigungen der ehemaligen Hauptstadt nichts Gutes verhiessen, entschlossen sie sich, Gozo und seine weniger stark verteidigte Hauptstadt Rabat anzugreifen. Die Stadt konnte sich nur ein paar Tage lang verteidigen. Fast die ganze Bevölkerung wurde in die Sklaverei abgeführt. Die Insel soll ihr demographisches Niveau erst 150 Jahre später wiedererlangt haben.

Die Ordensritter hatten noch keine Zeit gehabt, Malta gebührend zu befestigen. Sie waren ja noch nicht entschlossen, sich dort ständig niederzulassen. Die weitere Folge der Ereignisse brachte sie dann dazu, um doch auf der Insel festzusetzen.

Jetzt wandten sich die Türken gegen Tripolis. Der Platz wurde von dem Marschall Valies, der Auvergne sprachzugehörig, verteidigt. Jeder Widerstand war sinnlos, denn der Geiz des aragonischen Hochmeisters Juan d'Homedes war, so sagte man, für die Schwäche der Befestigungen verantwortlich. Die Zitadelle kapitulierte am 14. August 1551. Der Gesandte Frankreichs in Konstantinopel hatte einen Teil der Verhandlungen zwischen den Kämpfenden geführt. Den Ordensrittern wurde Leben und Freiheit zugesichert ihre Soldaten sollten die moslemischen Galeeren bemannen. Valies, den man für diese Kapitulation verantwortlich machte, wurde bis zum Tod des Hochmeisters, der zwei Jahre später erfolgte, ins Gefängnis geworfen. Seine Ordenskleidung wurde ihm entzogen. Zwischen Franzosen und Spaniern fand eine Polemik darüber statt, welcher von beiden Seiten die Verantwortung für die Ereignisse zuzuschreiben war.

1555 machten die Türken einen neuen Versuch; sie stiessen aber auf die neuen Befestigungen, die vom Hochmeister Claude de la Sengle errichtet worden waren, und nach dem das jetzige Viertel vor Senglea benannt wurde.

Kurze Zeit nach dem grossen Raid gegen Gozo und der Landung in der Bucht von Marsamxett beschloss man, die Halbinsel, auf der sich jetzt Valetta erhob, zu befestigen. So erbaute man ein sternförmiges Fort, das von hohen Mauern umgeben war: das Fort Saint-Elme, das später eine so wichtige Rolle spielen sollte und das der Ordensritter während der grossen Belagerung von 1565 eine Atempause verschaffte.

Im Verlaufe einer ihrer Expeditionen hatten die Ordensritter die Stadt Madhia in Tunesien besetzt, die früher die Hauptstadt eines arabischen Königreiches gewesen war. Karl V. schlug den Ordensrittern vor, die unschlüssig darüber waren, ob sie sich in Malta niederlassen sollten, es zurückzunehmen - und das um so mehr, da sie ja noch Tripolis verloren hatten.

Die letzte Expedition war die gegen Djerba (Februar 1690). Da man von der Idee, sich in Madhia niederzulassen, abgekommen war, beschloss La Valette, der seit drei Jahren Hochmeister war, im Einvernehmen mit den Spaniern, das immer noch nicht besser befestigte Tripolis zurückzunehmen. Dragut, dem dieses Gebiet unterstand, war abgezogen, um die Revolte einiger Nomadenstämme niederzuschlagen.

Anstatt Tripolis in einem Ueberraschungsangriff zu nehmen, befassten sich die Ordensschiffe mit zweitrangigen Angelegenheiten. So konnte Dragut wieder Oberwasser bekommen, und die Christen griffen die Insel Djerba an, wo der Chef der Seeräuber seit langem sein Hauptquartier aufgeschlagen hatte. Djerba, das reich an Oel und Getreide war, war schon oft der Zielpunkt der christlichen Streitkräfte gewesen. Doch diesmal mussten sie sich schnell wieder einschiffen, da Dragut und Ali Pascha, der Befehlshaber der türkischen Flotte, sich der Küste näherten. Einige tausend Mann bewachten die Zitadelle. Zwei Monate später mussten sie den Kampf aufgeben. Ungefähr dreissig Galeeren - die Hälfte der Schiffe, die das Expeditionskorps bildeten - wurden bei dem überstürzten Rückzug der Soldaten Philipps II. von Spanien, dem Nachfolger Karls V., verloren.

So blieb Malta die einzige Basis des Ordens. Es hiess jetzt, es schnellstens zu befestigen, denn es drohte Gefahr. *(photos p.107)*

JEAN PARISOT DE LA VALETTE

Dragut, der La Valette auf einer türkischen Galeere angekettet gesehen hatte, ist der Meinung, dass dieser "der grösste Krieger seiner Zeit" war.

Er diente dem Orden fünfzig Jahre lang, davon elf Jahre als Hochmeister. Dank ihm konnte Malta die zahlreichen Angriffe der Moslems zurückschlagen. Drei Jahre nach dem Fall von Tripolis hatte er vergeblich versucht, den Hochmeister davon zu überzeugen, dass es unumgänglich wäre, die Verteidigungskette der Insel zu verstärken. Dieser klarsehende Soldat hatte ebenfalls vorgeschlagen, eine Festung auf dem Sceberras-Berg anzulegen; dieses Projekt realisierte er nach der Belagerung von 1565 mit dem Bau von Valetta.

Er war als kaltblütiger Mensch bekannt; er feuerte seine Leute beim Kampfe an und stellte sich an ihre Spitze, um den Feind zurückzuschlagen. Er war nicht nur ein mutiger Mensch, sondern auch ein grosser Taktiker, der die Türken sich beim Ansturm, auf das Fort Saint Elme erschöpfen liess und der von diesem Aufschub profitierte, um neue Befestigungen anzulegen.

Wenn auch wohl die Chronik die Rolle des Inspirators der grössten aller befestigten Städte etwas verschönt haben mag, so war doch Jean Parisot de La Valette "der rechte Mann am rechten Platz".

DER KARNEVAL

Die Belagerung der Insel im Jahre 1565 gilt als grosse Waffentat der Ordensritter; sie ist gleichfalls ein historisches Datum. Konnten doch die Türken im Zaume gehalten werden, dank des Einsatzes von Tausenden von Maltesern, die sich, sei es als reguläre Soldaten, sei es als Freiwillige, engagiert hatten. Die Volksfeste nehmen oft auf diesen Sieg Bezug, und der Karneval bietet gleichfalls Gelegenheit, die verschiedensten Szenen der Epoche wieder darzustellen, wie hier oben, wo man kleine Mädchen die "Faldetta" tragen sieht; es ist das eine Art schwarzes Cape, das heute noch von den alten Mütterchen getragen wird; es erinnert etwas an die Röcke, die die türkischen Frauen - und auch manche Tunesierinnen - über ihren Kopf stülpen. *(photo p.121)*

DIE GROSSE BELAGERUNG VON 1565

Am Ende des Jahres 1564 schickten Geheimagenten des Ordens, die in Konstantinopel arbeiteten, alarmierende Berichte, in denen sie den Bau einer grossen Anzahl Galeeren mitteilten.

Für welch neue Expeditionen waren diese Schiffe bestimmt? Es war wohl kaum mit einem Angriff mitten im Winter zu rechnen, denn die Galeeren, die flach auf dem Wasser liegen, konnten sich bei schlechtem Wetter nicht aufs Meer wagen. In der Wintersaison gab es übrigens nie Kämpfe zu Wasser. Die Schiffe wurden repariert, die Zimmerleute bauten neue, kurz, man bereitete sich auf die Sommerkampagne vor.

Ohne absolut sicher zu sein, dass diese Vorbereitungen es selbst beträfen, so beunruhigte sich Malta sich doch. Die ganze Christenheit wurde um Hilfe angerufen, besonders der benachbarte Monarch, Don Garcia von Toledo, Vizekönig von Sizilien. Uebrigens hatte man sich schon seit mehreren Jahren auf einen Grossangriff vorbereitet. Das auf dem Sceberras-Berg gelegene Fort Saint-Elme war beendigt und die Forts Saint-Michel und Saint-Ange in Le Bourg und Senglea waren aufs schnellste konsolidiert worden.

Die Verteidiger verfügten über 9000 Mann, davon 5000 Malteser und nicht ganz 600 Ordensritter. Die acht Galeeren der Flotte konnten natürlich nichts gegen eine ganze Armada ausrichten.

Am 18. Mai 1565, frühmorgens, erschienen die zweihundert Schiffe der türkischen Flotte am Horizont. Nachdem sie den Tag über an der Küste entlaggekreuzt war, auf der Suche nach einer Landungsstelle, entschieden sie sich für die Bucht von Marsa-siroco, die bisher fast immer von den Eroberern der Insel als Landungsplatz benutzt worden war. Die auf dem Feldern arbeitenden Bauern, für die die plötzlichen Einfälle der türkischen Seeräuber nichts Neues waren, glaubten, dass diese wie sonst wie Heuschrecken über das Land herfallen würden, um dann ebenso plötzlich wieder zu verschwinden. Sie versteckten sich also an Ort und Stelle und dachten nicht daran, hinter den Befestigungen von Mdina oder des Hafens Zuflucht zu suchen. Da die Türken das Land aber drei Monate lang besetzten, verloren viele Bauern ihre Freiheit, wenn nicht gar das Leben.

Die türkische Armada hatte die Bucht von Marsaxlokk ausgesucht, um dort zu landen. Die Verteidiger setzten ihnen keinen starken Widerstand entgegen. Was konnte man schon gegen eine so zahlreiche Armee ausrichten? Man war auf jeden Fall entschlossen, den Türken hinter den Mauern Widerstand zu leisten. Die geringfügige maltesische Kavallerie konnte wohl hie und da einige Handstreiche ausführen, aber die zahlreichen kleinen Steinmauern, die die Felder von einander trennten, verhinderten sie zu manövrieren. Sie suchte in Mdina Zuflucht und machte von dort einige Ausfälle.

Die moslemischen Streitkräfte wurden von Mustafa Pascha kommandiert und die Flotte von dem Admiral Piali Pascha, dem Schwiegersohn des Sultans. Dessen Hauptsorge war es, seine zweihundert Schiffe kampfbereit zu machen. Er setzte deshalb, gegen die Meinung Mustafas, der zuerst Le Bourg und Senglea angreifen wollte, die Uebergabe von Fort Saint-Elme durch, bevor er irgendein anderes Manöver ausführte. So stände ihm dann die Bucht von Marsamxett offen. Das war ein Irrtum, den die Verteidiger auszunutzen wussten.

Die Türken schlugen ihr Hauptquartier in dem alten phönizischen Hafen Marso auf, weit hinten in der Bucht, die jetzt die hauptsächliche Hafenanlage von Valetta bildet. Sie dachten so, von der Höhenlage des Sceberras-Berges profitieren zu können, um das verschanzte Lager zu bombardieren. Das hiess aber, die strategische Lage des Forts Saint-Elme zu verkennen, das ungefähr zwölf Jahre vorher von Pietro Prado, dem spanischen Ingenieur, erbaut worden war. Für die damalige Zeit war das Fort das "nec plus ultra" der militärischen Verteidigungsbaukunst. Sein sternförmiger Grundriss und seine hohen Mauern sollten es uneinnehmbar machen. Seine Hauptrolle - die der Gegner unterschätzt hatte - bestand darin, die Einsetzung von Artillerie auf dem Sceberras-Berg, Le Bourg und Senglea gegenüber, zu verhindern. Mit ihren drei Forts konnten die Ordensritter jegliche dauerhafte Festsetzung im Bereich des grossen Hafens unmöglich machen.

Um ihre Kanonen zu schützen, hatten die Türken dem Fort gegenüber eine Stein- und Erdmauer aufgerichtet. Der erste bedeutende Angriff fand am 22. Mai statt mit einer Artillerievorbereitung, die mehrere Tage dauerte; es gelang ihr aber nicht, an den Befestigungen grosse Schaden anzurichten. Nach einer Woche machten die Belagerten einen Ausfall, der Unordnung in das gegnerische Lager brachte.

Die Türken konnten sich, im Gegenangriff, einiger ausserhalb des Forts gelegener Verteidigungswerke bemächtigen. Durch ihren Erfolg ermutigt, versuchten die Muselmänner die Mauern zu erstürmen, doch waren ihre Leitern oft zu kurz; die Brandpfeile und sonstige komplizierte mörderische Projektile, die die Christen von den Mauerzinnen auf sie hinunterwarfen, verursachten den Türken schwere Verluste. Die Türken sollten an diesem Tag zweitausend Tote - andere sagen wieder fünfhundert - gehabt haben. Das Fort Saint-Elme verlor an die hundert Mann, davon zwanzig Ordensritter.

Zweitausend Mann Verstärkung kämen aus Nordafrika mit dem furchterregenden Dragut an ihrer Spitze. Ihm schien es, dass das Fort Saint-Elme ohne grosse Schwierigkeiten genommen wurde, und dass nur die Anwendung einer ungeeigneten Taktik der Grund zu diesem Fehlschlag gewesen war. Er setzte neue Batterien ein, davon eine in einem Punkte, den man seitdem den "Angriffspunkt Dragut" nennt; dieser Punkt ist auf einem Kap gelegen, das sich am äussersten Ende von Sliema befindet, und das die Einfahrt der Bucht von Marsamxett kontrolliert. Von diesem Tag an nahmen die Bombardierungen an Intensität zu.

Während der ganzen Dauer der Belagerung konnten die Verteidiger des Forts Saint-Elme mit dem Hauptquartier der Ordensritter und ihrem Hochmeister La Valette in Verbindung treten; diese setzten die Befestigungsarbeiten in Le Bourg und Senglea fort. Da die Türken die Bucht nicht kontrollierten, konnte man ziemlich leicht nachts an das andere Ufer gelangen.

Dragut wurde tödlich verletzt, als er versuchte, den Verteidigern diesen Verbindungsweg abzuschneiden.

Doch das Fort gab allmählich nach, und die Verteidigungswerke wurden stark beschädigt, was den Türken schwere Verluste einbrachte. Zweitausendfünfhundert Soldaten, die als Nachschub aus Nordafrika gekommen waren, wurden kurze Zeit nach ihrer Ankunft niedergemetzelt. Dasselbe Schicksal wurde tausend Janitscharen zuteil, die versuchten, an Bord einiger Schiffe eine befestigte Brücke zwischen Le Bourg und Senglea zu erstürmen. Nur ein einziges Schiff kam heil davon. An diesem Tag waren die Verluste der Angreifer zehnmal höher als die der Ordensritter.

Am 23. Juni überwältigte ein Generalangriff die Verteidiger. Es gab nur einige Überlebende: ein paar maltesische Soldaten, denen es gelang, das befestigte Lager schwimmend zu erreichen. Einige Ordensritter fielen den Seeräubern in die Hände. Ihre Leichen wurden, auf grosse Holzkreuze genagelt, in den Hafen geworfen. Die Köpfe der Gefangenen dienten als Kanonenkugeln.

In dieser Schlacht um das Fort Saint-Elme verloren die Christen ungefähr 1500 Soldaten und 130 Ordensritter; die Türken wahrscheinlich mehr als 8.000.

Doch war die Sache noch längst nicht entschieden. Die Muselmänner hatten, weit von ihrer Basis eine Schlacht gewonnen, doch waren sie stark geschwächt. Sie wussten sehr wohl, das es schwer sein würde, den Sieg davonzutragen.

Die Verteidiger der Befestigungslinien wurden jedoch immer stärker bedrängt. Es gab immer häufigere Breschen, die schwer zu verteidigen und schwer zu reparieren waren. Eine von ihnen, grösser war als die vorhergehenden, erlaubte es den Türken, in die Umfassungsmauer von Le Bourg einzudringen. Sie stürzten sich darauf, indem sie Siegesrufe ausstiessen. Sie befanden sich aber plötzlich einer zweiten Umfassungsmauer gegenüber, die die Verteidiger inzwischen erbaut hatten, und der von dieser nun auf die Angreifer mörderische Projektile hinunterhageln liessen: Pech, Steine, usw.

Trotzdem gelang es ihnen, das Fort Saint-Michel einzuschliessen. Aber die beste Gelegenheit war nun für die Türken verloren. Die von Don Garcia von Toledo versprochenen Hilfstruppen waren auf dem Wege. Der König von Sizilien hatte gewartet, bis es ihm gelang, die notwendigen Streitkräfte zu versammeln, um keinen Fehlschlag zu erleiden.

Die gerade aus Sizilien angelangten Soldaten waren in dem von den türkischen Truppen verlassenen Lager eingefallen und hatten es zerstört und verbrannt, wobei ihnen die in Mdina verschanzte Kavallerie zu Hilfe kam.

Am 6. September schifften 30 Galeeren die Hilfstruppen in Mellieha aus, und zwei Tage später hielt es Mustafa für geraten, die Belagerung aufzuheben.

Malta war gerettet. Man hätte ihm viel schneller zu Hilfe kommen können, wenn die politischen Meinungsverschiedenheiten der Europäer nicht das schnelle Zusammenziehen der nötigen Truppen verhindert hätten.

(photos p.111)

189

DER JOHANNITERORDEN VON JERUSALEM

Während seines Aufenthalts in Rhodos wurde der Johanniterorden zu einer kolossalen militärischen und religiösen Institution Die Ritter, die im Anfang nur die Beschützer der Pilger im Heiligen Land gewesen waren, wurden nun zu Anführern der Christenheit im Kampfe gegen die türkische Hegemonie im Mittelmeergebiet. Sie verpflichteten sich, die Religion Jesu zu verteidigen und niemals feindliche Handlungen gegen irgendeine christliche Nation vorzunehmen.

Die Mitglieder des Ordens waren in drei Gruppen geteilt: die Ritter der Gerechtigkeit, die Kaplane und die dienenden Brüder.

Unter den Rittern befanden sich die grössten katholischen Adelsfamilien Europas. Von den Deutschen wurden sechzehn Ahnen verlangt, von den Franzosen nur acht. Jede Familie war stolz auf ihren Sohn, der in den Reihen des Ordens kämpfte. Ritter, die geringeren Ranges waren, konnten wegen ihres ausserordentlichen militärischen Wertes kooptiert werden.

Die Kaplane waren Feldgeistliche und hatten im allgemeinen nur religiöse Funktionen.

Die dienenden Brüder mussten nur beweisen können, dass sie honorablen Ursprungs waren; sie konnten sowohl Krieger als auch Krankenwärter in den Hospitälern des Ordens sein.

Die Mitglieder des Ordens trugen ein schwarzes Gewand und einen Mantel von gleicher Farbe aus Kamelhaar. Er erinnerte an den Mantel, den Johannes der Täufer trug. Dieser Mantel wurde nur bei Zeremonien getragen. In Herzenshöhe vergegenwärtigte ein achtspitziges Kreuz die acht Verpflichtungen oder Aspirationen:
- der Wahrheit leben
- den Glauben haben
- seine Fehler bereuen
- demütig sein
- die Gerechtigkeit lieben
- barmherzig sein
- aufrichtig und reinen Herzens sein
- Verfolgungen auf sich nehmen.

Sie folgten der Regel des Heiligen Augustin und legten die drei Gelübde ab: das der Keuschheit, des Gehorsams und der Armut. Doch eine betonte Strenge, denn, von den Kaplanen abgesehen, waren sie vor allem Soldaten, denen es sogar anempfohlen war, sich gut zu ernähren und sich in bester Form zu erhalten, um den Feind unter den besten Bedingungen bekämpfen zu können. Bart und Haare mussten sie kurzgeschoren tragen, damit sie während der Schlacht nicht behindert wurden. Im Waffenmuseum von Valetta kann man ihre Waffen sehen, die ohne besondere Verzierungen, aber von eindrucksvoller Solidität sind.

Alle, die es wünschten, in den Orden einzutreten, mussten sich einem von religiösen und ritterlichen Symbolen strotzenden Ritus unterziehen.

Der Kandidat präsentierte sich zunächst vor dem Altar mit einer Kerze und einem langen Gewand ohne Gürtel, um zu zeigen, dass er frei von jeglichem Band sei. Der beisitzende Ritter übergab ihm ein vergoldetes Schwert, das kundzutun, dass er die Religion verteidigen müsse "im Namen des Vaters, des Sohnes und des Heiligen Geistes". Der Gürtel, den er nun umband, bedeutete, dass er jetzt an die Gelübde des Ordens gebunden sei. Er zückte das Schwert über seinem Kopf zum Zeichen der Herausforderung an die Ungläubigen und steckte es dann wieder in die Scheide, nachdem er es abgewischt hatte, wie um anzudeuten, dass er makellos zu bleiben habe.

Man legte ihm vergoldete Sporen an, damit er die Reichtümer dieser Welt mit Füssen trete. Ihn, der die brennende Kerze in der Hand hielt, fragte man, ob er verheiratet sei, ob er Schulden hätte und ob Mitglied irgendeines Ordens sei. Dann führte man ihn zum Altar, wo er seine Gelübde auf das Messbuch ablegte. Jeden Tag musste er eine gewisse Anzahl von Gebeten hersagen, zu Ehren Gottes und der Mutter Gottes und für die Seele der verstorbenen Ritter.

Der Orden war in acht "Sprachen" eingeteilt, deren jede an ihrer Spitze eine "Stütze" oder Klostervogt hatte. Es gab da "die Sprachen" von Kastilien, England, Italien, Aragon, Deutschland und die drei französischen: Provence, Frankreich und Auvergne. Vergessen wir nicht, dass der erste Hochmeister der Provenzale Gérard de Martigues war. Von den achtundsechzig Hochmeistern waren vierundvierzig französischen Ursprungs. Die Sprache Englands war nicht mehr vertreten seit der Trennung dieses Landes von der katholischen Religion.

Jeder Vogt bekleidete traditionsgemäss ein ganz bestimmtes Amt. Der von Aragon kümmerte sich um die Gewänder des Ordens; der Vogt der "Sprache" von Frankreich betreute die Spitäler; der von England kommandierte die Küstenverteidigung; der Grossadmiral war immer von italienischer Sprache; der Grossvogt der deutschen Sprache sah darauf, dass die Befestigungen in gutem Zustand blieben.

Die "Sprachen" hatten zur Gewohnheit, eine Art Hauptquartier für jede von ihnen erbauen zu lassen: die Herbergen, die sehr bald miteinander rivalisierten, was die Schönheit ihrer Baukunst anbetraf. Mit den Kathedralen sind das die bedeutendsten Monumente, die uns geblieben sind. Fast die Hälfte von Maltas Herbergen sind während des letzten Krieges zerstört worden.

Der Hochmeister wurde auf Lebenszeit gewählt, spätestens drei Tage nach dem Versterben seines Vorgängers. So dachte man, das Eingreifen des Papstes zu vermeiden, sowie jegliches politische Aushandeln vonseiten der europäischen Mächte.

Diese "Eminenz", wie man sie nannte, hatte das Recht, eigenes Geld zu prägen. Die Unabhängigkeit des Ordens war eine gegebene Tatsache, und er war durch eigene Diplomaten bei mehreren europäischen Monarchen vertreten.

(photo p.105)

DIE HOCHMEISTER VON MALTA

Die Hochmeister waren über zweihundertfünfzig Jahre lang die tatsächlichen Herrscher des Archipels. Sie wurden auf Lebenszeit gleich nach dem Ableben des vorhergehenden Hochmeisters von allen Ordensrittern gewählt; ihnen standen sämtliche Hoheitsrechte zu. Sie trugen den Titel Eminenz und durften ihr eigenes Geld prägen.

Die Hochmeister hingen nicht mehr von ihrem Herkunftsland ab; sie hatten sozusagen eine doppelte Nationalität, sodass ihre Wahl stets mit Interesse diskutiert wurde. Die Regel, dass die Wahl des Nachfolgers binnen drei Tagen erfolgen musste, verhinderte so jedwede äussere Einflussnahme. Da es immer einer gewissen Zeit bedurfte, wurden die ausländischen Herrscher erst nach einigen Tagen, manchmal sogar erst nach mehreren Wochen, von der Wahl des neuen Hochmeisters unterrichtet.

Jeder Hochmeister hat der Insel sein Gepräge aufgedrückt, sowohl durch den Bau neuer Befestigungen (La Valette, Cottoner, Redin), öffentlicher Gebäude, von Aufenthaltsstätten des Ordens, wie auch durch die Inauftraggebung von Kunstwerken (Bilder, Fresken).

(photo p.151)

Philippe Villiers de L'Isle Adam (Frankreich)	1530-1534
Pietro del Ponte (Italien)	1534-1535
Didier de Saint Jaille (Frankreich)	1535-1536
Juan d'Homèdes (Aragon)	1536-1553
Claude de la Sengle (Frankreich)	1553-1557
Jean de la Valette (Provence)	1557-1568
Pietro del Monte San Savino (Italien)	1568-1572
Jean l'Evêque de la Cassière (Auvergne)	1572-1581
Hugues de Loubens Verdalle (Provence)	1581-1595
Martin Garzes (Aragon)	1595-1601
Alof de Wignacourt (Frankreich)	1601-1622
Louis Mendes de Vasconcellos (Kastilien, Leon, Portugal)	1622-1623
Antoine de Paule (Provence)	1623-1636
Jean-Paul de Lascaris Castellar (Provence)	1636-1657
Martin de Redin (Aragon)	1657-1660
Annet de Clermont de Chattes-Gessan (Auvergne)	1660
Rafael Cotoner (Aragon)	1660-1663
Nicolo Cotoner (Aragon)	1663-1680
Gregorio Carafa (Italien)	1680-1690
Adrien de Wignacourt (Frankreich)	1690-1697
Ramon Perellos y Rocaful (Aragon)	1697-1720
Marcantonio Zondadari (Italien)	1720-1722
Anton Manoel de Vilhena (Kastilien, Leon, Portugal)	1722-1736
Ramon Despuig (Aragon)	1736-1741
Manoel Pinto de Fonseca (Kastilien, Leon, Portugal)	1741-1773
Francisco Ximenes de Texada (Aragon)	1773-1775
Emmanuel Marie de Rohan-Polduc (Frankreich)	1775-1797
Ferdinand von Hompesch (Deutschland)	1797-1798

VALLETTA
DIE GEBURT EINER STADT

"Bruder Jean de la Valette, Hochmeister des Johanniterordens von Jerusalem, in der Erinnerung an die Gefahr, der seine Ritter und das maltesische Volk ausgesetzt gewesen waren, während der Belagerung der Türken im vergangenen Jahr und nach Konsultierung der Verantwortlichen des Ordens über die Möglichkeit der Erbauung einer neuen Stadt und deren Befestigung durch Mauern, Wälle und Wachttürme, die jedem Ansturm gewachsen wären und ihn zurückschlagen könnten oder wenigstens dem Angriff des türkischen Feindes standhalten könnten, legte am Donnerstag dem 28. März 1566, nach Anrufung des allmächtigen Gottes, der heiligen Jungfrau, des Schutzpatrons Johannes der Täufer und der sonstigen Heiligen, damit das unternommene Werk der Gesamtheit der christlichen Gemeinschaft Reichtum und Glück bringe, und damit dem Orden nur das Beste daraus erwachse, den Grundstein zur Stadt auf dem Hügel, den die Einwohner der Insel Sceberras nennen, und nach dem er ihr als Wappen einen goldenen Löwen auf rotem Grund gegeben hatte, äusserte er den Wunsch, das, sie seinen Namen, La Valette (Valletta) annähme."

So lautet die Inschrift auf einem der Grundsteine der neuen Stadt, deren Erbauung Jean de la Valette gewünscht hatte, die gemäss dem Plan von Francesco Laparelli, dem italienischen Militärarchitekten, der aus Cortone stammte, ausgeführt worden war. Der Malteser Girolamo Cassar nahm ebenfalls an der Erbauung der Stadt teil; er leitete den Bau von Gebäuden wie dem der Kathedrale des Heiligen Johannes.

Zwar hatte sich Europa lange bitten lassen, bevor es den belagerten Malteserrittern zu Hilfe eilte; aber die Gaben für den neuen Bau strömten von den zahlreichen europäischen Höfen zusammen. Der König von Frankreich gab 140.000 Pfund, von allen Gaben die bedeutendste.

Der Hochmeister war sich während der langen Belagerung des Grossen Hafens der strategischen Lage des Berges Sceberras und der wichtigen Rolle, die das Fort Saint Elme gespielt hatte, bewusst geworden. Warum nicht eine Stadt auf dieser Stätte selbst gründen? Das heroische kleine Fort wurde wieder aufgebaut. Was die Stadt anbetraf, so verlangte man die letzten Neuheiten der Militärarchitektur. Es existierten zahlreiche Projekte für befestigte Städte, denn je mörderischer die Waffen wurden, desto höher und breiter mussten die Befestigungen werden. Man goss immer grössere Kanonen, man baute immer grössere Schiffe, und wenn auch der Malteserorden sich noch während eines Jahrhunderts der Galeeren bediente, so fingen doch die Hochseeschiffe, die während der ozeanischen Entdeckungsreisen erprobt wurden, an, das Mittelmeer zu durchqueren.

In ganz Europa wurden die Städte mit neuen Befestigungssystemen versehen. Ein Projekt des Architekten Pietro Cataneo sah eine in Sechseckform befestigte Stadt vor, von der jeder Winkel und jede Seite mit Befestigungen versehen war, die sie theoretisch uneinnehmbar machten.

Die Strassen Vallettas, die sich im rechten Winkel schneiden, sind wie mit der Kordel gezogen. Der Bau schritt munter fort, was erklärt, dass man kaum Zeit hatte, ihr Relief umzumodeln. Die Stadt macht sozusagen einen Buckel mit ihren Strassen, die direkt zum Meer hinuntergehen, von Zeit zu Zeit von unerwarteten Treppen unterbrochen.

Die Türken waren zwar zurückgeworfen worden, aber nichts liess darauf schliessen, dass sie nicht wiederkommen würden. Ein Jahrhundert später lastete ihre Bedrohung immer noch auf Europa. Die neue befestigte Stadt wurde schnell fertig. Die Projekte Laparellis wurden keineswegs auf das Genaueste ausgeführt. Die Teile der Stadt, die ans Meer grenzen, werden mit einem hohen und dichten Festungsgürtel umgeben. Das vollständigste System betrifft den Abschnitt, der sich über die ganze Breite des Sceberras-Berges erstreckt, des schwächsten Punktes der Anlage. Ein einziges Tor mit einer Fallbrücke gestattete es, in die Stadt zu dringen. Ein tiefer in die Felsen gehauener Graben und Bastionen auf beiden Seiten trugen noch zur Verstärkung des Ganzen bei.

Nicht ganz hundert Jahre später wurde ein anderer Teil des Sceberras-Berges mit einem anderen Befestigungssystem überzogen, so dass so die Befestigungen Vallettas (1657) noch verstärkt wurden.

Die beiden Brüder Cottoner, die sich als Hochmeister folgten, bezogen in das gesamte Befestigungswesen die Städte Vittoriosa, Senglea und ein neues Viertel : Cospicua (Cottonera line 1680) mit ein.

Jeder neue Hochmeister trug so sein Scherflein dazu bei, indem er, sei es eine Schanze, sei es eine neue Befestigung errichten liess.

So wurde Valletta die meistbefestigte Stadt der Welt. Doch stellte sich jetzt ein neues Problem. Wo konnte man die Männer finden, die zur Verteidigung dieser riesigen Werke nötig waren? Man hätte dazu ungefähr vierzigtausend Mann benötigt. Man hat nie feststellen können, wie sich ein solches Verteidigungssystem im Falle einer Belagerung bewährt hätte.

Zur grossen Verzweiflung der Militärsachverständigen wagten es die Türken nicht mehr, neue Grossoffensiven gegen Malta zu starten. Die Mächte, die die Insel kontrollierten, beherrschten auch das Mittelmeer.

(photos p. 122)

DIE JOHANNESKIRCHE

Jean de la Valette war seit fünf Jahren tot, als man zur Grundsteinlegung der Klosterkirche schritt, die den Namen des Heiligen Johannes, des Schutzpatrons des Ordens, bekam. Der Architekt war der Malteser Gerolamo Cassar.

Der Hochmeister de la Cassière, der möglichst schnell die neue Stadt zum Sitz des Ordens machen wollte, schöpfte in seiner eigenen Kasse, damit das religiöse Gebäude möglichst schnell vollendet werde. Das, was später eine Kathedrale werden sollte, wurde aber erst dreissig Jahre später vollendet. Sowohl durch ihre Dekorationen wie auch durch die Elemente, die später im Laufe der Jahre hinzugefügt wurden, vergegenwärtigt sie einen wichtigen Teil der Geschichte der Ordensritter. Mehrere Hochmeister haben Kapellen erbaut und dekoriert. Der Boden ist mit marmornen verschiedenfarbigen Grabplatten bedeckt; sie schildern auf sehr realistische Weise hervorstechende Tatsachen aus dem Leben der verstorbenen Ritter.

Quentin Hughes, dem Architekturprofessor an der Universität von Malta nach, ist es eine der seltsamsten und eindruckvollsten Kirchen der Christenheit.

Dieses primitive Barock, das manchmal gerade erst die Gotik überstanden hatte, lässt beim geringsten Sonnenstrahl die später erst hinzugefügten Zierate erstrahlen.

In seiner ganzen Länge wird das Gewölbe von einer ungeheuren Freske gebildet, die Mattia Pretti zu verdanken ist. Ein System von mobilen Gerüsten auf Schienen gestattete es, jederzeit die gute Instandhaltung zu gewährleisten und - falls nötig - Restaurationen vorzunehmen. Der kalabrische Maler, dessen Hauptwerk diese Fresken bilden, richtete diese Arbeit auf Verlangen der Gebrüder Cotoner aus. Er gebrauchte dazu fünf Jahre.

Die Kapellen der verschiedenen Sprachen rivalisieren in den Verzierungen und den Ausführungen der Denkmäler. Diese Kapellen enthalten die Leichen der Hochmeister. Die ersten Hochmeister - und unter ihnen Jean de la Valette - liegen in der Krypta begraben.

Das Oratorium der Kathedrale enthält die berühmte "Enthauptung des heiligen Johannes" von Caravaggio. Caravaggio wurde tatsächlich vom Hochmeister Alof de Wignacourt 1608 nach Malta eingeladen. Ausser dem riesenhaften Bild, das die ganze Mauer dieses grossen Saales einnimmt, malte er noch ein Porträt seines Gastgebers, das sich im Louvre befindet.

(photos p. 133)

DER HOCHMEISTER-PALAST

Die geräumigste dieser Herbergen ist der Hochmeister-Palast in Valletta. Dort befindet sich heutzutage die Residenz des Präsidenten der maltesischen Republik. Ihr Bau begann im Jahre 1571. Man kann dort das grosse Eingangstor sehen, sowie den mit grossen schattenspendenden Bäuen bestandenen Innenhof. In einem Flügel dieser Herberge befindet sich die grosse Rüstkammer, wo eine grosse Anzahl von Rüstungen und Waffen aller Art und aller Epochen ausgestellt sind. Dort ist auch die einfache aber eindrucksvolle Rüstung Vallettas zu sehen, allerdings ohne sein Schwert, das im Louvre zu sehen ist. Hier befindet sich auch der Thronsaal mit seinen grossen, von Perez d'Aleccio gemalten Fresken, die die hauptsächlichen Episoden der grossen Belagerung von 1565 darstellen.

(photo p. 144)

DIE HERBERGEN

Seit ihrem Aufenthalt in Rhodos hatten die Malteserritter sich daran gewöhnt, ihre gleichsprachigen Mitglieder in grossen Herbergen zu gruppieren. Als Valletta erbaut wurde und die Stadt zum Ordenssitz wurde, mussten neue Gebäude errichtet werden. Mit der Johanneskathedrale waren diese die Kleinodien der neuen Stadt. Leider wurden mehrere der schönsten Herbergen 1942 während der Belagerung von deutschen Flugzeugen zerstört.

Der maltesische Architekt Cassar wurde beauftragt, die sieben Herbergen zu bauen. Jede Herberge gliederte sich in den Teil der Befestigungen ein, die die jeweiligen Sprachzugehörigen zu verteidigen hatten.

Die Herberge der Provence, die nicht gerade einen effektvollen Eindruck macht, beherbergt das Nationalmuseum, wo sich die meisten wesentlichen Objekte der maltesischen Vorgeschichte und Geschichte befinden. Nur selten hat eine so kleine Insel einen so grossen Reichtum seiner Vergangenheit entfalten können.

Die Herberge von Kastilien und Leon wurde im 18. Jahrhundert vollkommen umgeändert, unter dem Hochmeister dieser Sprache, Manuel Pinto de Fonseca, der die Geschicke des Ordens von 1741 bis 1773 leitete. Der Architekt, Domenico Cachia, war durch Lecce (Italien) gekommen, und die Herberge trägt das Gepräge dieses Aufenthalts. Sie ist das eleganteste der öffentlichen Gebäude dieser Art. Man bemerkt vor allem die Fassade und den herrlichen Balkon über dem grossen Eingangstor mit dem Wappen des Hochmeisters.

(photo p.130)

DIE VERTEIDIGUNG DER INSELN

Es genügte nicht, Valletta zu erbauen und eine Menge Befestigungen anzulegen. Die traditionelle Strategie wollte, dass man zuerst eine uneinnehmbare Bastion konstruierte, wie die Forts Saint Elme, Saint Michel oder Saint Ange. Die eigentlichen Städte, die wegen Menschenmangel oder der Schwäche ihrer Festungswerke nur schwer verteidigt werden konnten, hielten den Angriffen mit mehr oder weniger Glück stand.

Später wurden auch Städte zu Festungswerken, die von hohen Schutzmauern und tiefen Gräben umgeben waren. Der Bau von Valletta, das dazu bestimmt war, an die Stelle von Le Bourg, dem früheren Sitz des Ritterordens zu treten, verfolgte keinen anderen Zweck als eine befestigte Stadt zu gründen, die alle Sicherheitsbedingungen erfüllte. Während der Jahre, in denen sich die Ordensritter dort befanden, wurden neue Linien im Vorgelände der zuerst errichteten Bastionen aufgeworfen, so dass die Stadt so gut wie uneinnehmbar wurde (Konstruktion von Floriana). In Vittoriosa und Senglea wurde eine neue Mauerführung vorgenommen, die neue Viertel umfasste oder neue Urbanisierungsmöglichkeiten schuf dank des Schutzes, den sie bot (die Cotoner Linien).

Dank der zunehmenden Sicherheit, die der Archipel genoss, nahm die Bevölkerung schnell zu; teils durch das Aufhören der traditionellen Razzien, teils durch das Kommen von Seeleuten und Geschäftsleuten aller Art. Auch das Land entwickelte sich und die Bauernwirtschaft, die bisher autark eingestellt war, wandte sich nun den Märkten zu, die die neuen Stadtviertel darboten. Das war auch notwendig, denn der undankbare Boden hatte bisher die Autoritäten gezwungen, zumindest für die Stadtbevölkerung, einen grossen Teil der Produkte zu importieren. Die Sicherheit, die nun auf dem Lande herrschte, ermöglichte es, diese Abhängigkeit gewissermassen zu vermindern.

Kleine Burgen wurden überall auf der Insel errichtet, auf Anhöhen und gegenüber dem Meer. Davon waren einige rein militärisch (die roten Türme von Mellieha, Fort Saint Lucien) oder gemischt (der Sommerpalast des Verdalla-Palastes; eine Institution für die früheren Sklaven, wie der Selmun-Palast). Sie alle erwecken ein gewisses Interesse.

Um einer eventuellen Landung von Türken oder Piraten vorzubeugen, wurden zahlreiche Wehrtürme angelegt, und das kurz nach dem Eintreffen der Ordensritter. Vielleicht wurde so eine auf den Mittelmeerinseln althergebrachte Gewohnheit wieder lebendig, da diese ständig Razzien ausgesetzt waren. Diese Türme konnten den Umkreis von zwei Inseln überwachen. Sie konnten miteinander durch ein Signalsystem in Verbindung treten (Rauch- oder Flaggenzeichen). Sie bestanden aus einer oder mehreren Etagen, die untereinander durch einfache Leitern verbunden waren, die man beim geringsten Alarm heraufziehen konnte. So konnten sie eine Zeitlang der Belagerung durch eine Piratenbande standhalten, die nur mit Flinten ausgerüstet war, und so auf Hilfe warten. *(photos p.138)*

MDINA

Mdina, Citta Vecchia, Citta Notabile, die Stadt des Schweigens, ist die ehemalige Hauptstadt Maltas, die der Araber, der Römer und der Normannen, bevor die Ordensritter, Seeleute seit ihrem Aufenthalt in Rhodos, Le Bourg und später Valletta zum Sitz und hauptsächlichen Hafen des Ordens auserkoren.

In Mdina findet man noch die bedeutendsten Überreste aus der normannischen Epoche. Die Wälle, deren Grundmauern von den Arabern aufgeführt wurden, wurden von den Ordensrittern befestigt und erhöht. Bastionen wurden an den schwachen Stellen erbaut und ein Graben gezogen.

Das Haupttor wurde von dem Hochmeister de Vilhena 1724 erbaut, doch gibt es noch ein anderes Tor, das weniger auffällig ist; es befindet sich unten an den Wällen, und man nennt es "das Tor der Griechen".

Mdina ist wirklich eine Stadt des Schweigens, vielleicht weil jetzt das ganze wirtschaftliche Leben sich auf Valletta konzentriert, sowie auf das nicht weit entfernt liegende Rabat. Obwohl Mdina noch die letztem Abkommen einer Adelskaste, die sich bis zu den Normannen und Spaniern zurückverfolgen lässt, beherbergt, vermittelt es doch den Eindruck einer Stadt, in der die Zeit stehengeblieben ist. Man findet dort nur noch die Ruhe der Häuser und öffentlichen Gebäude vergangener Zeiten vor.

Die Kathedrale ist nicht mehr die, die der Graf Roger im Jahre 1100 von aus Sizilien gekommenen Maurern erbauen liess. Sie ist trotzdem die bedeutendste der Insel und wurde im Jahre 1419 vergrössert. Ein Erdbeben hat sie im Jahre 1693 zerstört. Das neue Gebäude war das Werk des Architekten der Kirche von Victoria-Rabat, Lorenzo Gafa (1697). Nach der Klosterkirche des heiligen Johannes ist sie die interessanteste des ganzen Archipels. Ebenso bemerkenswert ist der Schatz der Kathedrale, der Gegenstände enthält, die noch der Urkirche angehörten.

Von den Wällen Mdinas geniesst man einen herrlichen Ausblick über das ganze maltesische Land, das Valletta umgibt. *(photos p.148)*

VICTORIA –

Die bedeutendste Stadt von Gozo war oft heimgesucht und dann wieder neu bevölkert worden. An die Stelle seines ersten Namens: Rabat, trat im vorigen Jahrhundert der der grossen Königen Victoria.

Während der "Grossen Belagerung" nahmen die Türken, die die Hauptstadt belagerten, ihr Versprechen, die Stadt zu schonen, das sie dem Mönch Bartolomé Bonavia gemacht hatten, wieder zurück, nachdem dieser eine ehrenvolle Übergabe ausgehandelt hatte. Die Stadt wurde zerstört, die Archive verbrannt und die Bevölkerung deportiert. Der Gouverneur zog für seine Frau und seine Kinder lieber den Tod vor, als dass er sie in die Sklaverei abgeführt gesehen hätte.

Inmitten der Befestigungen erhebt sich die Kathedrale, die im Jahre 1711 von Lorenzo Gafa im italienischen Barockstil erbaut wurde. Man kann dort eine Kuppel in Augentäuschung sehen, die ziemlich einzigartig in ihrer Art dasteht und die dem italienischen Künstler Pozzo zu verdanken ist; sowie eine Madonnenstatue, die bei der jährlichen Prozession am 15. August ausgetragen wird. Der silberne Sockel, der von beträchtlichem Wert ist (man spricht von 30.000 DM), wurde von zwei Bewohnern der Insel aus Dankbarkeit gestiftet, nachdem sie aus einer schlimmen Situation im Meer errettet worden waren.

Auf dem Platz der Kathedrale befindet sich der ehemalige Bischofspalast, der im Jahre 1620 erbaut wurde. Er ist eines der ältesten Gebäude von Gozo.

Eine andere ehemalige Wohnstätte, der Bondi-Palast, beherbergt jetzt das Museum. Dort wird ein Überblick über die Geschichte und die Vorgeschichte der Insel gegeben: Tempel von Giantija, römische Ausgrabungen, arabische und christliche Geldstücke, der Grabstein von Majmuna und ein schöner vollkommen verzierter Schrank, der aus dieser Gegend stammt. *(photos p.146)*

FLORIANA

Der Name Florianas rührt von dem Namen des Architekten Paolo Floriani her, der vom Papst geschickt worden war, um Lösungen für den verstärkten Schutz Vallettas vorzuschlagen. Denn die Stadt, die nach der Belagerung von 1565 wieder aufgebaut worden war, hatte sich nicht über den gesamten "Mont Sceberras" erstrecken können, da es an Männern für ihre Verteidigung mangelte. 1634 hatte die Furcht vor einem türkischen Angriff zur Folge, dass eine neue Linie mit gigantischen Befestigungen erbaut wurde, die die Halbinsel vollkommen abschloss. Im Innern entwickelte sich ein neues Viertel, in dem man die Kirche des heiligen Publius errichtete und vor dieser Kirche ungeheure Speicher, die man heute noch sehen kann. Man gelangt dorthin durch ein Tor in Triumphbogenform, la Porte des Bombes (das Tor der Bomben), das in den Jahren 1697 und 1720 errichtet wurde; eine jede Säule stellt eine Kanone dar.

(photos p.142)

BONAPARTE

Auf dem Wege nach Ägypten stiess Bonaparte natürlich auf die Insel Malta. Schon 6 Monate früher, während der Rückkehr aus Italien, hatte er daran gedacht, sich dieser Befestigung zu bemächtigen und hatte schon deswegen bei dem Direktorium um Ermächtigung nachgesucht. Nachdem er eine Zusage erhalten hatte, konnte er am 9. Juni 1798 Valletta ins Blickfeld nehmen. Er kommandierte eine mächtige Flotte (300 Schiffe, davon ein Drittel Kriegsschiffe).

Die Befestigungen dienten zu nichts. Die Übergabe wurde auf dem diplomatischen Wege erzielt, und auch weil der Hochmeister von Hompesch einsah, dass die Sache verloren war.

Drei Tage später gab der Hochmeister dem Kaiser nach. Die Beute war beträchtlich: 1500 Kanonen, der Schatz des Ordens (3 Millionen in Gold und Silber) und an die 3500 Gewehre. Schon seit langem war der Kampf gegen die Türken beendet und "das Bündnis der Kirche und der Ordensritter, des Krieges mit der Religion", erlag so den Einflüssen der Revolution.

Der Archipel wurde annektiert und dem französischen Gesetz und den französischen Institutionen unterstellt. Die Kokarde trat an die Stelle des Ordenskreuzes, und alle Sklaven wurden als Kriegsbeute betrachtet.

Bei den Maltesern, die von Anfang an Frankreich günstig gesonnen waren, fand man so Spuren von Unzufriedenheit. Die Besatzungstruppen hatten Plünderungen vorgenommen, und die lokalen Institutionen waren missachtet worden. Die Bevölkerung geriet in Aufruhr.

Die kleine französische Garnison von Mdina wurde massakriert. Die restlichen Truppen, die sich in Valletta verbarrikadiert hatten, waren zwei Jahre lang der Blockade der Malteser und der Engländer ausgesetzt, deren Flotte alle Hilfsunternehmungen verhinderte. Einem Schiff jedoch gelang es die Blockade zu brechen. Es war mit Wein und Schnaps beladen . . .

(photo p.152)

DER ABZUG DES ORDENS

Mittlerweile war der französische Einfluss vorherrschend geworden. Im Anfang des Jahres 1789 waren zweidrittel der sechshundert Ordensritter französischer Herkunft und mehr als die Hälfte der Schiffe, die in Valletta anlegten, französischen Ursprungs.

Unabhängig unter der Flagge des Ordens, wurde Malta von den Grossmächten begehrt. Das auf Frankreich neidische England brauchte eine neue Basis im Mittelmeer, seitdem es Spanien Minorca überlassen hatte, und auch Russland hielt aus ähnlichen Gründen nicht mit Intrigen zurück.

Die maltesische Bourgeoisie, die sich dank der Handelsfunktionen der Insel beträchtlich entwickelt hatte und die sich von jeder politischen Verantwortung ausgeschaltet sah, hatte sich von einer Institution abgewandt, die sich weigerte, sie in ihre Reihen aufzunehmen. Daher soll man sich nicht wundern, dass sie, sowohl wie die übrige Bevölkerung, gewisse Ideen der französischen Revolution mit Begeisterung aufnahm.

Obwohl der grösste Teil der Ordensritter für das frühere Regime war, so waren doch einige von ihnen in Frankreich als Abgeordnete der Generalstände gewählt worden.

Als sich Bonaparte der Insel bemächtigte, war der gewählte Hochmeister seit ungefähr einem Jahr im Amt. Ferdinand von Hompesch war Deutscher. Die Schwäche der Streitkräfte über die er verfügen konnte und das geringe Vertrauen das er zu den lokalen Truppen hatte, die ziemlich unzufrieden waren, führte dazu, dass es zu einer wenig glorreichen Kapitulation vor Bonaparte kam. Er erhielt zur Entschädigung eine Pension von 30.000 Franken und die französischen Ordensritter lebenslängliche Pensionen, die sich ihrem Alter gemäss staffelten.

(photo p.153)

DIE ENGLÄNDER

Gemäss den Friedensabkommen, die von Frankreich und England im Jahr 1802 unterzeichnet worden waren, sollte die Insel dem Malteserorden wieder übergeben werden. Doch weigerten sich die Engländer unter den verschiedensten Vorwänden, was die Wiederaufnahme der Feindlichkeiten zwischen den beiden Ländern zur Folge hatte.

Nachdem es den Archipel annektiert hatte, konnte England ihn weiterentwickeln und Malta zu seiner militärischen und kaufmännischen Basis machen. Er gewann noch beträchtlich an Bedeutung durch die Eröffnung des Suezkanals im Jahr 1869 und durch die wirtschaftliche Entwicklung des brittischen Empires im Fernen Osten. Alle Schiffe, die sich nach Indien begaben oder von dort zurückkamen, konnten in Valletta haltmachen, dort ihre Waren löschen und vor allem nötiggewordene Reparaturen vornehmen. Die Ausbeutung der Erdölvorkommen im Nahen Osten hob noch diesen Schiffsverkehr. Im Jahr 1888 hielten zwölftausend Schiffe in Valletta an.

Zahlreiche Warenlager wurden gebaut. Sie sind noch zu Füssen der jetzt unnützgewordenen Wälle zu sehen. Die Stadt war ebenfalls der Heimathafen der britischen Kriegsflotte im Mittelmeer.

Sie entwickelte sich beträchtlich und nahm zahlreiche Dörfer in sich auf. Augenblicklich nimmt die Residenzzone die beiden Buchten vom Grossen Hafen und von Marsamxett vollkommen ein, mit der neuen Stadt von Sliema.

Der Bau eines gigantischen Arsenals genügte nicht, um das Arbeitsproblem in diesem kleinen Territorium zu regeln, dessen demographisches Wachstum so stark war, dass von zwei Maltesern einer augenblicklich im Ausland lebt. Von 25.000 im Jahre 1530 ist die Bevölkerung auf 100.000 im Jahre 1798 angestiegen, auf 205.000 im Jahre 1906 und auf mehr als 300.000 im Jahre 1970.

Auf der Insel fanden im Verlauf der europäischen Revolutionen in der Mitte des 19. Jahrhunderts mehrere Revolten statt. Während der englischen Besetzung versuchte man mittels politischer Kämpfe eine bessere Volksvertretung zu erlangen. Sie hatten den Verleih von verschiedenen Verfassungen zur Folge, die aber ständig wieder in Frage gestellt wurden.

(photos p.154)

DIE BELAGERUNG VON 1942

Der strategische Wert Maltas wurde bei Ausbruch des zweiten Weltkrieges in Frage gestellt. Gewisse brittische Strategen waren der Meinung, dass die Insel, die während der vorhergehenden Kriege eine grosse Rolle gespielt hatte (Krim-Krieg, 14-18), aufgegeben werden sollte, da sie zu nahe am italienischen Feind lag. Es genüge, die beiden Einfahrtsstrassen ins Mittelmeer bei Suez und Gibraltar zu blockieren, was nicht weiter schwierig wäre. Andere Militärs wieder waren der entgegengesetzten Meinung; nämlich, dass der Besitz dieses Meeres die englischen Olterritorien im Nahen Osten sichern könnte und dass man sich dort um jeden Preis behaupten müßte, und das um so mehr, als der Weg ums Kap viel zu lang war, um mit Aussicht auf Erfolg das zur Kriegsführung nötige Erdöl herbeizubringen.

Der Eintritt Italiens in den Krieg und die Operationen gegen Rommel in Nordafrika brachten es schliesslich dazu, dass Malta als Zitadelle beibehalten wurde. Von Valletta und von den Flugplätzen aus, die man in aller Eile konstruiert hatte, konnte man die feindlichen Geleitschiffe beheiligen, die den deutschen Streitkräften Proviant und Munition zuführten.

So wurde Malta zwei schreckliche Jahre lang angegriffen (vom 10. Juni 1940 bis 8. November 1942). Es fanden unzählige Operationen auf dem Wasser und in der Luft statt; die Insel wurde ständig bombardiert. Die Lebensmittelzufuhr wurde abgeschnitten und die Achsenmächte arbeiteten einen Landungsplan in der Bucht von Marsaxlokk aus.

Unaufhörlich fielen Bomben auf Valletta, den Grossen Hafen und die Flugplätze. Die Zivilbevölkerung erlitt schwere Verluste. 14000 Tonnen Bomben wurden so abgeworfen.

Ausser dem Tribut an Menschenleben waren zwanzigtausend Häuser zerstört und mehrere Herbergen der Ordensritter, wenn auch nicht vollkommen zerstört, so doch schwer beschädigt worden, wie zum Beispiel die Herberge der Provence. *(photos p.157)*

DIE KIRCHENERBAUER

Malta ist wohl das einzige Land, in dem die Bevölkerung - wie im Mittelalter für die Kirchen und Kathedralen - als Gemeinde einer kleinen Stadt oder eines Dorfes beschliesst, ein religiöses Gebäude zu bauen. Die dabei aufgewandte Zeit spielt dann natürlich keine Rolle.

Die Malteser waren von jeher sehr religiös. Waren sie nicht berühmte Baumeister von Tempeln in den vorgeschichtlichen Epochen? Der Kampf gegen die moslemischen Türken fand ebenso aus wirtschaftlichen und gewaltpolitischen, Europa betreffenden Gründen statt, wie auch zum grossen Teil aus religiösen Gründen.

Die Johanneskathedrale, die von einem maltesischen Architekten gebaut wurde, kann die ganze Welt nur mit Stolz erfüllen. Das gleiche gilt für die erst kürzlich gebaute Mosta-Kirche, deren Kuppel die dritte der Welt sein soll. Das Gebäude wurde 1860 errichtet mit Hilfe von Emigranten, die die Stadt verlassen hatten. Es heisst, dass der Architekt weder lesen noch schreiben konnte. Während des letzten Krieges fiel eine Bombe von 400 Kilo auf die Kuppel und rollte vor die Füsse der verängstigten Gläubigen. Das Objekt des "Wunders" ist jetzt entschärft in der Sakristei ausgestellt.

Das Heiligtum von Ta' Pinu, in Gozo, wurde von 1920 bis 1936 an der Stelle erbaut, an der sich früher eine Kapelle des 16. Jahrhunderts erhob. Dieses imposante Denkmal wurde infolge eines 1883 von der Bäuerin Carmella Grima erlebten spirituellen Ereignisses erbaut; sie hatte eine Stimme gehört, die von ihr verlangte, das Gebet der Madonna aufzusagen. Auf dem Vorhof kann man in natürlicher Grösse einen vollkommen in Marmor ausgeführten Leidensweg besichtigen.

Auf dem Land, in der Umgebung von Siggiewi, hat ein Bauer in die Felsen eines Steinbruchs grosse Statuen von Christus, der heiligen Jungfrau und des heiligen Michel gemeisselt.

(photos p.162)

EMSIG WIE EIN MALTESE

Da die Arbeitslosigkeit heute eines der Hauptprobleme Maltas bildet, kann man wohl verstehen, dass viele Einwohner in Länder mit einem umfassenderen und in voller Entwicklung begriffenen Wirtschaftswesen auswandern, wie zum Beispiel nach Kanada und vor allem, seit einigen Jahren, nach Australien.

Im Archipel wird jede nur mögliche Parzelle Erdboden bebaut und mehrere Ernten pro Jahr sind keine Seltenheit, aber die Wasserversorgung ist ein Problem, das in hohem Masse die Entwicklung der Bewässerung begrenzt.

Der nach und nach erfolgte Abzug der britischen Truppen hat die Devisenzufuhr stark vermindert, sowie auch die Beschäftigungsmöglichkeiten in den Stützpunkten. Durch die Schliessung des Suezkanals ist auch der Schiffsverkehr stark zurückgegangen, was eine Verminderung der Arbeit in den Reparaturwerkstätten zur Folge hatte. Deshalb wird die Wiedernutzbarmachung dieses Wasserweges mit Ungeduld erwartet.

1965 deckte die nationale Produktion weniger als 1% der Bedürfnisse. Die Landwirtschaft repräsentiert 7% des Brutt-onationaleinkommens und die Industrie 17,7%. Die Dienstleistungen stellen 20% des Bruttonationaleinkommens dar.

Nach seiner Unabhängigkeit Mitglied des "Commonwealth geworden, hat Malta bisher von den Investierungen und der Finanzhilfe Grossbritanniens profitiert. Seit einigen Jahren versucht es nun, seine Beziehungen zu anderen Ländern zu erweitern.

Wie bei vielen anderen Inseln, wo die Sonne einen grossen Teil des Jahres strahlt, hat man den Tourismus entwickelt und ganz besonders den Wintertourismus. Zahlreiche Hotels wurden besonders am Meeresufer, gebaut. 1974 erhielt der Archipel genausoviel Besucher wie er Einwohner zählte; das heisst, mehr als dreihunderttausend. *(photos p.159)*

DIE MALTESER IM AUSLAND

Seit dem 19. Jahrhundert wurden die Malteser, wegen der Ueberbevölkerung und dem Mangel an lokalen Ressourcen zur Emigration gezwungen.

Sie wandten sich natürlich den Ländern in Nord-Afrika mit französischer Kolonisation zu: vor allem Algerien und Tunis. Einige Gemeinschaften befanden sich dort schon seit langer Zeit. Die Neuankömmlinge, die nicht nur gut arabisch verstanden - Sprache die ja mit der ihren verwandt war - befanden sich so ebenfalls unter der Jurisdiktion einer katholischen Macht, nämlich Frankreichs.

Im Anfang dieses Jahrhunderts waren die Malteser fest in Tunis verwurzelt, sowie auch in Ost-Algerien (Bône, Bougie, Philippeville, Constantine). Zum grössten Teil waren sie Arbeiter (Steinschleifer oder Kaufleute. "In den starkbevölkerten Vierteln der grossen Städte verbrüderten sie sich mit den anderen Elementen mittelländische Herkunft, besonders mit den Italienern; sie schlossen sich sogleich der neuen französischen Gemeinschaft an, die eine Mosaik verschiedener Ethnien bildete, und in Algerien. Jedoch bewahrten sie in zahlreichen Domänen ihre eigene Personalität. So figuriert eine grosse Anzahl Malteser in Romanen, die von grossen französischen Schriftstellern Nord-Afrikas während der Jahre 1910 bis 1930 geschrieben wurden." (Pierre DIMECH)

DIE UNABHÄNGIGKEIT

Die Eroberer oder 'Besucher', die im Laufe der Geschichte die Insel betraten, haben dort ihre Spuren hinterlassen in Form von archäologischen Resten. Sie haben auch der lokalen Kultur ihren Stempel aufgedrückt. Der Sprachstreit ist sehr oft erwähnt worden. Es handelte sich letzten Endes darum zu wissen, ob Malta kulturell zu Italien gehörte.

Seit der Ankunft der Malteserritter haben die Malteser einen historisch originalen Weg verfolgt, der tiefe Spuren bei ihnen hinterlassen hat. Maltesisch wurde lange Zeit als ein Dialekt betrachtet, der bis zum Ende des 18. Jahrhunderts ungeschrieben war. Es ist nichtsdestoweniger eine Sprache, in der zahlreiche Werke gedruckt wurden. Mehrere lokale Zeitungen wurden herausgegeben. Maltesisch ist jetzt zur Nationalsprache geworden. Auf der Universität werden mehrere Kurse auf maltesisch gehalten.

Der politische Kampf für die Autonomie erschien zur gleichen Zeit wie die Autonomiekämpfe in Europa, d. h. im letzten Jahrhundert. Wirtschaftliche und demographische Probleme verstärkten noch die Scheidung zwischen der Bevölkerung und der Tutelarmacht.

Nach der Annahme einer Verfassung im Jahre 1947 wurde eine Volksabstimmung durchgeführt, um zu erfahren, ob Malta zu Grossbritannien gehören wollte. 75 % der Wahlteilnehmer, die aber tatsächlich weniger als die Hälfte der wahlberechtigten Bevölkerung ausmachten, stimmten dafür. Die englische Arbeiterpartei hatte das 'Ja' befürwortet; die Kirche hatte sich für das 'Nein' ausgesprochen. Infolge der schwachen Wahlbeteiligung zog Grossbritannien die erzielten Resultate nicht in Erwägung.

Im Jahre 1959 liess eine neue Verfassung den Engländern nur die Verantwortung für die Verteidigung und das Auswärtige Amt. Infolge der Verweigerung finanzieller Hilfe wurde eine Volksabstimmung organisiert, und am 21 September 1964 wurde dem maltesischen Archipel die Unabhängigkeit zuerkannt. Malta hat ein parlamentarisches politisches System. Die Macht liegt in den Händen des Ministerpräsidenten und der anderen Mitglieder des Kabinetts. Der Ministerpräsident ist der Chef der Mehrheit. Die Abgeordneten werden von der ganzen Bevölkerung gewählt. Die Insel ist nicht in Wahlbezirke aufgeteilt. Die Wähler haben die Wahl zwischen zwei Wahllisten: eine der konservativen Patei und eine der Arbeiterpartei.

Seit Dezember 1974 hat Malta die letzten Bande, die es an Grossbritannien knüpften, gebrochen und ein Präsident der Republik, Herr Anthony Mamo, ist ernannt worden. Der Ministerpräsident ist Herr Dom Mintoff.

Nach Jahrtausenden ihrer Geschichte, während derer sich praktisch alle Mittelmeermächte in der Machtausübung folgten, erhielten die Malteser endlich ihre nationale Unabhängigkeit.

(photo p.165)

Bibliographie

Es gibt nur wenige französische Bücher über die Geschichte Maltas, abgesehen von dem sehr umfassenden Werk von J. Godechot im Verlag "Que Sais-je?". Auf englisch dagegen gibt es eine grosse Anzahl solcher Werke. Doch lassen fast alle die bedeutende vorgeschichtliche Periode Maltas im Schatten, obwohl diese den meisten seiner Nachbarn in nichts nachsteht. Es gibt zahlreiche Bücher über die Malteserritter in allen Sprachen. Sehr alte Werke kann man in den grossen Bibliotheken finden.

T. Zammit:	Prehistoric Malta, the Tarxien temple, Oxford 1930
J.D. Evans:	Malta, London 1959
B. Blouet:	The Story of Malta, London 1967
A.J. Agius:	Guide Books, Feedom Press Valetta
J.D. Evans:	The Prehistoric Culture Sequence in the Maltese Archipelago, Prehistoric Society, London 1954
	The Prehistoric Antiquities of the Maltese Islands, London 1971
D.H. Trump:	An Archeological Guide, London 1972
J. Godechot:	Histoire de Malte, P.U.F. 1970
Quentin Hughes:	Fortress, Architecture and Military History in Malta, London 1969
	The Building of Malta, 1530-1795, London 1956
Claire-Elaine Engel:	Les Chevaliers de Malte, 1961
J.-L. Miège:	Histoire de Malte, 3 vol., Paris 1840
Pierre Dimech:	Contribution à l'étude de l'Histoire Constitutionnelle et Politique de Malte, Eveil du Nationalisme Maltais (1800-1936) Thèse de doctorat, Paris, 1973

Cet ouvrage a été realisé par les Editions
DELROISSE 113, rue de Paris - 92100 - BOULOGNE - France
Imprimé sur les presses des Editions DELROISSE
Textes, Photographies et Maquette: Bernard NANTET
Traduction anglaise: Colin NORRIS (sauf pour les p.37 et 166)
Traduction allemande: Helmut LEIBHOLZ
Exclusivité pour la France: VILO - Paris
Dépôt légal n° 695

ŻEBBUĠ

MARSALFORN

GĦARB

CALYPSO'S CAVE

XAGĦRA

ĠGANTIJA

VICTORIA

NADUR

QALA

XLENDI

MĠARR

TA'ĊENĊ

Gozo

COMINOTTO

Com

MARFA

Marfa Ridge

SE

MELLIEĦA

Mellieħa Ri

MANIKATA

Baida Ri

GĦAJN TU

SKORBA

MĠARR

Malta